Shakespeare's Comedies

University of Delaware Press Awards

General John Burgoyne
By Richard J. Hargrove

Time and the Artist in Shakespeare's English Histories
By John W. Blanpied

Small Georgian Houses in England and Virginia: Origins and Development through the 1750s
By Daniel D. Reiff

Shakespeare's Comedies: From Roman Farce to Romantic Mystery
By Robert Ornstein

Shakespeare's Comedies

From Roman Farce to Romantic Mystery

Robert Ornstein

Newark: University of Delaware Press
London and Toronto: Associated University Presses

© 1986 by Associated University Presses, Inc.

Associated University Presses
440 Forsgate Drive
Cranbury, NJ 08512

Associated University Presses
25 Sicilian Avenue
London WC1A 2QH, England

Associated University Presses
2133 Royal Windsor Drive
Unit 1
Mississauga, Ontario
Canada L5J 1K5

Library of Congress Cataloging-in-Publication Data

Ornstein, Robert.
Shakespeare's comedies.

Bibliography: p.
Includes index.
1. Shakespeare, William, 1564–1616—Comedies.
I. Title.
PR2981.O76   1986   822.3'3   85-40851
ISBN 0-87413-298-3 (alk. paper)

Printed in the United States of America

To Suzy, Lisa, and Adam

Contents

Preface

I have written this book on the comedies for all who love, study, and teach Shakespeare. Except in the discussion of *The Taming of the Shrew,* which clashes directly with current assumptions about the play, I deal with controversial issues primarily in endnotes, which also indicate the variety of critical responses the comedies have elicited. My own responses have been shaped by the many fine articles and books that have been written about these plays in recent decades. Some of my deepest obligations are to those with whom I take issue; chief among them is the late C. L. Barber, whose splendid book on the comedies set a standard for all later criticism.

To afford a comprehensive view of Shakespeare's achievement in comedy, I trace his artistic progress from *The Comedy of Errors* to *The Tempest.* I omit *The Merry Wives of Windsor* for reasons that are made clear in the Introduction. I discuss *Measure for Measure* only briefly in relation to *All's Well That Ends Well* because I have written more fully about it in *The Moral Vision* of *Jacobean Tragedy.* I omit *Pericles* because its unique problems of text and authorship set it apart from the other comedies.

A research fellowship from the National Endowment for the Humanities enabled me to begin work on this book. I am also indebted to Hallett Smith, who put aside his own work to read and criticize my manuscript.

I dedicate this book to my children, who know how to laugh and have done their best to rescue me from academic solemnity.

Shakespeare's Comedies

1

Introduction

If Shakespeare's early comedies seem to imply that there is no anguish greater than a lover's sigh, his early history plays leave no doubt of the ugliness of political contention and the agony of civil war. But we do not have to read the First Tetralogy to have a proper perspective on the romantic comedies because their laughter does not depend on naive optimism or unexamined, idealistic assumptions about human nature. They do not ask us to believe that this is the best of possible worlds; they ask us only to rejoice in honest affection and to share in the good-natured laughter that chastens the emotional extravagances and self-conscious posturings of lovers.

Like the history plays, the romantic comedies belong to the remarkable first decade of Shakespeare's career, when his artistic powers matured so swiftly that only a few years separate his first attempts in comedy and history from his earliest masterpieces. If he is not quite certain of his artistic direction in *The Comedy of Errors, Love's Labor's Lost,* and *Two Gentlemen of Verona,* he is clearly master of the genre in *A Midsummer Night's Dream,* and his inspiration soars in *The Merchant of Venice, Much Ado About Nothing, As You Like It,* and *Twelfth Night.* After *Twelfth Night* few of Shakespeare's plays can be called comedies, and none resemble plays like *A Midsummer Night's Dream* and *Much Ado About Nothing. All's Well that Ends Well* is a puzzling and not particularly attractive play that is different in tone, theme, and characterization from the comedies of the 1590s. *Measure for Measure* is not, as some would have it, a tragedy manqué; but its somber mood, its sense of the ironies of human judgments, and its emphasis on the power of sexual appetite and the cynicism of commercialized vice convince some critics that, like *Troilus and Cressida,* it expresses a personal disillusion from which Shakespeare did not easily recover.

If we resort to biographical conjectures to explain the unpleasantness of the dark comedies, it is because they apparently lack the balance and proportion of Shakespeare's other plays and do not seem to share any common artistic ground either with the romantic comedies that preceded them or the romances the followed them. I devote a chapter to *All's Well* because it is a Janus-like work that looks back on and transforms the drama of courtship presented in the romantic comedies even as it anticipates the marital and familial drama of *Cymbeline* and *The Winter's Tale*. I also include a chapter on *Cymbeline*, although it has only one scene that is clearly intended to be comic, because its first two acts take up again the themes of slandered innocence and sexual jealousy that are central in *Much Ado* and *Othello* and thereby anticipate the daring treatment of these themes in *The Winter's Tale*. For want of a better name, we call *The Winter's Tale* and *The Tempest* late romances, but they have their moments of boisterous and genial comedy and clowns who are first cousins to the Dromios, Launce, Speed, and Touchstone. Shakespeare concludes his artistic journey in comedy where he began, by paying homage in *The Tempest* to the dramatic structure of Roman farce even as he imitates Plautus's *Menaechmi* in *Errors* very early in his career.

Because Shakespeare had an extraordinarily original imagination and his development as poet and playwright was very swift, some of the comedies that will be discussed in succeeding chapters hardly seem to resemble one another, but in one crucial respect they are alike. These are the plays of Shakespeare in which women share the center of the stage with men as dramatic protagonists; indeed, the heroines are usually more interesting and memorable than the heroes.[1] Because the drama of politics is played out in the great public arenas of the world, in halls of state and on battlefields, few female characters have significant roles in the history plays. Except for Juliet and Cleopatra, the heroines of the tragedies also play supporting roles; the tragic protagonist is Othello, not Desdemona; Lear, not Cordelia; Macbeth, not the wife who goads him into a career of savagery. *The Tempest* is the only play I include here in which a heroine plays a subordinate role. Often the female characters are the preeminent figures of the comedies and the choric interpreters of their dramatic worlds. For each time Shakespeare adapts an existing story or play in a comedy he amplifies the roles that the women play and enhances their stature. He turns the shrewish wife of *Menaechmi* into the sympathetic Adriana of *Errors* and creates two additional female characters who have important roles in the dramatic action. He makes Kate more sympathetic than her counterpart in *A Shrew* but coarsens Petruchio. He transforms the deceitful mercenary Widow of *Il Pecorone* into Portia and places Nerissa by her side; he makes Helena of *All's Well* far more complex and interesting than Boccaccio's Giletta, but he makes Bertram far less noble than Beltramo. Although *Cymbeline* supposedly deals with international political conflict, its protagonist is Imogen, and the drama of her betrayal is the only coherent strand of plot. The protagonist of *The Winter's Tale* is Leontes, but his destiny lies in the hands of Paulina and Hermione, who make possible his redemption. As we shall see, the heroines or their female allies preside over the denouements of *Love's Labor's, The Merchant, As You Like It, All's Well,* and *The Winter's Tale,* and frequently they are the contrivers of the comic conclusions.

We look in vain for Portias, Beatrices, Rosalinds, or Violas in the comedies of Shakespeare's contemporaries. There are memorable heroines in the tragedies of Webster, Middleton, and Ford but few in their comedies. Indeed, the marriage quest is often as unromantic or antiromantic in Elizabethan and Jacobean comedy as it is in Roman comedy, in which the heroine is the sexual prize for which men compete and women are otherwise customarily depicted as shrewish wives, comic servants, and courtesans. Female characters play more important roles in Lyly's comedies, but his heroines are never as attractive as Shakespeare's, and his view of love is ambivalent and often threaded with satirical denigration.[2] Only a few plays by Greene, Chapman, and Dekker deserve the name of romantic comedy, and very few of their heroines are interesting and strong dramatic personalities.[3] In short, the often perfunctory use of the marriage quest as a plot device in Elizabethan and Jacobean comedy does not explain the prominence of the heroines in Shakespeare's comedies, who owe more to his romantic imagination and sensitivities than to any convention of Roman or Renaissance drama. We could say that these heroines are creatures of fable and fairytale, except that they are almost invariably more level-headed and realistic than the heroes, who may have more experience of life but seem less mature and capable of fending for themselves.

Where Elizabethan love poetry gives voice to the vagaries of masculine passion, the memorable speeches about love in Shakespeare's comedies express the ardor and wit of heroines like Portia, Viola, Olivia, Imogen, and Perdita. Fortunately the success of the romantic heroes does not depend on their facility as love poets, for some are barely competent versifiers, others are merely conventional or overblown in their sentiments. Their raptures often seem second hand and they rarely escape self-consciousness because they know how lovers are supposed to act and enjoy the self-indulgence and self-absorption of romantic angst. They play a variety of roles in the comedies: neoplatonic casuists, bristling rivals, gentle swains, sexual predators, and jealous lovers and husbands. Not many of them, however, transcend their romantic roles and become, like the heroines, memorable dramatic figures in their own right. Only Berowne among the heroes of *Love's Labor's* can match the French Princess in wit and insight. Only Benedick and, to a lesser degree, Bassanio, among the later heroes have a gift of poetry or wit equal to Portia's and Beatrice's. The other heroes are usually amiable and endearing enough to engage sympathy, but some scarcely rise above the norm of masculine gallantry in love and some sink below the level of common decency. It is Touchstone, not Orlando, who is Rosalind's rival in satiric humor, just as it is Feste, not Orsino, who matches Viola in quickness of wit and insight.

Where the romantic heroes incline to earnestess and often lack a sense of irony or humor, the heroines are usually able to see the comedy of a difficult situation and they are the inventors of the charades that teach the heroes something of the nature of love or generosity. Indeed, if Benedick seems the most attractive of the romantic heroes, it is because his manliness is graced by a humor and sensitivity that is far more characteristic of the women than the men in the comedies. In the comedies of Jonson and Middleton as in most Roman and Italian comedies, wit is often cynical and almost always masculine and contriving; it is the province of cunning servants, con men, and ingenious manipulators of others. In Shakespearean comedy wit is more often feminine than masculine, and it is gentle and understanding of folly and frailty. The most inspired gambit of *Twelfth Night*, the letter that gulls Malvolio, is Maria's invention; Toby's games are less attractive and genial.

Given the number of comedies in which heroines are preeminent and even arbiters of the plot, it is remarkable that modern critics should try to convince us that Shakespearean comedy is by and large a man's world. In his often reprinted and cited essay, "The Argument of Comedy,"[4] Northrop Frye defines the archetypal plot of classical and Elizabethan comedy as an oedipal conflict between a young man and his father (or an elderly suitor) over the love of a young woman. C. L. Barber argues implicitly for the masculine character of Shakespearean comedy by identifying its festive spirit with saturnalian indulgence and with robust country sports and entertainments such as mummings, sword dances, and May games.[5] Indeed, he identifies the comic "clarification and release" that Shakespearean comedy allows with the overthrow of priggish restraint in holiday cheer[6] even though the masters of the comic revels are Portia, Beatrice, Rosalind, and Viola, not Falstaff and Poins. It is worth noting that the only play in which saturnalian cheer is evident is *Twelfth Night*, which alone among the comedies ends with broken pates and shattered friendships, anger and recrimination. Other comedies end on a more optimistic and loving note, but none provide even a glimpse of the new dispensation, the "green world" that, Frye suggests, is envisioned in the happy denouements of Shakespearean comedy.[7]

Oedipal rivalry scarcely exists as such in Shakespeare's comedies. Although tyrannical and possessive fathers sometimes appear, they are less of an obstacle to the fulfillment of love than are the rivalries of the romantic heroes. Except perhaps in *A Dream*, youth does not triumph over age in Shakespearean comedy; on the contrary, those who are young require the counsel and protection of older characters in *Errors*, *Two Gentlemen*, *Much Ado*, *All's Well*, *Cymbeline*, *The Winter's Tale*, and *The Tempest*. In *Much*

Ado as in *The Tempest* it is the father of the heroine who assures her happiness by denying his vindictive impulses. The ending of Shakespearean comedy is a time when different generations are reunited, not separated, and an occasion that promises continuity with the past, not significant change; at the close the lovers take their places again in the social order of Athens or Messina, and friends and relatives gather to celebrate their marriages. After anxious misadventures and misunderstandings, the fulfillment of love is metaphorically if not literally identified with "going home," with reunion with a lost brother or sister, father or mother, and with the restoration of the intrinsic ties of family life.[8] I do not mean that Shakespearean comedy defends the status quo; more often than not it comments pointedly on conventional assumptions that do not bear too close examination. I mean only that the security of comedy depends on an assurance (or a hope) that top side is right side, that communal life is nurturing despite the blusterings of fathers and the hypocrisies of ordinary standards of sexual morality.

The sense of holiday in Shakespearean comedy that Barber would trace back to Tudor social observances is characteristic of many Roman and Italian comedies in which lovers must assume new identities or disguises to woo a maiden.[9] In Gascoigne's *Supposes*, a translation of Ariosto's *I Suppositi*, love makes the hero a truant to his studies and a partner with his clever servant in a series of contrivances and masquerades. Forever in the toils of circumstance he is too busy trying to outwit the heroine's father and his wealthy rival to enjoy the comic confusion his schemes engender. Shakespeare's romantic protagonists have more opportunity to enjoy the adventure of love because they do not inhabit the crass world of Roman farce in which the pursuit of love is often a cunning as well as mercenary enterprise. Nobly born and amply provided for, they have the leisure to devote themselves to the game of love and to debate its nature in prose and poetry, in dialogue, soliloquy, and sonnet. If they are lords of Navarre, their titles and estates afford a perpetual freedom from mundane occupation; if they are Venetian merchants they have world enough and time between their commercial ventures for music, masking, and feasting. When tyranny drives the characters of *As You Like It* into exile, that exile turns to holiday because the only activities possible are banqueting under the boughs, hunting, singing, sonneteering, philosophizing, and making love. No doubt some sheep can be found in the sheepcote Celia purchases, but Corin and Silvius see to them when they are not engaged in the dialogues appropriate to shepherds in pastoral eclogues.

The essential spirit of Shakespearean comedy is romantic, not festive; it is more closely allied to the wonder of antique romance than to Elizabethan holiday observances.[10] That wonder is dimly, briefly glimpsed in the recognition scenes of Roman comedy, in which scattered families are reunited and parentless heroines identified as long-lost heiresses. It is reborn and celebrated anew in Shakespearean comedies that tell of disguised maidens,

desperate flights, exiles, shipwrecks, conspiracies, and encounters with outlaws, fairies, mountaineers, and monsters. The adventure of romance is one
that heroines share with those they love, for by choice or necessity they put
aside the usual decorums of maidenly dress and conduct and for a time enjoy
the freedom of action men have. Because Shakespeare's characters are flesh
and blood, they can give themselves to the tremulous adventure of romantic
love without becoming romantic clichés. Indeed, to appreciate the unconventionality of Shakespeare's treatment of romantic love, we need only listen
to Orsino, a self-proclaimed expert on the subject, who has read widely in
Elizabethan love poems and treatises on the passions. He knows that no
woman can love as he does because women are either too delicate to have
powerful passions—they are the rose-madonnas of the sonnets—or they are
too cold—cruel fairs who prove fickle in their affections. For Orsino as for
other votaries of passion in the comedies, love is a masculine sport and
dedication. Women may be enshrined and adored by such romanticists but
they exist as objects of male desire, prompters of male pain, and projections
of male fantasy. They are the justification for a hero's self-indulgent absorp-
tion in his own emotions. Elizabethan poets make us aware of the comedy
and egotism of a lover's complaint, but very few attempt to see the game of
love from a woman's point of view. Only in Shakespeare's sonnets and the
greatest love poems of Spenser, Sidney, and Donne does the speaker's response to a loved one become a mirror for her nobility and beauty of soul.
Much more common in sixteenth-century love poems is the speaker's anger
at a woman's coyness or fickleness. A mistress's changeableness is the subject
for many lines dipped in ironic scorn, while the speaker's exploits in love are
the subject of many lines of manly boasts—he has loved and got and told and
he is not averse to telling of it again even though this experience can create an
anxiety about the possibility of genuine and lasting love.

The only female character in the comedies who closely resembles the
stereotypes of Elizabethan poetry is Phebe, the pastoral nymph of *As You
Like It,* and she is less of a dramatic personality than a literary convention
brought to life. Orsino accuses Olivia of being proud and cruel, but she is
never coy and indeed is more forthright in denying his suit than he is in his
faint-hearted wooing. The heartless or faithless woman decried in many
Elizabethan love poems does not exist in the comedies. It is the heroes who
prove giddy in their affections and at times heartless in their abuse of the
women who love them. With very few exceptions, the heroines of the
comedies are more generous and steadfast in their love than the heroes are,
not because Shakespeare thinks women are nobler than men but because he
knows that they are raised with the expectation that fulfillment will come in
love and marriage, to which they can make an absolute commitment. Men,
on the other hand, are subject to a wider range of pressures and opposing
claims. Honor beckons them to prove themselves worthy in the great world,

and reputation demands that they measure themselves by the esteem they win from other men. Thus a callow Bertram hungers to prove his manhood in chivalric gestes and can regard a woman only as a clog or a scutcheon of sexual conquest. The ambivalence of Elizabethan love poetry is reflected in many of the comedies, and it is paradoxically most vivid in those heroes who pronounce themselves love's votaries but cannot imagine the love of a woman as the be-all and end-all of their existence because that would be unmanly. Quite often a trace of anxiety accompanies the hero's hyperbolic yearnings. He needs to exaggerate the beauty and purity of his mistress just as he needs to think of her as delicate and fragile and therefore in need of his protective love, because unless she is a saint, nay a goddess, she is mere woman and unworthy of devotion. He may hesitate to invest his sense of self in a romantic union because in doing so he risks losing it and making himself the target of other men's jests.

Shakespeare's heroines are not plagued by these unacknowledged fears; they face more immediate dangers if they give their hearts too easily, for they may gain the reputation of wantonness, which is as devastasting as the actual loss of a maidenhead. Because they are chaste in spirit as well as body, the heroines can jest broadly, and even greasily about sex, and they tease their lovers and husbands about the danger of cuckoldry; when the heroes joke about horns it is often with a slightly nervous laughter. Claudio and Posthumus are victimized not only by cunning slanders but also by their readiness to believe the worst about the women they love. Leontes does not have to be duped by a Don John or Jachimo because he can create his own tormented fantasies about the gracious Hermione. In contrast, the heroines who have reason to be envious of a rival—Julia, both Helenas, and Viola— are almost free of jealousy and capable of sympathy for the women they should dislike.

The comedies do not create the impression that men are naturally or peculiarly susceptible to sexual jealousy. If they are more vulnerable than women, it is because the suspicion of cuckoldry touches their manhood and because they think themselves justified in acting on jealous suspicion, which too quickly becomes "fact." It is their duty, they tell themselves, to expose and punish a cunning wanton who pretends to virginal modesty or marital fidelity. The poignant sense in the comedies of the emotional dependence of women on men helps to explain why they are reluctant to blame whereas men are quick to lash out—why they want to believe in and are loyal to the men who wrong them. And yet their acceptances are not motivated by timidity or ignorance of the inequities of their status in society. Adriana complains bitterly of the double standard that allows her husband's wanderings in *Errors,* but what she desires is his love, not a similar freedom from the marriage bond, which she regards as a spiritual and physical union. When the heroines laugh at romantic protestations it is not because they are skeptical of the possibility of fidelity but because they love so completely and ardently that they cannot stand conventional attitudinizings. At times they seem too forgiving, or incapable of the anger that Beatrice feels toward Claudio in *Much Ado,* but none of the comedies depends for its resolution on a heroine's Griseldan self-denial; more often than not the heroes rather than the heroines are humbled in the final scenes. The comedies leave little doubt that men as well as women are victimized by the conventional hypocrisies of sexual morality, but they also affirm the fundamental decencies that the social order promotes—the civilities that lend humanity and grace to daily life and that contribute importantly to the emotional resolutions of the comedies.

To dwell at length on the vulnerability of the heroines and the failings of the heroes is to risk turning the romantic comedies into dark comedies and the dark comedies and late romances into tragedies manqué. Although Dr. Johnson thought that Shakespeare was more successful in his comedies than in his tragedies, which he found labored and wanting in poetic justice, later critics have found it more difficult to accept the happy endings of *The Merchant, Much Ado,* and *All's Well* than to accept the harrowing conclusions of *Othello* and *King Lear.* They cannot put the treatment of Shylock out of their minds and they are doubtful that Claudio deserves the gentle Hero or that *All's Well* ends well when Bertram is no more attractive in its final scene than in earlier ones. The temptation, of course, is to argue away the difficulties and declare that the endings of the comedies are cheerful and sunny even if they do not seem so because they *have* to be—because it is the nature of comedy to end with joy, release, and reconciliation. One can smile urbanely at those who worry over a comic denouement, as if it were pedantic to ask for anything more than that every Jack gets his Jill, but this urbanity is as patronizing of Shakespeare's artistic intention as it is of critical solemnity because it suggests that he did not seek to do more in his comedies than entertain and only by accident included something that touches the heart or troubles the mind.

Shakespeare's comedies do not achieve their denouements by sacrificing their seriousness of theme or integrity of characterization. They do not ask us to believe in sudden repentances or sentimental transformations of personality. Indeed, they trouble us at times because they are unsentimental and uncompromising in their presentation of human behavior. They will not let us believe that beneath every hard exterior beats a compassionate heart, nor do they try to persuade us that the turmoil of a comic plot leads to remarkable transformations of character and acquisitions of wisdom. We would have Claudio more conscious of his crime against Hero and might wish Orsino were more levelheaded at the end of *Twelfth Night* than he seems to be. We do not think it enough that every Jack gets his Jill if the Jack seems, like Proteus or Bertram, a bit of a knave. On the other hand, we cannot prescribe how happy a happy ending should be in comedy because plays vary, and the sense of satisfying resolution depends on the emotional expectations each comedy creates, not on the formulations of literary critics. Renaissance literary theorists made absolute distinctions between the genres of tragedy and comedy, which would overlap only in the somewhat bastard genre of tragicomedy.[11] The theorists did not know or could not imagine a play like *Richard III,* in which political treachery is presented to the audience as a sardonic farce by a winking hunchbacked villain. Nor could they imagine a tragedy like *Romeo and Juliet,* which has so much comedy in its early scenes that an audience does not quite believe the Chorus's insistence on the inevitability of catastrophe. My point is not that Shakespeare's comedies (or *Richard III* and *Romeo and Juliet*) are mixed forms; they do not, like Fletcherian tragicomedy, teeter on the edge of calamity here and descend to farce there. Even when a Shakespearean denouement mingles joy and sorrow as in the late romances, the fundamental tonality of the play is never in doubt. The irrepressible humor of a clown, the confidence of a heroine, or the touch of absurdity in a would-be villain shapes the expectation that the worst will not happen; the decency of minor characters exerts a gravitational pull that bends the course of the dramatic action away from the edge of disaster.

Had Shakespeare been willing to accept the donnés and plot formulas of Plautine comedy, there would be no critical debates over his comic denouements. For all to end well in Plautus no character need be chastened or enlightened because no moral issues are raised, and no regret or sorrow is possible in characters who are fixed forever in their stereotypical natures: the parasite must be greedy, the wife shrewish, the servants cunning, the courtesan unscrupulous. In this farcical universe whatever is, is right and most of the difficulties are merely illusory—the result of some "error" or "suppose," a misunderstanding about the identity of a hero or heroine. In *Menaechmi,* which Shakespeare adapts in *The Comedy of Errors,* comic antagonism and muddle contain their own solutions because the donné of plot (the presence of identical twins) that creates wholesale confusion also ensures that it must end. Sooner or later the two brothers will appear together on stage or their presence in Ephesus will be grasped by one of the characters. Indeed, only Plautus's ingenuity keeps the inevitable discovery scene from occurring too soon, because the more the twins become accidentally entangled in each other's affairs, the likelier it is that someone will pluck out the heart of this comic mystery. The art of the Roman farceur is to sustain and elaborate a fundamental suppose so that the difficulties of the protagonist mount up to the instant of the discovery of the true identity of hero or heroine, when all antagonisms dissolve and the play ends with the triumph of love and happy reunions. The more turbulent the plotting becomes in Roman farce, the closer it is to its happy resolution and to the characters' recognition that nothing of consequence was ever at stake—it was all ado about nothing.

In writing *Errors* Shakespeare accepts Plautus's comic conception and often follows the plot of *Menaechmi,* but he rejects Plautus's comic assumptions about human nature. He would have a note of sadness in his comedies, and since it does not exist in *Menaechmi* he creates it in the unhappiness of the neglected Adriana and in the sorrow of Egeon, who faces execution because of his search for his lost family. The note of sadness recurs in the denouement of *Love's Labor's,* in Julia's discovery of Proteus's faithlessness in *Two Gentlemen,* and so on in each succeeding comedy. Since the possibility of disaster is inherent in the romantic vision of life, Shakespeare could be engrossed in his early romantic comedies at the same time that that he was absorbed by Brooke's tragic poem *Romeus and Juliet.* His borrowings from Brooke are most explicit in *Two Gentlemen;* they are less emphatic in later comedies, but the clash of youthful passion and parental authority is also significant in the plot of *A Dream,* in Quince's dramatization of "Pyramus and Thisbe," and in *The Merchant,* where love and hate clash and two heroines must decide whether to follow their heart or abide by their father's will.

Because Shakespeare's romantic impulse prevails after *Errors,* he does not again write a play that depends on a farcical donné for its happy ending. The survival of Sebastian, Viola's twin brother, and his appearance on stage with her do not guarantee that *Twelfth Night* will end well because the chief complications of plot are not simply caused by mistaken identities as in *Errors.* Orsino thinks he loves Olivia, who hungers for Cesario, who secretly adores Orsino. For the play to end well, this emotional triangle must dissolve and the wranglings of the minor characters be sorted out. Where Plautine comedy derives its comic security from its artificiality of plot, Shakespearean comedy depends far more on characterization than coincidence for its resolution. For a brief time the comic security of *Much Ado* seems to be embodied in the bumbling Watch, which apprehends Borachio before the denunciation of Hero is to take place, but once she is savagely denounced, the proof of her innocence, which the Watch can provide, is not enough to set all right again. Here as elsewhere in the comedies the confidence that all will be well rests on a belief in human kindness, not on a discovery of the identity of a heroine or the wickedness of a villain.

It was easier for Shakespeare to abandon the formulas of Plautine comedy than to discover his own way in the comedies that followed *Errors.* The static plotting of *Love's Labor's* almost denies the heroes and heroines an opportunity to meet either as romantic antagonists or as lovers. The plot of *Two Gentlemen* is energetic but shapeless and finally self-parodying. Even before he solves the problem of comic plotting, however, Shakespeare is able to create memorable heroes, heroines and clowns; indeed, in the earliest comedies the portrayal of motive and emotional response is far more sophisticated and satisfying than Shakespeare's handling of his comic fables. Only in *The Taming of the Shrew* and *The Merry Wives of Windsor* do the characterizations seem in the main shallow and conventional, but these plays are also different from the other comedies in other intrinsic ways. I omit *The Merry Wives* from this study because it seems to me a skillful perfunctory exercise in comedy by a Shakespeare so bored by his assignment that he is willing to reduce the Falstaff of the Henry IV plays to a vain would be seducer fatuous enough to be thrice duped by the wives of Windsor. *The Shrew* is also uninspired work and, I think, like *The Merry Wives* a play Shakespeare was asked to write rather than chose to write.[12] Nevertheless, it demands attention because its treatment of love and marriage seems to contradict the romantic view that is present in every other comedy.

One hesitates, of course, to distinguish between what is "characteristic" and "uncharacteristic" in Shakespeare's plays because such distinctions were used to rationalize the disintegration of the texts by nineteenth-century critics. Yet we cannot make Shakespeare "the best critic of Shakespeare"— that is, use a cumulative knowledge of his artistic practice to illuminate a particular crux of interpretation—if we do not have a clear sense of the values that inform his comedies. Shall we laugh at Petruchio's humiliation of Kate if we do not laugh at Solanio and Salerio's humiliation of Shylock, who cries out for justice in the streets of Venice? Is Petruchio's baiting of his wife more amusing than the baiting of Malvolio, who is locked in a dark room and treated as a lunatic by Feste and Toby? To answer such questions is to decide whether Shakespeare would have us believe that a bit of ridicule or torment improves the character of the comic victim or the comic manipulator. I would say that Shakespeare lacks the satirist's impulse to inflict a little pain— for therapeutic purposes only—and he does not, like Jonson, ask us to admire those who amuse themselves by making puppets of others. One can argue that Petruchio and Kate are a special case because their Punch-and-Judy relationship is too farcical to be taken seriously by an audience. But once we label something in the comedies "unreal" and therefore innocuous we stand on very slippery ground, for Petruchio is more "real" in his coarse bullying of a woman than Bottom and Dogberry are in their unwavering courtesy to others.

It is only when artistic inspiration flags that the artificiality of a comic plot oppresses us and dramatic situations seem to us "unreal." Since all plots are contrived, and few if any mimic the mundane reality of life, the verisimilitude of a comic moment must depend on whether, despite its elements of fantasy or fairytale, it speaks to us of human truths. The earnest improbabilities of prose romance will not stand the slightest breath of satiric realism or ironic humor because these would blow away the cardboard unreality of character and plot. Shakespeare's comedies can join ironic wit and romantic fancy because they never ask an audience to suspend its common sense, much less its disbelief. Rosalind's romantic ardor is not threatened by Touchstone's satiric wit because she has no illusions about love. With wise humane skeptics like Rosalind shaping the plots of Shakespearean comedy there is no need for divine intervention ("the god out of the machine") to ensure happy endings and no need for critics to ignore what is profoundly serious and occasionally disturbing in these plays.

2

The Comedy of Errors

Although there is fairly general agreement that *Errors, Love's Labor's,* and *Two Gentlemen* were written early in the 1590s and are probably Shakespeare's earliest comedies, no records of performances, contemporary references, or topical allusions exist that permit us to date them precisely or establish their order of composition. It is impossible, moreover, to argue that one of these plays is obviously an apprentice work and another more mature in its artistry. *Errors* has the most coherent and unified plot, but it owes its skillful design to *Menaechmi. Love's Labor's* has the most vivid dramatic personalities, but its plotting is—or seems to be—more primitive than that of *Errors. Two Gentlemen* crystallizes the romantic themes of Shakespearean comedy but it meanders to a self-parodying conclusion and is less effective and satisfying in performance than either *Errors* or *Love's Labor's.*

Since these plays are very different from one another in form and substance and seem to be discrete artistic experiments by a playwright still seeking his own metier in comedy, I see no point in arguing about their chronology. I begin with *Errors,* not because it is more primitive artistically than the others, but because it seems to me probable that Shakespeare began his career in comedy by imitating and adapting Plautus, and struck out on his own in *Love's Labor's* and *Two Gentlemen* after exploring the possibilities and realizing the limitations of Roman farce.[1] The fluent verse of *Errors* suggests that like the other early comedies it was written after Shakespeare had already served his apprenticeship as a dramatic poet in the Henry VI plays. Its lines are never stiff or leaden as are many in *1 Henry VI* and never quite as inspired as the finest passages of *2 & 3 Henry VI.* At its best the poetry of *Errors* has a colloquial ease and raciness that is not achieved in the history plays until the Bastard enters in *King John.* One memorable example is Antipholus E.'s description of how he was tormented by a quack physician:

> . . . Along with them
> They brought one Pinch, a hungry lean-fac'd villain,
> A mere anatomy, a mountebank,
> A threadbare juggler and a fortune-teller,
> A needy, hollow-ey'd, sharp-looking wretch,
> A living dead man.
>
> (5.1.237–42)[2]

This has the verve of the slanging matches in *The Alchemist* and may have been in Jonson's mind when he wrote Face's description of Subtle as a walking anatomy,

>   pinn'd up in the several rags
> Yo' had rak'd and pick'd from dunghills, before day;
> Your feet in mouldy slippers, for your kibes;
> A felt of rug, and a thin threaden cloak,
> That scarce would cover your no-buttocks.
>
> (1.1.33–37)[3]

The most powerful lines in the play belong to Adriana and Luciana, who speak eloquently of the ways that men mistreat women. Mistaking her brother-in-law for her husband, Adriana appeals for his love. When he responds with bewilderment she tries to hide her sense of humiliation behind a self-ridicule that is all the more touching for its attempt at casualness:

> Come, come, no longer will I be a fool,
> To put the finger in the eye and weep,
> Whilst man and master laughs my woes to scorn.
> Come, sir, to dinner. Dromio, keep the gate.
> Husband, I'll dine above with you to-day,
> And shrive you of a thousand idle pranks.
>
> (2.2.203–8)

Compared to Gascoigne's Englishing of Ariosto's *I Suppositi* in *Supposes*, Shakespeare's adaptation of *Menaechmi* is an ambitious recreation of the original, one that significantly elevates its tone and humanizes its characterizations. Yet Shakespeare is largely content to follow in Plautus's footsteps scene by scene so that the dramatic action of *Errors* rarely rises above the level of farce, and the farce depends upon the ingenious complication of a single "suppose" or "error": namely, the confusions of identity that arise when twin brothers and twin servants are mistaken for one another by those they meet. Most of the characters are mere sketches; some are ciphers of the plot and all must be hurried along from one perplexing event to the next lest they have time to reflect on the sudden irrationality and irresponsibility of those they have known for many years. If Antipholus E. had Viola's thoughtfulness he might like her guess that his twin has survived and is being mistaken for him, but that would undermine the plot; moreover, Antonio's accusation of Viola in 3.4 of *Twelfth Night* gives her a reason to believe in her brother's survival that the Antipholi lack. Shakespeare shows considerable skill in making the responses of his characters seem plausible. Although Antipholus S. has come to Ephesus in search of his brother, he has little hope of finding him alive, for that would be as likely, he says, as for one drop of water to "find his fellow forth" in the ocean. Therefore it does not occur to him that he receives strange courtesies from the Ephesians because he is being mistaken for his twin. He congratulates himself on his good luck and when that luck turns, he rails against these Ephesians, who have a reputation for engaging in witchcraft. He is also so accustomed to the incompetence of his servant that it does not astonish him when Dromio lies about his behavior. The Dromios, in turn, are accustomed to being treated as whipping boys by their masters and are therefore not surprised by the unwarranted scoldings and beatings they receive.

By providing twin servants for the twin brothers, Shakespeare multiplies the rough and tumble comedy—the confusions, arguments, threatenings, and thrashings—of *Menaechmi*. He also multiplies the farcical complications of the plot by adding to the cast of characters the goldsmith who sets officers of the law on Antipholus E. Thus the bewildered husband is hounded on all sides and forced at last to take refuge in an abbey. Shakespeare's skill as a farceur makes the concluding scene of *Errors* far more intricate and hilarious than Plautus's denouement, but this somewhat wild-eyed climax does not justify the current stagings of *Errors* as an Elizabethan *Hellzapoppin'*. The supposed rediscovery of the "Elizabethan vitality" of *Errors* is a modern vulgarization of Shakespeare's artistic intention, for he carefully eliminated all that was coarse and scurrilous in the language and characterizations of *Menaechmi*. Plautus's characters are an unattractive lot, some greedy, others callow, whining, or small-minded; but they are not singled out for ridicule or condemnation because they are the typical inhabitants of the crass bourgeois world of Roman comedy, in which there is almost no conception of the ideal, no sense of nobility or aspiration. The only character capable of some kind of dedication is Menaechmus Sosicles, who has roamed the Mediterranean for six years in search of his lost brother. He explains to his servant that he will continue to search until he is certain that his brother has died: "Little knowest thou, Messenio, how near my heart it goes."[4] Naturally enough, his servant finds this dedication as ridiculous as "washing of a blackamore" and offers practical reasons why it must be abandoned. The momentary note of romantic pathos in Sosicles' speech is made a leit-motif in *Errors*, which opens as Egeon, the aging father of the twins, tells the sad story of his life and his fruitless search for his sons. He is less anguished by his impending execution than by the memory of the shipwreck that apparently took the life of his wife and one of his twins; and now his other son has vanished in search of his brother.

Shakespeare did not invent Egeon to expedite his plot. On the contrary, Egeon's overly long tale of woe delays the start of the comic action until the second scene and tries an audience's patience in a seemingly gratuitous fashion, for Egeon will not again appear until the final scene, when he is rescued from the block by a fortuitous meeting with his wife and sons. The opening scene of *Errors* is clearly not a casual artistic miscalculation by an inexperienced playwright; it is rather a very deliberate attempt to invest the farcical action of *Menaechmi* with some of the pathos of ancient romance. Shakespeare willingly risks his audience's attention at first to introduce a nobility of motive and depth of emotional response absent in Plautus. At the same time that the first scene softens the brittle tone of Shakespeare's source, it places an emphasis on the bonds of kinship that parallels the emphasis on familial bonds in the Henry VI plays, in which the horror of civil war is emblemized by twin tableaus of a father killing his son and a son killing his father in battle. In *Menaechmi* familial ties have little meaning; the Senex is not much attached to his daughter, the Wife, and one cannot tell if her marriage is good or bad because she is a stereotype of shrewish jealousy and her husband, Menaechmus, is accustomed to enjoying his pleasures outside his home. The Wife gets no sympathy from her father when she complains that her husband prefers the Courtesan to her. How can she complain, the Senex asks, when her husband provides her with apparel, servants, meat, and drink—all things necessary? She must expect her husband to dine out and spend money on harlots, he continues, because her nagging makes his house intolerable. In other words, men will be men in Roman comedy, and women will be nagging wives or courtesans when they are not young desirable prizes for which men compete. The Senex changes his tune, however, when he learns that Menaechmus has stolen his wife's cloak and jewelry to give to the Courtesan. This theft of valuables is no laughing matter and the father-in-law who will not rebuke Menaechmus's philandering hastens to chide him for snitching his wife's property.

There is no place in the dramatic world of *Errors* for Plautus's gluttonous Parasite or for the crass Senex, who is replaced as a sounding board for the Wife's complaints by Luciana, Adriana's sister, and later by the Abbess. The presence of these sympathetically drawn intelligent women radically alters the nature of the dramatic action because Ephesus is no longer a man's world in which women exist as household scolds or harlots, but one in which men and women are equally prominent, and the latter are more interesting and fully developed as dramatic personalities. Refusing to see her marriage as simply a domestic arrangement, Adriana regards the bond between husband and wife as intrinsic as that which links father to child. Indeed, when she speaks of her oneness with Antipholus E., it is with the same metaphor that

Antipholus S. uses to describe his impossible search for his brother.[5] For her the marriage vow is like a tie of birth and blood in that her sense of self depends on her husband's love and fidelity and she feels defiled by his adultery:

> For if we two be one, and thou play false,
> I do digest the poison of thy flesh,
> Being strumpeted by thy contagion.
>
> (2.2.142–44)

These lines evoke the noblest Renaissance ideal of love—one soul in body twain—and do not allow us to dismiss Adriana's complaints as shrewish jealousy.[6]

The lack of any scene in which Adriana directly confronts her erring husband is striking because her misery and insistence on the inequity of her situation give *Errors* much of its emotional ballast. First she complains to her sister, then to her husband's twin, and lastly to the Abbess, but her husband is not present to hear any of these speeches. Perhaps Shakespeare feared that any direct confrontation of husband and wife would make the other farcical misunderstandings of the play seem trivial by contrast, and he was not prepared to jettison the farcical supposes that keep his plot moving. And yet he allows Adriana to make a powerful indictment of the double standard that must affect an audience even though her speech is directed to the wrong man—her husband's twin. She protests the conventional attitudes that allow men their casual philandering but condemn an unchaste wife to her husband's pitiless revenges:

> How dearly would it touch thee to the quick,
> Shouldst thou but hear I were licentious,
> And that this body, consecrate to thee,
> By ruffian lust should be contaminate?
> Wouldst thou not spit at me, and spurn at me,
> And hurl the name of husband in my face,
> And tear the stain'd skin off my harlot brow,
> And from my false hand cut the wedding-ring,
> And break it with a deep-divorcing vow?
>
> (2.2.130–38)

Although some critics have suggested that Adriana alienated her husband by a jealous possessiveness, she is not the eternally suspicious comic shrew that other dramatists portray. Her manner is never strident or undignified; her requests are never unreasonable. Balthazar, a voice of sanity in the play, speaks of her "unviolated honor," of her "wisdom, / Her sober virtue, years, and modesty"— hardly the attributes of a jealous nag. The worst that

Antipholus E. can say of her is that she is shrewish if he "keeps not hours"—
that is, if he is not home at a reasonable time. Even Luciana, who at first
accuses her sister of "self-harming jealousy," stoutly defends her against the
Abbess's intimation that her shrewishness caused Antipholus E.'s derangement.[7] Where Plautus's husband is indifferent to his wife's continual complaints, Antipholus S. seems ignorant of his wife's unhappiness and is guilty,
so it seems, of insensitivity rather than habitual infidelity. He is obtuse and
quick-tempered, ready to engage in a flyting match with his servants or to
tear down the gate to his house with a crowbar, but he is not loutish in the
manner of his Plautine counterpart. He intended to give the necklace to his
wife and presents it to the Courtesan only when he is locked out of his
house. Although he is familiar with the Courtesan he does not boast of her
sexual favors to Balthazar. She is, he claims, "a wench of excellent discourse,
/ Pretty and witty; wild and yet, too, gentle." This circumspect description
does not come from the lips of a libertine; Antipholus E. is a successful
businessman who uses his wife's mistreatment of him as an excuse for a night
on the town. Because he is too coarse-grained and attached to his comforts
to spend years in search of a lost brother, one doubts that he would
understand Adriana's ideal of marriage even if he heard her pleas.

Antipholus S. is a more interesting character who not only embarks on a
hopeless quest for his twin but also demonstrates his romantic temper by
falling in love with Luciana at first sight. Like many later romantic heroes he
is a rapturous wooer, one who has read many sonnets and knows by heart
the literary language of love, the appropriate conceits and hyperboles with
which to declare a boundless passion. He protests that Luciana is "our
earth's wonder, more than earth divine"; nay, she is a very deity. Like many
later heroines Luciana seems wiser than the man who woos her, even though
she seems at first priggish in advising her sister to accept her unhappy lot
without complaint. A man is master of his liberty, she explains, and his
liberty is necessarily greater than a woman's because he is the provider and
must be away from the home. To this practical reason, Luciana adds the
metaphysical argument that a husband is the rightful bridle of his wife's will
because of his superior position in the universe. If Luciana's sermon on order
and degree smells a bit of the lamp, it is nevertheless seriously offered,
complete with the usual commonplaces about the hierarchy of nature that all
animals recognize and obey:

> Man, more divine, the master of all these,
> Lord of the wide world and wild wat'ry seas,
> Indu'd with intellectual sense and souls,
> Of more pre-eminence than fish and fowls,
> Are masters to their females, and their lords.

(2.1.20–24)

These high sentences are deflated, however, as soon as they are delivered. "This servitude," Adriana dryly responds, "makes you to keep unwed." "Not this," Luciana says, "but troubles of the marriage-bed." "Were you wedded," Adriana suggests, "you would bear some sway." Luciana's lame response is, "Ere I learn to love, I'll practice to obey," a tacit confession that she will have to school herself to the submissiveness that she claims is natural to women. When Luciana says that she would forbear a husband's wanderings, Adriana loses all patience with such pieties:

> Patience unmov'd! no marvel though she pause [in marrying]—
> They can be meek that have no other cause:
> A wretched soul, bruis'd with adversity,
> We bid be quiet when we hear it cry;
> But were we burd'ned with like weight of pain,
> As much, or more, we should ourselves complain.
>
> (2.1.32–37)

Inevitably Adriana has the last word because here as elsewhere in Shakespeare's plays, platitudinous counsel and painted comforts shatter against the hard reality of suffering and anger.[8] Moreover, Luciana is not simply a spokesman for conventional pieties; she knows too much about the world to have any illusions about the way men treat women. When Antipholus S. woos her, she is not horrified even though she thinks him Adriana's husband. Indignant at his advances, she does not, however, threaten to expose his "adulterous' (indeed, "incestuous") lust to her sister and she does not rebuff him with pious sentences. Instead she pleads with him to be circumspect in his philandering and thereby considerate of his wretched wife. She would have him be prudent if he cannot be faithful:

> If you did wed my sister for her wealth,
> Then for her wealth's sake use her with more kindness:
> Or, if you like elsewhere, do it by stealth,
> Muffle your false love with some show of blindness:
> Let not my sister read it in your eye;
> Be not thy tongue thy own shame's orator:
> Look sweet, speak fair, become disloyalty;
> Apparel vice like virtue's harbinger.
>
> (3.2.5–12)

On other lips this might seem Machiavellian advice, but Luciana's anger shows through her seeming acceptance of the cynical way of the world. She knows too well the emotional dependence of women on men and their willingness to deceive themselves about their marriages if their husbands will give them half a chance:

> . . . make us but believe
> (Being compact of credit) that you love us;
> Though others have the arm, show us the sleeve;
> We in your motion turn, and you may move us.
>
> (3.2.21–24)

It is remarkable that the pathos of a woman's subservience in marriage should be made more explicit in *Errors* than any other comedy to follow. The issue is not explicitly resolved in the play, but then Shakespeare never assumes the role of social critic or reformer. On the other hand, the prominence that he allows Adriana, Luciana, and the Abbess in the denouement of *Errors* makes an important if oblique comment on the relations of women and men.

The concluding scene of *Errors* is a fairly dazzling performance for an apprentice dramatist because most of the characters in the play have active roles in it as pursuers and pursued or as accusers and accused, and most of the accusations are false. The darkness of comic confusion is greatest just before the dawn of comic enlightenment. Insults and threats of violence multiply until the noisy wrangling in the street attracts the attention of the entire cast of characters, including Egeon, who is being taken by the Duke to the place of execution. As ruler of Ephesus, the Duke would be the logical one to straighten out the tangled web of plot, but he is unable to make sense of the conflicting stories and mutual accusations. This muddle demands an arbiter with the fey humor and shrewd insight of the Abbess, who commands attention by force of personality as well as her religious office.[9] Even before she knew that Antipholus was her son, she protected him against his pursuers, and she is unwilling to surrender him until she has cured his seeming distraction. With a woman's instinct for the practical she questions Adriana about the origins of her husband's bizarre behavior. Perhaps he suffered a business loss—perhaps he is in the grip of an "unlawful love." When Adriana says the latter may be the case, the Abbess slyly suggests that Adriana was at fault in not reprehending him severely enough. When she has goaded Adriana into insisting that she reproved Antipholus day and night, in company and alone, the Abbess does an about-face and accuses Adriana of driving her husband mad by the "venom clamors of a jealous woman," which poison "more deadly than a mad dog's tooth."

The comedy of the Abbess's examination of Adriana is directed as much against her role of sage counselor as it is against Adriana, for she has a knack of clothing outrageous exaggerations in ancient saws:

> Thou say'st his sports were hind'red by thy brawls:
> Sweet recreation barr'd, what doth ensue
> But moody and dull melancholy,
> Kinsman to grim and comfortless despair,

and concern for his distracted state. Luciana, at first superior to her sister's
misery, draws closer to her as the play proceeds until she finally champions
her sister's cause to the Abbess and even complains that Adriana is too silent
when she should defend herself. Here, as again in the last acts of *All's Well*,
the growing solidarity of the women and their preeminent roles in determin-
ing the outcome of the play are very important precisely because the attitudes that Antipholus E. and Bertram have toward their wives leave much
to be desired.[11]

Although *Errors* is as successful a beginning in comedy as any playwright
could hope for, one understands why Shakespeare did not write another
comedy in the Plautine mode. His romantic impulse and interest in character
are at odds with the very nature of Roman farce. He will seek to create comic
designs responsive to his romantic imagination in later plays, but he will also
remember the clamorous accusations and perplexed judgments of the discovery scene of *Errors* when he fashions the denouements of *Twelfth Night*, *All's
Well*, *Measure for Measure*, and *Cymbeline*. He knew, of course, that he had
struck comic gold in the Dromios, who are cheeky comedians, not simply
grumbling servants born to be yelled at and thwacked by their masters.
Immediately after Antipholus S. offers his Petrarchan adoration to Luciana,
Dromio S. offers his parody-Petrarchan catalogue of the beauties of the
amorous kitchen wench, a woman of many parts, all of them greasy. The
first of a long line of exuberant clowns that includes Trinculo and Stephano,
the would-be Barnums of *The Tempest*, the Dromios have the last words in
Errors as they exit arm in arm rejoicing in a world that can produce two such
remarkable creatures.

And at her heels a huge infectious troop
Of pale distemperatures and foes to life?

(5.1.

By the time she has finished her explanation, Adriana's household
become a scene out of Hieronymus Bosch, and Luciana protests the di:
tion.[10] The Abbess, one suspects, has not spent all her life inside the wal
a convent. She knows something of men, women, and marriage, and
brisk confident manner is a happy contrast to the helplessness that is
pressed in the speeches of Adriana and Luciana. One doubts that she ev
viewed Egeon as her lord and master, and she takes charge of the denou
ment by inviting all to join in a happy feast of celebration in the abbey.

Although the knots of plot are untangled by ingenious use of accident and
coincidence, the emotional resolution depends on an assurance of the fundamental decency of the characters. The goldsmith graciously clears up the
confusion over the chain; Antipholus E. returns the Courtesan's ring; all
monies and possessions are accounted for and returned to rightful owners.
Antipholus E. also makes the noble gesture of pawning his ducats for his
father's life, and the Duke, ever sympathetic to Egeon, remits the fine.
Whatever the future holds for Antipholus E., he has been tried in the fire of
comic calamity. While his twin has been wined, dined, and showered with
jewels and money by strangers, he has been denied his house, hounded on
all sides, arrested, bound, declared lunatic, subjected to Dr. Pinch, and
abused by family, friends, and servants. Such misadventures could make any
man willing to spend his evenings at home with his wife.

Yet there is no explicit reconciliation of husband and wife in the final scene
of *Errors,* and there is little if any intimation that Antipholus has learned
something about himself during the play. Although the denouements of
Shakespearean comedy may depend on sudden revelations, they never depend on sudden "moral discoveries." They never ask us to believe that all
will be well because one or more of the characters has abruptly become more
sensitive or self-aware. It would not have taken many lines to suggest that
Antipholus E. will be a better husband in the future, but Shakespeare does
not offer this sentimental satisfaction here or in any of the comedies to
follow. An actor can perhaps make Antipholus E.'s parting words to the
Courtesan sound like a farewell, but it does seem tactless of him to return
her diamond with "much thanks for my good cheer." At best these words
are unnecessary; at worst they may seem a last thrust at Adriana, who made
him endure the ministrations of Dr. Pinch.

The reunion of the twins with their father and mother provides a joy that is
sufficient for any comic conclusion. Antipholus S.'s love of Luciana holds
out the possibility of a more loving and ideal marriage to come, and although
Antipholus E. does not draw closer to his wife, she loses her anger in pity

3

Love's Labor's Lost

Like most farces *Errors* has to be seen on stage to be fully appreciated, partly because of its slapstick scenes and partly because its ingenious plot is inspired by the stage—by a playwright's control of the lives of his characters, who enter and exit on cue and meet or avoid each other as his comic plan requires. The relation of *Love's Labor's* to the stage is more difficult to assess. Most scholars agree that it was influenced by Lyly's comedies,[1] but these comedies are undramatic as well as highly artificial and much too static and bloodless to succeed in the Elizabethan public playhouses. To the extent that Shakespeare follows Lyly he merely uses the stage as an arena for witty exchanges and debates that masquerade as dramatic dialogue but do not necessarily further the progress of a dramatic action or create an impression of opposing personalities. Yet Shakespeare's heroes and heroines do not weary us with arid euphuistic discourses. They are sometimes too clever but rarely arch; they are ready to display their ingenuity in puns and paradoxes, but unlike the minor comic figures, who try our patience with elephantine attempts at wit, the lords of Navarre and ladies of France are engagingly bright and entertaining.

The verbal brilliance and dullness of *Love's Labor's* are unique in the comedies. No later play so persistently aims at bravura displays of acrobatic wit and none devotes so much space to figures like Holofernes and Nathaniel, who preen themselves on their turgidities. Unable to account for the lengthy display of verbal pedantry in *Love's Labor's*, we hypothesize that it had a satiric purpose, and since we cannot document the supposed targets, we assume that the play was written for a special audience that could relish every rhetorical flourish, decipher every obscure allusion, and smile knowingly at palpable satiric hits. Few scholarly hypotheses have had so little foundation in evidence as the conjecture that *Love's Labor's* is a satire on the abstruse intellectuality of Chapman's circle, a conjecture that rests on a single puzzling line that may refer to a "school of night" or simply be a compositor's misreading of copy. It may well be that various puzzling and curious lines are topical satiric allusions, but this hypothesis does not account for the other peculiarities of the play or its other artistic shortcomings,[2] whereas the enduring appeal of its heroes and heroines requires no conjectures about arcane intellectual coteries and no footnotes whatsoever.

The static highly patterned scenes of *Love's Labor's* suggest that Shakespeare consciously sacrificed dramatic tension and excitement to an intellectual purpose. The title reinforces that impression by its deliberate, even defiant rejection of conventional expectations: here is a comedy that ends in separation, not reunion, in the postponement of marital joy, not the fulfillment of courtship. Yet this unconventional, unromantic denouement requires an extraordinary authorial intervention at the moment when the course of love can belatedly run smooth. Just when the Princess is beginning to soften her attitude, Marcade enters with news of the death of the French King. In other words, the dramatic action of *Love's Labor's* does not from the beginning lead us to expect that the heroes' passions will be frustrated; on the contrary, from the beginning we anticipate that love will subdue those who try to deny its power. But after showing how passion triumphs over asceticism in Navarre, Shakespeare allows only one scene of wooing in the play and that begins badly and is aborted by the arrival of Marcade. Thus love's labors are not so much lost as arbitrarily ended just as they have begun. The lords of Navarre and ladies of France meet in the third scene (2.1) and not again until the last scene of the play, which is mainly devoted to the heroines' ridicule of their lovers' bumbling attempts at courtship. Indeed, the various couples do not speak frankly to each other until the last two hundred lines. Act 4, scene 3 is devoted to the heroes' discovery that they are all in love and to the decision to renounce their ascetic vow, but almost as much space is given to Armado's passion for Jaquenetta, which unfolds its fantastic plumage in several scenes, and as many lines are given over to the tedious hair splittings of the minor characters.

It is possible that Shakespeare grew so absorbed in writing the Armado and Nathaniel-Holofernes scenes that he failed to realize the lack of movement in his main plot toward its resolution (or antiresolution). More likely, however, he elaborates the pedantries of his minor figures because he needed their bombast to fill out a dramatic conception that does not develop beyond its original premise and become more complex scene by scene. Although Shakespeare turns away from Plautine farce, he substitutes his own simplistic donné for the suppose of identical twins when he shows the lords of Navarre agreeing to an ascetic vow just before the arrival of the French princess. As we expect, the ladies are annoyed by the edict that bars them from the court and the lords fall in love despite their vow. Thus the stage is set for a variety of romantic encounters and rebuffs. But the possibilities inherent in the plot of *Love's Labor's* are never realized because the heroes and heroines are not allowed to pair off in scenes or even moments of individual wooing. Dumaine and Longaville exchange less than a dozen lines with their ladies during the play; the King and Berowne have longer (and sharper) encounters with the Princess and Rosaline but always in the company of others. Since the heroes and heroines speak with one another only very briefly and acrimoniously, the memorable *debats* of the play pit heroine against heroine and hero against hero; they do not allow the men and women to match wits with one another.

By not allowing his lovers to pair off, Shakespeare dooms his play to a certain repetitiousness. The quadrille pattern is amusing, of course; it offers the simple childlike delight of "follow-the-leader." What one hero does, all do; what one heroine says, the others repeat with variations. But wooing and disdain *à quatre* becomes a bit tiresome after a while, and one wonders why Shakespeare bothered to create such intelligent, spirited heroes and heroines if he was not going to allow them independence of action or statement. Although there are more vivid characterizations in *Love's Labor's* than in *Errors,* the persistence of the quadrille pattern robs Longaville, Dumaine, Maria, and Katherine of their individualities; even the glorious verve of Berowne is a gratuitous flourish as far as the plot is concerned because it does not affect the outcome of events. Despite an initial reluctance, he joins the other heroes as anchorites, falls in love when they do, and woos and is rebuffed with them. Like clockwork figures the lords of Navarre and ladies of France move in unison when the hour of love strikes. The repeated patterns of movement would be sufficient if Shakespeare were fashioning a courtly dance rather than a play, but surely he must have known that the formal, restricted, repetitious patterns of a courtly dance do not hold a viewer's attention for long unless the dancers vary and subvert the formality of their prescribed steps by glances and whisperings, an embrace or a kiss.

In a sense the donné of ascetic vows has nothing to do with individuality of character; it is a variation of the ancient literary joke of Cupid's revenge on those who would deny his sovereignty over the human heart. The reason for the denial or defiance does not really matter—any motive from asceticism to cynicism will suffice; all that matters is the ironic peripeteia in which the scoffer is humbled by passion. The earnest Navarre would improve the minds of his youthful companions by mortifying their flesh, but we know that a royal court is a dubious substitute for an anchorite's cell, especially when the court is set in a park and a garden is a traditional milieu for medieval romances and allegories of love. *Love's Labor's* turns the conventional allegory of love upside down, for at Navarre the men are cloistered and protected from the importunities of suitors, and the women are the would-be encroachers who seek to enter the park and are rebuffed by the edict rather than by Honor and Shame.

Berowne's sensible opposition to the plan of a "three year's fast" immediately calls attention to its naiveté, and the impracticality of the venture is underlined by his reminder that an embassy from the French Princess is momentarily expected. As soon as the edict is promulgated, Dull appears with Costard, whom he has arrested for consorting with Jaquenetta. It is not very likely that Navarre and his companions will have greater success in denying the flesh. They are more worldly than spiritual, and their edict to bar women from the court under pain of losing their most precious possession—their tongue—is a schoolboy sneer at chattering females. If one may judge by their naive attempt at courtship, the heroes are almost as innocent of the pleasures of love as they are of the disciplines of asceticism. What they lack in suavity they make up for in enthusiasm; they are incompetent rather than insincere, as the French ladies would soon recognize if they were not more disingenuous in their rejection of their suitors than the heroes are in their amorous protestations.

Navarre's ambition to make his court a world-renowned center of learning could be taken more seriously if his proposed academy were modeled after the ducal academies of Italy in which poetry, music, drama, and neoplatonic philosophy flowered. Trappings of neoplatonism are ubiquitous in the dialogue of *Love's Labor's* but only as themes for ingenious quibbling, as, for example, about light and darkness, or fairness (light complexion) and darkness, or sexual lightness and the heaviness it may produce in women. Like the lords of Navarre, the French ladies have read Ficino and Castiglione; they can be equally clever in their neoplatonic equivocations and they are considerably franker in their double-entendres than their suitors. They could be the ladders by which their lovers ascend from earthly passion toward the knowledge of spiritual truths, but Shakespeare will not allow them the honored place at Navarre that women had in the academies of Renaissance Italy. For his plot demands that Navarre's academy have more of the cold ascetic flavor of the northern Renaissance than the warm expansiveness of Florentine humanism.

A search for Hermetic truths was of course one of the currents of Renaissance thought. Navarre's desire to know "things hid and barred . . . from common sense" is echoed in some of Donne's greatest poems, which yearn for the hidden essence of love, and in alchemical philosophy, which also assumes a spiritual purity in the seeker.[3] But Navarre's philosophy is retrograde in temper, for its goal of cloistered mortification of the flesh was one that Renaissance intellectuals associated with an outworn medieval monasticism.

One cannot imagine the ladies of France desiring to lose themselves in arcane studies. Like most of the heroines of the comedies, they have a firm grasp on reality. And unlike Adriana and Luciana of *Errors*, they have a confident sense of their dignity and worth as women, which they will not let men compromise. Wary of the biological consequences of sexual love, about which they broadly jest, they are not eager to give their hearts away, but neither are they antagonistic at first to the lords of Navarre. The edict that bars them from the court insults their womanhood, however. It is doubly insulting to the majesty of the Princess, who comes as a royal ambassador; and she is further angered by Navarre's unwillingness to take her word about the repayment of the debt France owes. If she finds Navarre attractive, she will not admit it, and she will not allow her ladies to fall in love with Navarre's companions, whom they already admire.

If we remember that the Princess is not an idealized figure—that she has a personal reason to take Navarre down a notch or two—we will not over-simplify the action of *Love's Labor's* by turning the heroines into wise tutors of their somewhat shallow wooers. When the heroines gain the upper hand they do not use their advantage graciously, and since they are bent on enjoying their lovers' discomfort, they are not particularly qualified to give lessons in frankness and moderation. Indeed, their scorn is finally more excessive than the heroes' initial discourtesy. Some have suggested that the lords of Navarre must learn plain-speaking from the ladies of France, but that is to ignore the heroines' continual strivings for wit, their pleasure in wordplay, and their readiness to "abuse" language in the manner of the heroes. If Shakespeare's purpose is to protest excessive verbal cleverness, he protests it excessively by providing hundreds more examples than his didac-tic intention requires. He also commits the blunder of making the verbal high-wire acts the chief glory of the play.[4] If Nathaniel and Holofernes are meant to be cautionary figures, they do not persuade us that the desire for verbal cleverness is reprehensible; they merely demonstrate that a simpering or leaden wit is exceedingly tiresome. Moth, on the other hand, is amusing even though he cannot resist a quibble because his wit is quicksilver. He also makes us think better of his master Armado, whom he mercilessly rags, because any fantastico who would hire Moth as a page cannot be all bad.

Unlike Holofernes's pedantic vanities, Armado's affectations are gifts of nature. The only end of his rodomontade is clarity. He gilds the lily of factual description so that there can be no doubt of his meaning, not even a shadow of a doubt, nor the barest scruple of a shadow of a doubt. His passions are genuine, however inflated his manner of expressing them. He loves Jaquenetta beyond reason, and necessarily so, because she was taken consorting with Costard, whose child she is carrying. He loves by the book because all lovers are supposed to derive inspiration from literary sources: witness the lords of Navarre, who express their intimate yearnings in poems that look suspiciously like those in *Tottel's Miscellany*. The only plain speaker in a world of wits and would-be wits is Costard, a worthy successor to the Dromios and progenitor of Launce and Speed. He is incapable of affectation, but he is too capricious to give a sober answer to any question. He also has a talent for equivocation that makes it difficult for the King or Berowne to get the truth out of him, even though he never tries to impress anyone or seem cleverer than he is; like Pompey in *Measure for Measure* he is as honest a reprobate as one would desire to do business with.

Whether Berowne's flights of poetic fancy are less honest than Costard's utterances is hard to say. Artificiality of style expresses native wit and genuine exuberance of feeling at Navarre; verbal ingenuity is for the heroes and heroines a friendly competitive sport that confirms the opposing players' affinities as well as differences. Unlike some Shakespeareans, the lords of Navarre do not take their casuistries too seriously. They have no doubt read some of Shakespeare's sugared, highly conceited sonnets and know what clever punning *will* accomplish. The Hotspurs of the world, unaware of the poetry of their personal idiom, would have truth bluntly spoken, but Hotspur is not a useful model of decorum. Knowing that imaginative play of language is intrinsic to the pleasure of poetry, Shakespeare never insists that sincerity demands plain speaking. Romeo's apostrophe to Juliet's beauty at Capulet's ball is, if anything, more artificial and richly conceited than his earlier lines about Rosaline.[5] Juliet's love is similarly expressed in very elaborate conceits. Since hypocrisy can be blunt and plain-spoken in manner (witness Iago's gruff "honesty"), we have to judge the sincerity of poetic statement by its imaginative conviction and intensity, not its lack of adornment.

Costard knows that words are not in themselves deceptive; on the contrary, the more obviously affected they are, the more they reveal about sham and evasion. The smaller a reward is, the fancier is the name given to it. A guerdon is necessarily worth more in currency than a remuneration because it has, shall we say, less ring to it: tokens of gratitude, like inexpensive presents, are best delivered in elaborate boxes.

After love poems, masked and unmasked embassies, and entertainments fail to soften the hearts of the French ladies, Berowne announces his intention to woo frankly in "russet yeas" and "honest kersey noes." Repeated humiliations have taught him, he says, never again to

>   trust to speeches penn'd,
> Nor to the motion of a schoolboy's tongue,
> Nor never come in vizard to my friend,
> Nor woo in rhyme, like a blind harper's song!
> Taffeta phrases, silken terms precise,
> Three-pil'd hyperboles, spruce affection,
> Figures pedantical—these summer flies
> Have blown me full of maggot ostentation.
>
>   (5.2.402–9)

It does not matter that this dedication to utter simplicity flows forth in a stream of metaphors because the metaphors are instinct with Berowne's contempt for preciosity. To speak more plainly than this, Berowne would have to change his nature, seel up his poet's eye, and lose his sensitivity to the texture of "taffeta phrases" and "silken terms precise." Despite his pledge to reform his hyperboles, Berowne later attributes the wantonness of the heroes' behavior to love rather than conceit and is as casuistic as ever in pleading for forgiveness:

> Therefore, ladies,
> Our love being yours, the error that love makes
> Is likewise yours. We to ourselves prove false,
> By being once false for ever to be true
> To those that make us both—fair ladies, you;
> And even that falsehood, in itself a sin,
> Thus purifies itself and turns to grace.
>
> (5.2.770–76)

What could be plainer!

The heroes are vulnerable to the heroines' scorn, not because they are too ingenious and sophisticated, but because they are too impetuous and un-guarded in their emotions. As soon as they fall in love, they retire to write love poems to their mistresses, as soldiers, statesmen, courtiers, and scholars are supposed to do. Their poems are fairly conventional and derivative but no more so than most Elizabethan love lyrics. Although they will not win any laurels as poets, the lords of Navarre are more competent versifiers than Hamlet, whose rhymes to Ophelia are stumbling; or Orlando, who is absolutely sincere in his love of Rosalind though absolutely pedestrian as a sonneteer. At least Berowne and his colleagues are skilled enough to ra-tionalize their stunning change from anchorites to amorists. They also can wax metaphysical and impress their mistresses with subtle equivocal plays on the meaning of faith and apostasy in love. Since Berowne was most dubious of the monastic vow, it is appropriate that he be the first to confess his love; it is also fitting that he be skeptical of romantic infatuation and unwilling to surrender easily to Dan Cupid, "dread prince of plackets," that comic figure he so often mocked. He will not lose himself in Petrarchan raptures or exaggerate the beauties of Rosaline, she of the velvet brow with two pitch balls for eyes. He knows that his attraction is sexual—he desires her as one who "will do the deed"—and yet he seeks a wife, not a courtly mistress. He looks forward, not to the excitements of wooing, but to the irritations of married life. If he does not achieve Benedick's charm as a lover, it is because he has no opportunity to express his feelings to a Beatrice who tempers her wit with affection. His Beatrice is a Rosaline determined to remain Lady Disdain.

Although Berowne does not bow to convention, it bothers him that by conventional standards Rosaline is the least attractive of the French ladies.

When his secret passion for her is revealed, he labors to prove that her dark complexion is dazzlingly fair, indeed, that only dark is fair, only black is white. No one takes this casuistry seriously, least of all Berowne, who threatens to prove Rosaline fair or talk to doomsday. These heroes are not deceived by their cleverness; no more hyperbolic in their enthusiasms than the usual run of smitten versifiers, they know the difference between verbal extravagance and romantic commitment. Dumaine and Longaville pay fairly conventional tributes to their goddesses, the former in a pretty, garlanded May song, the latter in an earnest sonnet that argues the virtue of breaking his monastic vow. Navarre, attempting a higher metaphysical vein, out-Donnes Donne in elaborating a conceit of a lover's tears. The scene in which the heroes read their love poems aloud does not expose their shallowness of feeling; it frees them from the folly of the ascetic regimen. This is their one brief moment "alone" on stage, their one opportunity to escape or nearly escape the group pattern. It is also one of the few moments in *Love's Labor's* that is intrinsically dramatic in inspiration, for its comedy of multiple eavesdropping depends on the use of the stage as a place to play hide-and-seek, not simply as a platform for witty exchanges.

The heroes are too fond of each other and too good-humored to resent being spied on or exposed, especially when it allows them to love openly and unabashedly. Berowne summons them to the hunt of love, and as earnestly as he had argued that white is black, he proves that they remain true to themselves by breaking their ascetic vows:

> [Let] us once lose our oaths to find ourselves,
> Or else we lose ourselves to keep our oaths.
> It is religion to be thus forsworn:
> For charity itself fulfills the law,
> And who can sever love from charity?
>
> (4.3.358–62)

If this be foolery, it is an honest, forward-looking chop logic that replaces the dusty monasticism of the proposed academy with a neoplatonic credo that is intellectually à la mode;

> From women's eyes this doctrine I derive:
> They sparkle still the right Promethean fire;
> They are the books, the arts, the academes,
> That show, contain, and nourish all the world.
>
> (4.3.347–50)

The wheel has come half-circle: no longer a distraction and bar to learning, women have become the source of all wisdom.

Where the heroes vie with one another in justifying their true affections, the heroines vie with one another in mocking their suitors, and that mockery is less honest than the love poems they receive. For Rosaline, Maria, and Katherine knew the virtues of their suitors and openly praised them at first; afterward, they dutifully take their cue from the Princess's disdain and strain their wits to make a joke of their wooers. "O, he hath drawn my picture in this letter," Rosaline says of Berowne's epistle. The Princess asks, "Anything like?"

> *Ros.* Much in the letters, nothing in the praise.
> *Prin.* Beauteous as ink—a good conclusion.
> *Kath.* Fair as a text B in a copy-book.
> *Ros.* Ware pencils [ho!] let me not die your debtor,
> My red dominical, my golden letter:
> O that your face were not so full of O's!
>
> (5.2.39–45)

Katherine carries the game a step further by describing Dumaine's poem as

> Some thousand verses of a faithful lover.
> A huge translation of hypocrisy,
> Vildly compiled, profound simplicity.
>
> (5.2.50–53)

Is this plain-hearted candor? Or a brittle slander that is falser than Dumaine's expression of love, and a warning of worse to follow? "We are wise girls," the Princess says, "to mock our lovers so." Rosaline adds:

> They are worse fools to purchase mockery so.
> That same Berowne I'll torture ere I go.
> O that I knew he were but in by th' week!
> How I would make him fawn, and beg, and seek,
> And wait the season, and observe the times,
> And shape his prodigal wits in bootless rhymes,
> And shape his service wholly to my device;
> And make him proud to make me proud that jests!
> So pair-taunt-like would I o'ersway his state
> That he should be my fool and I his fate.
>
> (5.2.59–68)

It is hard to say which is more conventional and artificial: Berowne's poetry or Rosaline's determination to play the "cruel fair." The Princess applauds her scheme, "None are so surely caught, when they are catched, / As wit turn'd fool." Portia will express something like this scorn of deliberate fools, but her target is Arragon, whereas Rosaline and the Princess belittle suitors who are like Bassanio.

Let us say the insult of the edict that barred women from the court justifies the heroines' rudeness, and the suddenness with which the heroes turn lovers merits their skepticism. Perhaps this pack of schoolboy wooers, who regard courtship as a May game, deserve the schoolgirl tricks the heroines use to wreck the embassy of love. But then the score is even and some gentler response would seem appropriate. When the chagrined lords return without their vizards, however, the ladies do not relent; they continue to mock the apostasy of their suitors and their Muscovite embassy. Stung by Rosaline's gibes, Berowne confesses the folly of their wooing and declares his love is "sound, sans crack or flaw." When she responds with another clever thrust, one suspects that she and the Princess have come to enjoy this brittle game. It is not until she learns of her father's death that the Princess responds frankly and directly to the heroes' wooing:

> We have receiv'd your letters full of love;
> Your favors, the embassadors of love;
> And in our maiden council rated them
> At courtship, pleasant jest, and courtesy,
> As bombast and as lining to the time.
>
> (5.2. 177–81)

Dumaine rightly protests, "Our letters, madam, show'd much more than jest," and Longaville rightly adds, "So did our looks."

If *Love's Labor's* were by Lyly, it could appropriately end with noble reununciations of desire calculated to flatter a virgin queen. Such denials of human nature would sound ludicrous from the lips of Shakespeare's flesh and blood characters, who are so attractive and suited to one another that one anticipates a happy ending despite the play's ominous title. It will only be a matter of time, one assumes, before the ladies of France drop their roles of cruel fair and respond warmly to their deserving suitors. Unfortunately time runs out on the plot and the wooers of *Love's Labor's*, because the news of the King's death demands the immediate departure of the heroines even while the heroes are still smarting from their recent humiliations. Yet Shakespeare cannot abruptly and arbitrarily conclude his dramatic action by an extrinsic device,[6] and he cannot leave the romantic issues of his play unresolved, especially since he has created the impression that the heroines are a bit chill in their insistent mockery of their suitors. Even before Navarre and his comrades make their last desperate appeal for love, Shakespeare subtly creates the anticipation that their appeal will be answered. Since the Princess placed the chief obstacle in the path of love, she is the one who must remove it. Her innate gentleness and warmth begin to show when the suitors debate whether to allow the Pageant of Worthies to proceed. Navarre would abort the pageant lest it become another source of humiliation. Berowne would have it go on because it is "some policy / To have one show worse than the King's and his company." Navarre still says no, but the Princess "begs" to overrule him:

> That sport best pleases that doth [least] know how:
> Where zeal strives to content, and the contents
> Dies in the zeal of that which it presents.
> Their form confounded makes most form in mirth,
> When great things laboring perish in their birth.
>
> (5.2. 516–20)

This Thesean appreciation of honest amateur efforts contrasts with the readiness of the chagrined heroes to confound the actors of the pageant, while the ladies, all gibes before, are either demurely silent or sweetly sympathetic. Indeed, nothing that the heroines did to unnerve their suitors is quite as bad as the heroes' baiting of defenseless actors who do not deserve this "revenge." Although Berowne makes a shambles of Costard's presentation of Pompey the Great, the Princess pretends that it has given much pleasure: "Great thanks," she says, "Great Pompey." Astonished by Don Armado she asks Berowne, "Doth this man serve God? A' speaks not like a man of God his making"; yet she is all courtesy to him while the lords hardly permit him to speak. They also join forces to disconcert Nathaniel and Holofernes, who tries to keep to his part but finally justly complains, "This is not generous, not gentle, not humble." Moved to genuine sympathy the Princess remarks, "Alas, poor Machabeus, how hath he been baited!" By now it is evident that the impulse to belittle is as native to the quick-witted male as to the clever female. Yet Berowne is still unsatisfied and would have Costard/Pompey do battle with Armado/Hector, knowing that Armado's cowardice will make him ridiculous. This "sport" comes uncomfortably close to the "sport" of the comic duel that Sir Toby forces upon Viola and Sir Andrew. Marcade's entrance is welcome despite his sad news because it ends the baiting of the "worthies."

As if she expected her father to die, the Princess seems to know Marcade's news before he delivers it; now her angry response to Navarre's questioning of her father's word becomes understandable. Despite a heavy heart she greets the news royally, apologizes for the mistreatment of the suitors, and almost admits that she and her women have taken advantage of Navarre's courtesy by overboldness of speech. Now when Navarre makes one last stilted appeal for love, she simply answers, "I understand you not—my griefs are double." She will not "at the latest minute of the hour" grant her love, but her challenge to Navarre to prove the steadfastness of his love leaves no doubt that she loves in return. Indeed, her insistence on a trial of his devotion expresses the ideality of her view of love and marriage, not a dark suspicion about his truth. She will not plight troth with him now because the time, she thinks, is "too short / To make a world-without-end bargain in." These words make clear how sacred wedding vows are to her—a commitment that reaches beyond time itself. Now she speaks of Navarre's apostasy as a "dear guiltiness" to be absolved by a year in a "forlorn and naked hermitage."

> If this austere insociable life
> Change not your offer made in heat of blood;
> If frosts and fasts, hard lodging and thin weeds
> Nip not the gaudy blossoms of your love
> But that it bear this trial, and last love;
> Then at the expiration of the year,
> Come challenge me, challenge me by these deserts,
> And by this virgin palm now kissing thine,
> I will be thine.
>
> (5.2.779–807)

This invitation to love is as warm as that which Juliet extends to Romeo when at the ball she responds to his request for a holy kiss.[7] She seals with her hand a mutual commitment, for she will endure an equal time of religious retreat in grieving for her father.

After Navarre consents, Katherine and Maria also promise loving answers to their suitors in a year, and though the joy of marriage is to be postponed, the testing of love is in itself a romantic notion, indeed, an echo of the testing of chivalric heroes like Gawain in medieval romances. Desiring to be Rosaline's knight, Berowne asks, "What humble suit attends thy answer there. / Impose some service on me for thy love." Her reply is harshly different in tone from those of the other heroines, for she would have Berowne, the most reasonable of the lovers, spend his year of penance in visiting "the speechless sick" and conversing

> With groaning wretches; and your task shall be,
> With all the fierce endeavor of your wit,
> To enforce the pained impotent to smile.
>
> (5.2.851–54)

No wonder that Berowne, alone of the suitors, is dismayed by his lady's answer. Rosaline explains her grotesque demand as salutory to weed the wormwood from Berowne's brain and as a remedy "to choke a gibing spirit" and end his idle scorns. Alas, there is more wormwood in Rosaline's gibes than in Berowne's brain.[8] She enjoys her power over him to the last moment and that is almost too long for a satisfying ending to the play.[9] This sudden change in the emotional weather of the denouement would leave a sense of bitter impasse were it not for the reappearance of Armado to announce the lyrical debate of the Owl and the Cuckoo.

Although the minor figures of *Love's Labor's* are often tiresome, one welcomes their presence here because their songs bring the play to an enchanting conclusion. They turn our attention away from the artifices of courtly wooing to the homely facts of life as it is known to farmers, shepherds, dairymen, and their wives, who make their way to church in winter over icy roads. After so many clever exchanges and barbed remarks the good-natured innocence of the debate is doubly welcome.[10] One might think that the Owl's song should come first to symbolize the days of wintry trial that will end with the spring of love's fulfillment. Yet the Cuckoo rightly begins because he is not love's champion but rather a sophisticated lyricist who paints a somewhat enameled portrait of spring, in which flowers paint meadows and Meissenware shepherds pipe on oaten straws. Turtles tread, and so do unromantic rooks and daws; worse still, the Cuckoo has the last words, which are unpleasing to a married ear.

The Owl's song is no dreary account of wintry nights. It is a lilting celebration of the daily round of life in the countryside. Icicles hang by the wall, milk comes frozen in the pails, and roads turn slippery. Who indeed would know better than Nathaniel the curate the futility of preaching when the coughing of the congregation drowns out the sermon? Springtime is the only pretty ring time; winter is the season of domesticity. If love is not time's fool, it will survive long wintry days when noses turn red and hands greasy; and if the lords of Navarre are steadfast, "frosts and fasts, hard lodging and thin weeds" will not nip "the gaudy blossoms" and gaudy expressions of love. The winter of waiting will be the prelude not only to the joy of sexual union but also to years of contentment before the fire.

Although no later comedy is as artificial as *Love's Labor's*, it was not a sterile experiment in courtly wit. Shakespeare will remember and redeem the fiasco of the pageant of the Worthies in the triumphant performance of "Pyramus and Thisbe" in the last scene of *A Dream*. The bristling encounters of Navarre and France will be reenacted with more sweetness of humor and meeting of minds in the merry wars of Beatrice and Benedick.[11] The writing of *Love's Labor's*, I imagine, convinced Shakespeare of the need for more energetic plotting in his comedies, but he was not willing to abandon his romantic themes by turning back to the plot devices of Roman comedy. Instead he tried to incorporate the variety and excitement of romantic fabling in *Two Gentlemen,* one of the very few plays Shakespeare wrote that invites the scorn of critics by asking the audience to laugh at the actors as well as the characters in the final scene.

4

Two Gentlemen of Verona

Unlike *Errors* and *Love's Labor's*, which are frequently and successfully staged today, *Two Gentlemen* is not often produced and very rarely to critical acclaim. The play is interesting enough to hold an audience's interest despite an unaccountably silly final scene, but not if directors lack confidence in its artistic qualities or reduce its characters to clichés. Silvia often seems to step out of a pre-Raphaelite painting; almost invariably she is golden-haired, ethereal, and pensive. Julia strides forth as quintessential Elizabethan ingenue—sprightly, winsome, remorselessly girlish in doublet and hose. Proteus and Valentine usually appear as all-purpose Elizabethan gallants who are almost indistinguishable from one another in their romantic posturings. Where the low comedy of *Love's Labor's* is often a trial, the low comedy of *Two Gentlemen* often seems its crowning glory on stage because Launce and Speed steal every scene they are in and make their supposed betters look like cardboard figures.

Critics can forgive what is tedious in *Love's Labor's* for the sake of its witty heroes and heroines. They are less patient with the defects of *Two Gentlemen* because none of its characters are as vivid as Berowne or the Princess. Julia rises to poignancy in several scenes; Silvia does not seem to wear well; Proteus is unpleasant and Valentine is coolly observed. One can say that Shakespeare is less engaged in his task of artistic creation in *Two Gentlemen* than he was in *Errors* or *Love's Labor's*, but that impression may be mistaken. It is not easy to assess a play that offers a very romantic dramatic fable and a very detached point of view. We are likely to smile at the melodrama of *Two Gentlemen* and ignore the penetrating insight it offers into the psychology of male rivalry and romantic egotism. We may also fail to appreciate the comedy of crossed purposes and cunning machinations in *Two Gentlemen* because we do not expect to find this kind of ironic plotting in an early comedy, especially one whose heroines are less experienced and wary than the heroines of *Errors* and *Love's Labor's*.

Where other romantic heroines seem precociously wise and knowledgeable about the way of the world, Julia and Silvia seem very innocent and therefore vulnerable. At first Julia cannot imagine the possibility that Proteus may stop loving her or find another woman more desirable. If she is not a storybook heroine she is one who has gained her knowledge of men and women from romantic tales; she has at first the blushing modesty and naive ardor of a schoolgirl. Too prim to admit her love of Proteus, she pretends anger at his wooing and tears up his letter, only to piece it together when her maid Lucetta exits. Unable to bear separation from Proteus, she plans to fly to Milan on "love's wings" to be with him; that journey will be for her a pilgrimage to his "divine perfection." Threatened by an enforced marriage to a dolt, Silvia dares to show her preference for Valentine despite her father's glowerings. She is ready to elope with Valentine and to join him in banishment, but she is also given to lecturing Proteus in a relentlessly high-minded and ultimately comic fashion.

Compared to Julia and Silvia, Proteus and Valentine are worldly wise. They are not necessarily more experienced in love but they are much less innocent in attitude and speak knowingly and unpleasantly of the ways men win the hearts of women. Their emotional responses are also more sophisticated than the heroines' and threaded by egotism. They have read sonnet cycles and mastered the literary language of love; they can embroider their speeches with Petrarchan conceits and neoplatonic sophistries. It is ironic that Proteus, who declares himself love's votary, should prove fickle and predatory. It is more ironic that he does not struggle much against such unworthy desire or feel remorse at jilting Julia. As protean in his scruples he is in his romantic desires, he expounds a religion of love that allows him to worship one saint, abandon her for another goddess, and still remain a true believer. He is a bit more sensitive about his betrayal of Valentine's friendship, but he takes comfort in the romanticist's credo that all's fair in love and war. If he were an allegorical figure, his name alone would account for his giddiness of character; but he cannot be caddish by nature and still worthy of Julia's love and Valentine's friendship. If *Two Gentlemen* is to be a comedy, Proteus must be capable of redemption. He cannot seem morally shapeless; although he falls easily, he must be able to recover his initial nobility.

By reducing the octet of heroes and heroines in *Love's Labor's* to two pairs of lovers, Shakespeare can trace in some detail the emotional and psychological development of Proteus, Julia, and Valentine. At the same time, however, he is content to reduce dramatic setting to a kind of shadowy backdrop against which his romantic fable unfolds. While the proposed academy of Navarre is a literary joke, the court of Navarre is real enough: it has a king, noble lords, retainers, even a pedant, curate, constable, clown, and visiting Spanish fantastico. Similarly, the Ephesus of *Errors* has imaginary substance: streets, houses, inns, even an abbey with abbess, a quack doctor, merchants, a duke, courtesan, jailer, and jeweler. The Verona and Milan of *Two Gen-*

tlemen, however, are little more than place-names, or perhaps scenes on a painted cloth. Where Romeo and Juliet are surrounded in Verona by family, friends, servants, and local citizenry, Proteus and Julia are not part of any social milieu either in Verona or Milan.[1] Because she is not encumbered by family or friends, Julia is not subject to the pressures that continually weigh on Juliet. She can decide on the spur of the moment to steal away in disguise to Milan, and once there to enter into service as a page to Proteus; she is ready to follow her romantic destiny wherever it leads. Proteus's life is somewhat more complicated in that he must obey his father's command to join Valentine in Milan even though he wishes to stay in Verona with Julia. Yet his father exists only for the brief scene in which he sends Proteus off, and Proteus is victimized by his own cleverness, not by an overbearing father. Unwilling to declare his love of Julia, he protests his desire to join Valentine so convincingly that he is given leave, that is, told to do so—a comic irony prophetic of less amusing ironies to come. Silvia's father, the Duke of Milan, has a bit more substance, but he lacks the reality of Capulet although he plays Capulet's role to Silvia's Juliet. Where Capulet comes alive in his joviality and pride, his affection and blusterings, the Duke is the archetypal tyrannical father of legends and folk tale. Sir Thurio and Sir Eglamour are little more than dramatic speech-heads, and the outlaws Valentine meets are anonymous and indistinguishable one from the other, cutthroats supplied, as it were, by central casting. Only Launce, Proteus's comic servant, has a family history of any note. Though his relatives never appear on stage, they assume an almost Dickensian reality in his account of his farewell to his father, mother, sister, dog, and cat. Indeed, Launce's dog is one of the more vivid personalities in the play because we are privy to the intimate details of his canine existence, including his toilet habits.

The comedy of Launce and his dog is just one of the recurring motifs that lend an architectural unity to the episodic plot of *Two Gentlemen.* Montemayor's *Diana* tells of an exchange of letters between the hero, Don Felix/Proteus and the heroine, Diana/Julia, and one between Don Felix and Celia/Silvia, who rejects his wooing. Shakespeare makes the convention of the love letter a source of comedy and a structural device. Where Proteus is too clever for his own good in concocting a story about Julia's letter, she is ingenuous in pretending disinterest in his letter. Silvia is more artful in using the trick of a letter to reveal her love to Valentine, but he is not quick to grasp her intention. The letter motif recurs when the disguised Julia, sent to deliver a love letter from Proteus to Silvia, almost makes the "mistake" of giving her a letter she received from Proteus. The discovery of a letter ruins Valentine's plan to elope with Silvia, and Julia's habit of mixing up letters and rings precipitates the final moral discovery of the play—Proteus's realization of his dastardly behavior. Where Julia has difficulty delivering the correct letter,

Launce has difficulty delivering the correct present to Silvia, who refuses to accept Crab as a love token.

Unless a director draws attention to the letter motif by stage business, it is not likely that many in an audience will note its recurrence. The weightier dramatic and moral contrasts in the play are bound to impress, however. Proteus, the avowed votary of love, proves false in his devotion; Valentine, somewhat skeptical of love despite his name, proves a more flamboyant wooer than Proteus. When the skeptical Valentine turns ardent swain, the ardent Proteus turns Machiavellian schemer. By inventing the character of Valentine, Shakespeare makes Proteus's fall doubly shameful because he violates the bond of friendship as well as his vow of love. Yet there is no intimation that Proteus's affection for Valentine is shallow or suspect; on the contrary, theirs is at first the kind of friendship that Renaissance courtesy books idealize. The opening scene of the play shows two youths who have known one another for years and are completely open and trusting with each other. Playing Benvolio to Proteus's Romeo, Valentine would cure him of love-melancholy by persuading him to complete his education as a gentleman. His teasing is always affectionate; he does not deride Proteus's love of Julia even though he thinks that it prevents him from venturing forth and keeps him "living dully sluggardized at home." He can appreciate Proteus's devotion to Julia and hopes that he will love as deeply and truly himself:

> But since thou lov'st, love still, and thrive therein,
> Even as I would, when I to love begin.
>
> (1.1.9–10)

As his name intimates, Valentine is a romantic like Proteus despite his willingness to play the role of devil's advocate. Their discussion of love is filled with echoes of Elizabethan love poetry, as well it should be, because Valentine is like the unnamed friend of Astrophil who chides him for neglecting the claims of honor and ambition. To be in love, Valentine argues, is to buy scorn with groans,

> Coy looks with heart-sore sighs; one fading moment's mirth
> With twenty watchful, weary, tedious nights:
> If happ'ly won, perhaps a hapless gain;
> If lost, why then a grievous labor won;
> However—but a folly bought with wit,
> Or else a wit by folly vanquished.
>
> (1.1.29–35)

This rebuke is far gentler than the one that causes Astrophil to cry out in Sidney's Sonnet 14:

> Alas, have I not pain enough, my friend,
> Upon whose breast a fiercer gripe doth tire
> Than did on him who first stole down the fire,
> While Love on me doth all his quiver spend;
> But with your rhubarb words ye must contend,
> To grieve me worse in saying that desire
> Doth plunge my well-form'd soul even in the mire
> Of sinful thoughts, which do in ruin end?[2]

Like Astrophil's counselor, Valentine warns Proteus not to let love become his master. Proteus replies:

> Yet writers say: as in the sweetest bud
> The eating canker dwells, so eating love
> Inhabits in the finest wits of all.

Valentine uses the same sonnet imagery to describe the sickness of love:

> And writers say: as the most forward bud
> Is eaten by the canker ere it blow,
> Even so by love the young and tender wit
> Is turn'd to folly, blasting in the bud,
> Losing his verdure, even in the prime,
> And all the fair effects of future hopes.
>
> (1.1.42–50)

Although Proteus will not be argued out of love, he does not angrily deny Valentine's premises, for he shares to some extent Valentine's ambivalence about love, an ambivalence that can be found in Elizabethan sonnets that speak of love both as a sublime mystery and an affliction or unmanly dotage.[3] The term *folly* runs through Valentine's admonitions, as does the suggestion that the expense of spirit in love is not worth the fleeting ecstasy it may bring. It is a rose but also a canker that can blast the bud of youth. When Valentine leaves, Proteus admits his own divided "Sidneyan" thoughts:

> He after honor hunts, I after love:
> He leaves his friends, to dignify them more;
> I [leave] myself, my friends, and all, for love.
> Thou, Julia, thou hast metamorphis'd me,
> Made me neglect my studies, lose my time,
> War with good counsel, set the world at nought;
> Made wit with musing weak, heart sick with thought.
>
> (1.1.63–69)

Although this mood passes, Proteus is nevertheless afraid to tell his father that he loves and would stay in Verona, because the ideal of manhood to which Valentine and his father allude demands travel, study, and honorable accomplishments that win applause from other men.

Montemayor need not explain Don Felix/Proteus's wandering affections because such emotional vagaries are the sine qua non of romantic tales and the least of the trials a heroine must endure. For Shakespeare, however, Proteus's lack of fidelity is a crucial issue, one that deserves extended exposition. He does not attempt to give Proteus much psychological depth or complexity; rather, he implicates Valentine in Proteus's fall in a way that illuminates the nature of male egotism. Like Proteus, Valentine appears at his best in the first scene of the play, in which they are devoted friends. At the court of Milan he proves a sharp-tongued, aggressive rival to Thurio, whom he openly insults and baits. He generously praises Proteus to the Duke as a complete gentlemen, but when Proteus arrives at court, he preens himself on the possession of Silvia's heart. He asks her to confirm Proteus's welcome "with some special favor," and "entertain him / To be my fellow-servant to your ladyship."

Alone with Proteus Valentine speaks of himself as one humbled by love, but his praise of Silvia is arrogant. He would have Proteus agree that Silvia is a heavenly saint, divine, "sovereign to all creatures on the earth" including Julia, who

> shall be dignified with this high honor—
> To bear my lady's train, lest the base earth
> Should from her vesture chance to steal a kiss,
> And of so great a favor growing proud,
> Disdain to root the summer-swelling flow'r,
> And make rough winter everlastingly.
>
> (2.4.158–63)

Proteus, who can sympathize with Valentine's rapture, is astonished by this blatant egotism. He asks, "Why, Valentine, what braggadism is this?" Like many sonneteers, Valentine protests that his most extravagant praise is not adequate to his mistress's worth; then he proceeds to describe that worth as *his* treasure:

> Why, man, she is mine own,
> And I as rich in having such a jewel
> As twenty seas, if all their sand were pearl,
> The water nectar, and the rocks pure gold.
>
> (2.4.168–71)

While the sentiment is conventional, Valentine's lines become unpleasantly provocative in their dramatic context: they make an envious Proteus eager to win Silvia for himself. Hardly in the grip of irresistible desire, Proteus wonders in soliloquy if it is his eye

> or Valentinus' praise,
> Her true perfection, or my false transgression,
> That makes me reasonless, to reason thus?
>
> (2.4.196–98)

Proteus does not try to convince himself that Silvia is more beautiful than Julia. He knows that he desires her because Valentine adores her and boasts of her love. Abandoning Julia, he pursues Silvia for the same reason Demetrius will abandon Helena and pursue Hermia, who is Lysander's love. It is the thrill of rivalry that sets the price of the women for whom men compete. Proteus's knowledge of his motives is fascinating because he does not pretend to be overwhelmed by passion. He employs neoplatonic sophistry to justify a sober determination to be blinded by Silvia's "perfections":

> 'Tis but her picture I have yet beheld,
> And that hath dazzled my reason's light,
> But when I look on her perfections,
> There is no reason but I shall be blind.
> If I can check my erring love, I will;
> If not, to compass her I'll use my skill.
>
> (2.4.209–14)

When Proteus next appears, his "struggle" is over. He speaks coolly of his perjured state in lines that are free of anguish. The flatness of his statements leaves no doubt that his excuses are perfunctory. He knows that he should be torn by emotional and moral conflict, but he does not feel that turmoil, and thus his equivocations are as perfunctory as a classroom recitation:

> I cannot leave to love, and yet I do;
> But there I leave to love where I should love.
> Julia I lose, and Valentine I lose:
> If I keep them, I needs must lose myself;
> If I lose them, thus find I by their loss—
> For Valentine, myself; for Julia, Silvia.
>
> (2.6.17–22)

Although it is becoming fashionable to interpret Shakespeare's characters by reference to their linguistic idiosyncracies, as if the key to their behavior lay in the speech centers of their brains, Proteus is not duped by his verbal ingenuity any more than the lords of Navarre are duped by the witty paradoxes they use to rationalize their defection from monasticism. Unlike them, he takes no pleasure in his rationalizations, which flatly express his calculating egotism in a torrent of "I's." Julia is also extravagant in her rhetoric in the early scenes of the play; she declares her love of Proteus in literary hyperboles that closely resemble his.[4] Making a religion out of her love, she declares that when she rejoins Proteus in Milan, she will rest as "a blessed soul doth in Elysium." She speaks of herself as one who is unable to resist the hot fire of her need for Proteus even as Proteus says he is unable to resist love's commandment to betray Julia and Valentine. It is ironic, of course, that Proteus announces his treachery just before Julia insists upon his sincerity and truth, his inviolable oaths and immaculate thoughts, to the skeptical Lucetta. But Proteus's faithlessness does not make her devotion folly. If her hyperboles are naive, her faith in Proteus recalls the meaning of the romantic ideal that he betrays. We would not have Julia more sober and rational in love; we would have Proteus more worthy of a love that naturally speaks in poetic hyperbole.

The scenes of intrigue in act 3, in which Proteus, the Duke, and Valentine match wits, are not in Montemayor. They are composed by a Shakespeare who has Brooke's *Romeus and Juliet* immediately in mind and who is probably beginning to think through the design of *Romeo and Juliet*. In 2.7 Lucetta plays the Nurse to Julia's Juliet, whom she fears will find herself in a fool's paradise. In act 3 Silvia and Valentine play Juliet and Romeo to the Duke's Capulet and Thurio's Paris, and like Juliet and Romeo, they are separated from one another when Valentine is banished from Milan. Or, more correctly, they are not victimized by malicious fortune but by a dissembling Proteus who makes gratitude to the Duke an excuse for revealing their plan to elope. Tactful as well as two-faced, Proteus asks that his role as informer not be revealed to Valentine, who is, after all, his dearest friend; the Duke, a man of some delicacy, promises on his honor to keep secret Proteus's good deed, his "honest care." He also proves that he can be as cunning as Proteus when he undertakes to outwit Valentine. First he pretends to take him into his confidence; he solicits his help in revenging himself on his ungrateful daughter by disinheriting her and marrying again. Asked by the Duke for advice in wooing his lady, Valentine, who just before was breathless in adoration of Silvia, answers like an experienced roué who knows precisely how to conquer a woman:

> Win her with gifts, if she respect not words:
> Dumb jewels often in their silent kind
> More than quick words do move a woman's mind.
>
> (3.1.89–91)

Many men have sneered more openly at female vanity, but the cynicism of Valentine's advice deepens as he explains the psychology of feminine coyness. When a woman seems to deny, Valentine says, she does so to invite, because "the fools are mad, if left alone":

> Flatter and praise, commend, extol their graces;
> Though ne'er so black, say they have angels' faces.
> That man that hath a tongue, I say is no man,
> If with his tongue he cannot win a woman.
>
> (3.1.102–5)

This cynicism is not a pose that Valentine must adopt to deceive the Duke.[5] It is freely offered in response to the Duke's complaint that his Veronese lady is "nice and coy" and unresponsive to his "aged eloquence." The other side of the coin of romantic idealism, Valentine's patronizing view of women is expressed more darkly when Claudio turns on Hero in *Much Ado:* that is to say, men make goddesses of unsullied virgins because they must be absolutely unlike the women they can casually bed.

Proteus, who volunteers to slander Valentine on Thurio's behalf, also offers cynical advice on how to win Silvia. He would have Thurio "tangle her desires" with "wailful sonnets" filled with "serviceable vows"—a pretty play on words:

> Say that upon the altar of her beauty
> You sacrifice your tears, your sighs, your heart;
> Write till your ink be dry, and with your tears
> Moist it again, and frame some feeling line
> That may discover such integrity.
>
> (3.2. 72–76)

Donne, a great visitor of women, could testify to the soundness of this advice, for he writes of purchasing a woman's love with vows, tears, and letters.[6]

At moments like these the comic ironies of *Two Gentlemen* are almost as brittle as those of *Measure for Measure.* Indeed, the machinations in which Proteus, Valentine, and the Duke engage are the kind of ironic plotting more commonly found in Elizabethan tragedy than comedy. Knowing that Valentine intends to steal Silvia away with a "corded ladder," the Duke would have him suggest a device to have access to a lady kept from "resort of men." The too-confident Valentine recommends the kind of ladder he has concealed under his cloak, and is hoist by his own petard when the Duke borrows his cloak, ostensibly to see how it fits, and discovers the ladder and a letter to Silvia about their elopement. Valentine laments his fate in lines that anticipate Romeo's self-pitying complaints in Friar Lawrence's cell. Ever the good friend, Proteus offers sage Lawrencian counsel; he also promises to deliver Valentine's letter "in the milk-white bosom of thy love," a promise that mingles false friendship with barely concealed sexual desire.

For all his cleverness, Valentine cannot see the obvious evidences of Proteus's falseness; it never occurs to him that his dear friend was the only one who knew of his planned elopement and could have betrayed it to the Duke. Launce, however, knows that his "master is a kind of knave." Like Dromio S., he is also adept at parodying the romantic raptures of his master. Swearing that teams of horses will not pluck him from the identity of the woman he loves, he proceeds to tell who she is, and with Speed as his straight man he compiles a mock-Petrarchan catalogue of her excellencies. She is not attractive, chaste, intelligent, or sweet to kiss; on the other hand, she is not talkative, can spin, knit, and brew, and has more wealth than faults. Who could ask for anything more? Immediately after Proteus's extravagant farewell to Julia, Launce enters to describe his tear-drenched farewell to his family, one that was so moving his cat wrang her paws. Unlike Proteus, who sacrifices all to egotism, Launce sacrifices himself to protect his dog Crab, who had the bad manners to piss under the Duke's table. Crab may be a "cruel-hearted" cur, but Launce is a dog's best friend.

Like Launce, Silvia immediately recognizes Proteus's duplicity and rebuffs his wooing with earnest admonitions. Bad luck attends his every attempt to court her: Launce brings her the wrong dog; Julia nearly offers her the wrong letter. The exquisite song with which he serenades her succeeds only in exposing his disloyalty to the disguised Julia. The words of his love song have a significance he could not possibly understand, for they underscore his betrayal of his vow of love. Men may claim that they lie and scheme in pursuit of beauty but the song insists on the oneness of beauty and truth:

> Who is Silvia, what is she,
> That all our swains command her?
> Holy, fair, and wise is she;
> The heaven such grace did lend her,
> That she might admired be.
>
> (4.2. 39–43)

After Proteus, Valentine, and the Duke demonstrate their skill at dissimilation, Julia and Silvia demonstrate their nobility. A child when she left Verona to see her "saint," Julia must either be shattered by the discovery of Proteus's infidelity or learn how to deal with such realities. She faces the crisis of Proteus's faithlessness as Juliet faces her mother and father's importunities after the banishment of Romeo—with a courage and self-possession that allows poignant touches of humor.[7] At first her anguish shows and prompts the Host to ask, "How now, / Are you sadder than you were before?

How do you, man? The music likes you not.
Julia. You mistake; the musician likes me not.
Host. Why, my pretty youth?
Julia. He plays false, father.
Host. How, out of tune on the strings?
Julia. Not so; but yet so false that he grieves my very heart-strings.
Host. You have a quick ear.
Julia. Ay, I would I were deaf; it makes me have a slow heart.

(4.2. 55–65)

More affecting than her earlier declarations of love, Julia's restraint persuades us that she is stronger than the man who betrays her, strong enough to continue to love and even pity him because he does not know that his shame has been exposed.[8] She has the composure to enter into Proteus's service and become his messenger to Silvia just as Viola will serve as Orsino's ambassador of love to Olivia in *Twelfth Night.*

The proxy wooing scene in *Two Gentlemen* is almost as memorable as its analogue in *Twelfth Night.* Like Viola, Julia is determined to be an incompetent wooer; indeed, she very nearly discloses her true identity by giving Silvia the wrong letter to read. She cannot, however, regard her rival as an adversary because Silvia scorns Proteus's suit and speaks feelingly of the woman he has jilted. Thus even though Silvia does not know that she speaks to Julia, the heroines share a moment of intimacy and sympathy that is a vivid contrast to the ugly machinations that preceded it. Like Viola, Julia obliquely reveals the feelings she cannot openly express. She pretends to describe to Silvia how Proteus's jilted love exposed the roses of her cheeks to wind and sun, neglecting herself because her beauty had become meaningless to her.[9] Asked how tall Julia was, she answers:

> About my stature; for at Pentecost,
> When all our pageants of delight were play'd,
> Our youth got me to play the woman's part,
> And I was trimm'd in Madam Julia's gown,
> Which served me as fit, by all men's judgments,
> As if the garment had been made for me;
> Therefore I know she is about my height.
> And at that time I made her weep agood,
> For I did play a lamentable part.
> Madam, 'twas Ariadne passioning
> For Theseus' perjury and unjust flight;
> Which I so lively acted with my tears
> That my poor mistress, moved therewithal,
> Wept bitterly; and would I might be dead
> If I in thought felt not her very sorrow.

(4.4. 158–72)

After the height of inspiration reached in this scene, the fiasco of the last act of *Two Gentlemen* is all the more puzzling. It is as if Shakespeare, no longer interested in his play, patches together a denouement that is very close to burlesque. His lack of engagement in working out the plot shows in the flatness of Sir Eglamour, who helps Silvia to flee Milan; he is a literary shadow, a fairytale knight who vowed a life of chastity at the grave of his only love. If Sir Eglamour had more reality as a character he might convince us, despite Proteus and Valentine, that men are capable of nobility in love. But he is as fictitious as the outlaw band Valentine meets in exile. One part mafioso, one part Sigmund Romberg, with just a dash of D'Oyle Carte for comic flavor, they are refreshingly candid about their line of work. Valentine's suave manner does not take them in. When he addresses them as "my friends," they answer, "That's not so, sir; we are your enemies." Ah, but that deferential "sir" suggests a willingness to listen, especially since they find him "a proper man." A more ingenuous hero would have told them the true story of his banishment. Valentine, however, invents a tale that would win any outlaw's heart: namely, that he was exiled for killing a man. Here is a kindred spirit, someone they can trust and admire, although they do wonder that he was banished "for so small a fault." Since confessions are in order, one outlaw says that he was banished for practicing to steal away a lady; another "for a gentlemen / Who in my mood, I stabbed unto the heart"; a third, for "suchlike petty crimes as these." They make Valentine an offer he cannot refuse: either he will stay and be their general, or refuse and die. Since they are sensitive to rebuffs, they would not want him bragging to others that he turned them down. Like Valentine (and Proteus) the outlaws are romantics at heart—they love and hate at first sight.

The forest in which the outlaws live has a strange psychological effect on all travelers, for with few exceptions those who enter leave their common sense behind. It is not improbable that all the characters would meet in the forest or that Proteus should rescue Silvia from the outlaws almost in sight of Valentine. It is to be expected that Silvia will again reject Proteus's advances because she denied them before with tight-lipped disapproval. When he had finished his song, she told him to go home to bed:

> Thou subtile, perjur'd, false, disloyal man,
> Think'st thou I am so shallow, so conceitless,
> To be seduced by thy flattery,
> That hast deceiv'd so many with thy vows?
>
> (4.2.95–98)

In the forest Silvia's earnestness reaches new heights. Proteus, who has rescued her from cutthroats, asks for "one fair look." She replies:

> Had I been seized by a hungry lion,
> I would have been a breakfast to the beast
> Rather than have false Proteus rescue me.
>
> (5.4.33–35)

We may smile at such high-mindedness, but Proteus is willing to reduce his request from "one fair look" to "one calm look." Unwilling to negotiate, Silvia continues to harp on his betrayal of Julia and Valentine, and declares that having rent his faith to Julia, Proteus cannot have any faith left unless he began with two,

> And that's far worse than none; better have none
> Than plural faith, which is too much by one.
>
> (5.4.51–52)

Such flat-footed literalism and bad punning will sound comically right in the speeches of Helena in *A Dream*. Here it serves only to reduce Silvia to caricature. Proteus is not amused. He has tried to do the decent thing and been rewarded with pious rebukes. The only alternative left is to ravish her.

Since Valentine has been in the forest longer than Silvia, Proteus, and Julia, he proves more fatuous than they. He rescues Silvia from a fate worse than death only to lose himself in self-pity for having a friend as despicable as Proteus. Without a word to Silvia and without any rage at her attempted ravishment, he regretfully tells Proteus, "I am sorry I must never trust thee no more." Seared by these words, Proteus immediately repents of all his villainy and asks forgiveness; Valentine, ever the soul of courtesy, offers not only forgiveness but his interest in Silvia to prove that his love is "plain and free." Silvia is understandably speechless; Julia has the presence of mind to swoon and to remember afterward that she neglected to give Silvia Proteus's gift of a ring. By producing the wrong ring, Julia gains Proteus's attention and, revealing her true identity, she adds the strangest rebuke of all of those already leveled by Silvia and Valentine. She does not mention Proteus's fickleness, betrayals, lies, and so on. She calls attention to her page's habit, which she says should make him blush:

> Be thou asham'd that I have took upon me
> Such an immodest raiment—if shame live
> In a disguise of love!
>
> (5.4.105–7)

Struck to the heart by an awareness of how much Julia has sacrificed for him, Proteus becomes again her adoring lover.

Nothing remains but to reconcile the Duke to Silvia and Valentine, who

welcomes him cordially at the same time that he plays the roaring boy to
Thurio:

> Thurio, give back, or else embrace thy death;
> Come not within the measure of my wrath.
> Do not name Silvia thine; if once again,
> [Milan] shall not hold thee. Here she stands,
> Take but possession of her with a touch:
> I dare thee but to breathe upon my love.
>
> (5.4.126–31)

In the face of these hysterical threats, Thurio replies that only a fool would
risk his life for a girl who loves him not. This common sense infuriates the
Duke, who can stomach anything but a quitter:

> The more degenerate and base art thou
> To make such means for her as thou hast done,
> And leave her *on such slight conditions.* [emphasis mine]
>
> (5.4.136–38)

Perhaps the presence of Valentine's outlaw band, brandishing their knives,
has something to do with the Duke's decision to award Silvia to Valentine as
Valentine would have awarded her to Proteus. In any event, all ends well
even for the outlaws, who are pardoned by the Duke on Valentine's recom-
mendation of them as "reformed, civil, full of good / and fit for great
employment."

Whatever way one stages the concluding scene of *Two Gentlemen*—in
straight-faced or mock-heroic style—it turns out to be a bad joke on the
characters, the play, and the actors. The joke would be more understandable
if Shakespeare had allowed his plot to become so muddled or implausible
that there was nothing left to salvage by the final scene, but in fact he has to
go out of his way to make a travesty of the denouement by turning Valentine, Silvia, and the Duke into virtual idiots. The most obvious explanation
for this act of sabotage would be that while writing *Two Gentlemen,* Shakespeare became increasingly convinced that romantic melodrama was a blind
alley in comedy. Although he decided not to scrap what he had already
finished, he was indifferent to how he brought his play to a conclusion and
determined to amuse himself at its expense. But perhaps the opposite is
true—perhaps *Two Gentlemen* trails off into absurdity because Shakespeare's
inspiration leaped so far ahead of his immediate task that he found it
impossible to concentrate again on his original dramatic conception. The
title announces that the play is going to center on a pair of romantic heroes,
and the first three acts focus on their adventures in love. In writing the

fourth act, however, Shakespeare finds the emotional relationship of his heroines far more interesting then the rivalry of his heroes. Perhaps by accident he discovered what is to be an essential theme in succeeding comedies, the bond of friendship and love that unites their heroines: Hermia and Helena, Portia and Nerissa, Beatrice and Hero, and Rosalind and Celia. It is as if he suddenly understood the artistic impulse that made him create Adriana and Luciana even though their relationship is largely extrinsic to the plot of *Errors*. Suddenly he stands on the threshold of possibilities as splendid as the Olivia-Viola scenes of *Twelfth Night*, and he does not much care how he finishes *Two Gentlemen*.

He will create another pair of rivalrous heroes in *A Dream*, but their rivalry is only a single thread in the complex weave of the play. Indeed, it is less interesting in itself than in its effect on the friendship of Hermia and Helena, whose perplexity is the chief source of comic delight in the romantic scenes in the forest.

5

The Taming of the Shrew

Error's, Love's Labor's, and *Two Gentlemen* differ from one another in many artistic respects, but they agree that love is—or should be—a joyous mutual commitment. *The Taming of the Shrew* is unlike these early comedies, indeed unlike any of Shakespeare's comedies, in its depiction of courtship as a Punch-and-Judy farce in which a bully-boy hero imposes his will on a wild-eyed but ultimately supine heroine. It is one of the dependable box office hits of contemporary Shakespeare festivals because it can be pitched to the lowest denominator of audience taste with mugging and leering, shouting, thumping, and chasing across the stage, and it can therefore be warmly recommended by reviewers as an "Elizabethan romp." Since the slapstick is in the text and the comedy is not particularly subtle, there is something to be said for this approach, which by vulgarizing the action and reducing the characters to cartoon figures makes the taming too preposterous to offend.[1]

Reading the text of *The Shrew*, however, forces one to acknowledge and respond to the speeches that unfold Petruchio's coarseness of temper as well as those which suggest that Kate is not a virago who has to be subdued by coercion and humiliation. It is easy to rejoice when an overbearing termagant is put in her place, especially when she is humbled by her long-suffering husband. It is less easy to enjoy the abject submission of a wife to a man determined to make her obedient to his every whim. One way that critics have attempted to rescue *The Shrew* from its inherent unpleasantness is to claim that appearances are deceiving, that Petruchio is really sensitive and loving, and that Kate is a subtle manager of the husband she pretends to obey. The final solution to the problem of *The Shrew* is to follow Petruchio's example and insist that night is day, male is female, and that the knockabout quality of Petruchio and Kate's marriage is proof that their love is more genuine than the conventionally romantic wooing of Bianca and Lucentio.[2] It is certainly true that Kate and Petruchio kiss one another more often on stage than any other lovers in the comedies, and they do encounter each other—in an Esalen sense—more fully than do Beatrice and Benedick or

Portia and Bassanio. If lips, hands, and parts of bodies collide, can the meeting of true minds be far behind?

The most strenuous efforts of critical casuistry can not endow *The Shrew* with the humanity that characterizes every other comedy by Shakespeare. Although fierce, vindictive, terrible women are depicted in some of his tragedies and histories, Kate is the only shrew who appears in his plays, and the only female character of violent temper in any of the comedies. Helena and Hermia become adversaries only after Puck's magical charms have miscarried and Lysander and Demetrius have begun to bully Hermia in an ungentlemanly fashion; even then their spat is brief and restrained compared to the heroes' huffing and puffing. Other heroines incline to be patient and long-suffering, or, if they are outspoken, it is in the manner of Beatrice and the Princess of *Love's Labor's*. I do not mean that Shakespeare could not once have decided to write a comedy about a shrewish woman, even though he turns the nagging shrew of *Menaechmi* into the sympathetic Adriana. I mean rather that he would not have chosen to write a play as brittle as *The Shrew*, and I cannot believe that he asks us to applaud the means Petruchio uses to subdue Kate and the success he achieves. Although Kate is much meeker at the close of *The Shrew* than she is at its beginning, she does not grow in self-knowledge or maturity; she is not more sensitive to or more considerate of others in the last scene than before, even though she has been trained to heel, fetch, and carry. Petruchio's attitude toward Kate also does not change for the better by the final scene of the play. He never thinks of his wife as a loving companion or a helpmeet or as his other self. She is his house, his barn, and his chattel, and when her training is complete, she is his obedient hawk whose stooping at command wins him a handsome wager. He does not abuse and humiliate her because any milder effort would obviously fail to moderate her behavior. Almost from the start Petruchio's therapy is more violent than Kate's misconduct, and very soon it lacks any justification at all. At their first meeting he is very engaging; his refusal to admit her shrewishness, his supreme confidence, and his compliments disarm her completely. Afterward his methods are as subtle as hammer blows, and he would by using them bring most women to their knees.

The Shrew stands apart from all the other comedies, not only in its roughhouse treatment of love and marriage, but also in the fact that it alone very closely resembles another Elizabethan play, *The Taming of a Shrew*, which was printed in 1594. Nineteenth-century scholars generally assume that *A Shrew* was the chief source of Shakespeare's play, but in the twentieth century Peter Alexander and J. Dover Wilson argued that *A Shrew* is a bad quarto, a memorial reconstruction of *The Shrew*.[3] This view has gained currency even though R. A. Houk and G. I. Duthie, who made the most detailed analyses of the two texts, concluded that *A Shrew* is more likely to be a bad quarto of a lost play from which *The Shrew* derives than a bad quarto of *The Shrew.*[4] They thought it probable that the lost text was an earlier Shakespearean version of the play, but if one looks beyond the verbal parallels and the varying treatments of the subplots in both texts that Houk and Duthie chiefly examine, one realizes that Shakespeare's conception of the taming of the shrewish woman is significantly different from that in *A Shrew.*[5] Whether we regard *A Shrew* as a corrupt version of the play Shakespeare revised, or, as J. W. Shroeder has fairly recently claimed, as a direct source of *The Shrew,*[6] it sheds valuable light on Shakespeare's play precisely because it reveals that Shakespeare's version of the wife-tamer is both coarser and less attractive as a dramatic figure than his counterpart in *A Shrew.* And that very curious fact may provide a central clue to the other anomalies in the play.

Ferando, the Petruchio of *A Shrew,* decides to woo Kate before his friends approach him to undertake the task, and spurred on by her father's offer of a handsome dowry, he is determined to make her "yield to grant me love." Petruchio's attention is drawn to Kate by Hortensio, who describes her as very rich although so shrewish that he would not wish her to become Petruchio's wife. Whether his future wife will have a nasty temper or not does not matter to Petruchio, for he comes "to wive it wealthily in Padua; / If wealthily, then happily in Padua." It also does not matter to him if his bride be foul, old, or as curst as Xantippe as long as she be rich. *A Shrew* makes it clear that Ferando assumes a ruffian behavior to tame his shrew. At every stage of the taming, he explains in dialogue or aside what his aim is in behaving like a madcap and how he expects his gambits to succeed. He never thinks of breaking Kate's spirit and he does not enjoy bullying or intimidating her. He never plays the roaring boy in the manner of Petruchio. Questioned about the base attire he wears to his wedding, he explains that

> when my wife and I am married once,
> She's such a shrew, if we should once fall out,
> She'll pull my costly suits over mine ears;
> And therefore am I thus attir'd awhile.[7]

Asked the same question by Tranio, Petruchio offers no explanation except that Kate is being married to him, "not unto my clothes." When Ferando refuses to stay for the wedding feast, Kate exclaims, "I'll have my will in this as well as you." He amiably replies:

> Aye, Kate, so thou shalt, but at some other time.
> Whenas thy sisters here shall be espous'd,
> Then thou and I will keep our wedding day
> In better sort than now we can provide.
> For here I promise thee before them all,
> We will ere long return to them again.

> Come, Kate, stand not on terms. We will away.
> This is my day. Tomorrow thou shalt rule,
> And I will do whatever thou commands.

This dialogue takes a nastier turn in *The Shrew.* Tranio and then Gremio entreat Petruchio to stay for dinner, but he refuses. Kate adds her humble request, "Let me entreat you." He mockingly replies, "I am content." "Are you content to stay?" she asks.

> *Pet.* I am content you shall entreat me stay,
> But yet not stay, entreat me how you can.
> *Kath.* Now if you love me stay.
>
> (3.2. 200–204)

His answer is to call for his horse. Seeing his desire to humiliate her, she refuses to go:

> I see a woman may be made a fool,
> If she had not a spirit to resist.
>
> (3.2. 220–21)

Petruchio's reply is to command the other guests to go to the feast and "carouse full measure to [Kate's] maidenhead." When they hesitate, he warns them:

> Nay, look not big, nor stamp, nor stare, nor fret,
> I will be master of what is mine own.
> She is my goods, my chattels, she is my house,
> My household stuff, my field, my barn,
> My horse, my ox, my ass, my any thing.
>
> (3.2. 228–32)

Instead of promising to return to celebrate his wedding day when Bianca marries, Petruchio sweeps Kate off, threatening to strike anyone who stands in the way.

If one did not know that Kate is an intolerable shrew, one would think that her behavior at her wedding is remarkably restrained given the anxiety and humiliation she suffers from Petruchio's behavior. And if one did not know that Petruchio is loving and caring beneath his coarse exterior, one would think that he is an insensitive boor who enjoys his outrageous conduct regardless of whom it offends. Ferando blusters only at his servant in the wedding scene of *A Shrew;* Petruchio insults everyone in his determination to make a shambles of his wedding. According to Gremio, he swore at the priest, called for wine, which he caroused "and threw the sops all in the sexton's face" because he did not like his beard. Then "he took the bride about the neck / And kissed her lips with . . . clamorous smack." This conduct made Gremio so ashamed that he left the church. Compared to Petruchio, Kate was "a lamb, a dove" during the ceremony. So the lessons in moderation and restraint begin.

Shakespeare's decision to coarsen Ferando would be easier to understand if he also made Kate wilder and more intransigent and therefore in need of rougher treatment than she receives in *A Shrew*. She is readier to use her hands than the Kate of *A Shrew*; she breaks a lute over her tutor's head, binds her sister to a chair, and threatens her with worse. On the other hand, the Kate of *A Shrew* is cruder in thought and speech than Shakespeare's heroine. When Ferando's servants deny her food, she threatens, in true virago fashion, to tear the flesh from her face and eat it. It is hard to imagine such words from Shakespeare's Kate, who never rages like an animal and is capable of kindness to servants. Grumio tells how Petruchio beat him because Kate's horse stumbled on the journey and "how she waded through the dirt to pluck him off me." Curtius observes that "by this reck'ning [Petruchio] is more shrew than she." When Petruchio strikes a servant at supper she begs him to have patience with "a fault unwilling," and pleads with him to be less disquiet when he flings food and dishes at the servants. She beats Grumio for tormenting her about food when she is not given anything to eat, but she is courteous with the Tailor and Haberdasher. She likes the cap made for her, and when Petruchio refuses to let her keep it, she mildly replies:

> Why, sir, I trust I may have leave to speak,
> And speak I will. I am no child, no babe.
>
> (4.3. 73–74)

Although she is not terribly bright, Kate is intelligent enough to see that Petruchio wants "to make a puppet" of her. Docility, not civility, is the goal of his schooling, and when he has finished her education she does not speak unless he bids her open her mouth. More than once Ferando speaks of loving as well as taming Kate; he tells her that ere long "thou and I shall lovingly agree." When she joins with him in the madcap pretense that the traveler they meet is a young maid rather than an old man, Ferando praises her affectionately:

> Why so, Kate, this was friendly done of thee,
> And kindly too. Why, thus must we two live,
> One mind, one heart, and one content for both.

Petruchio also believes in "one mind, one heart, and one content for both"— his own. He never speaks of loving Kate except with obviously ironic hyperbole, and his view of marriage does not allow the possibility of mutual respect. Ferando explains that he will tame Kate as men tame hawks to "make her gently come unto the lure" despite her stubborn nature. The corresponding speech by Petruchio boasts at length of how he will tame his falcon, man his haggard, and watch his kite. His goal is not, like Ferando's, to teach his wife a gentle obedience; he would not have a gentle wife any more than he would have a gentle hawk. The art of taming a falcon is to make it utterly obedient to its master so that it will use its wild aggressive skill as a hunter only at his command. After Petruchio has tamed his hawk, he turns her loose in the final scene to fly at the other wives while he wagers on her absolute obedience.

If Kate were an independent, strong-minded woman, Petruchio's bullying would not so completely destroy her will. He is able to reduce her to abject submission because she is never unconventional or genuinely rebellious. Rather than a free spirit, she is a prisoner of insecurities that make her more sympathetic and more psychologically complex than the heroine of *A Shrew*.[8] She does not lash out against men because she refuses to accept the role and destiny society allots to women. Although she jeers at Petruchio's wooing, and once attempts to strike him, and swears she will see him hanged before she will marry him, she is silent when Petruchio and her father agree to the match and is wretched at the thought that Petruchio will not come to the church to marry her. Love and marriage are what she wants, and fearing that she will not be loved, she behaves in a way that makes men avoid rather than reject her. She lashes out at Bianca because she has suitors, and she complains that Bianca is her father's favorite although her behavior makes it impossible for Baptista to be close to her. Acutely self-conscious and always ill at ease, she fears that the world is pointing and laughing at her, that she will be alone and miserable while her sister is married and happy; the intensity of that fear provokes the rage that makes her a wretched outcast. And yet marriage is always on her mind: she lays hands on Bianca to make her tell which suitor Bianca loves best. It is not astonishing that Kate is so well-behaved at her wedding, even though Petruchio is an offensive lout, because marriage gives her all that she wishes—esteem, a place in society, perhaps even love. And therefore she wants to enjoy all the traditional pleasures of the wedding ceremony and the feast with family and friends. She is ready to be like other brides and other wives, but he wants something more special in a spouse and therefore the taming will proceed despite Kate's reasonableness.

Even after his insulting bully-boy conduct at the wedding, Petruchio might still turn from a frog—or perhaps a toad—into a prince of a fellow when Kate, delighted to have a husband, kisses him. When they do kiss, however, Petruchio does not reveal the true refinement and sensitivity that he hid beneath a facade of crudeness. He is the same as before, the same as he will always be: once a frog, always a frog. For only one brief moment are he and Kate equal partners in a witty charade. When, on the road back to Padua, she joins with him in pretending that Vincentio is a fair maiden rather than an old man, they both enjoy the role-playing.[9] But as R. B. Heilman notes, this mutuality does not last. When, in the next scene, Kate refuses to kiss Petruchio in the street, he cracks the whip again, threatening to drag her away from the wedding feast for her sister as he had dragged her away from her own wedding feast.[10] This moment does not exist in *A Shrew;* it is Shakespeare's way of making clear that Petruchio never relinquishes his command of Kate.

Dressed in suitable garb, Petruchio seems on his good behavior at the feast. But when Lucentio speaks of friendship and good cheer, he mutters, "Nothing but sit and sit and eat and eat." What a bore civility is. To relieve the tedium he quickly baits Hortensio about his bride, the Widow; and he shows that he is quite willing to banter with someone else's wife though he tolerates no back talk from his own.[11] Her education complete, Kate is silent but not more confident or social. She does not join in the conversation until the Widow's sparring with Petruchio opens up the old wound of her self-consciousness. Baited by Petruchio, the Widow refers to Kate's shrewishness. When Petruchio says that Hortensio is afraid of his wife, the Widow answers:

> He that is giddy thinks the world turns round.
> *Pet.* Roundly replied.
> *Kate.*   Mistress, how mean you that?
> *Wid.* Thus I conceive by him.
> *Pet.* Conceives by me! how likes Hortensio that?
> *Hort.* My widow says, thus she conceives her tale.
> *Pet.* Very well mended. Kiss him for that, good widow.
> *Kath.* "He that is giddy thinks the world turns round":
>   I pray you, tell me what you meant by that.
> *Wid.* Your husband, being troubled with a shrew,
>   Measures my husband's sorrow by his woe:
>   And now you know my meaning.
> *Kate.* A very mean meaning.
> *Wid.*   Right, I mean you.
> *Kate.* And I am mean indeed, respecting you.[12]

(5.2. 20–33)

Kate's temper is beginning to boil, and Petruchio, the famed teacher of good manners is delighted, not horrified. "To her, Kate," he yells.

In *A Shrew*, Bianca's husband suggests that the three husbands test their wives' obedience. In *The Shrew*, Petruchio suggests the wager that will confirm his genius at wife-taming. He knows that Kate will obey his com-

ᴊ, like a trained hawk, show her aggressive spirit when let fly. ᴊeaves the table when Petruchio threatens to "have at her for a bitter ᴊr two"; naturally, she is not eager to return and replies to Lucentio's ᴊnmons that she is busy and cannot come. The Widow suspects rightly that "some goodly jest" is in hand and also refuses to return. At Petruchio's summons, Kate immediately returns to the table and goes off again to fetch the other women, by force if necessary. Although Kate wins the wager for Petruchio, he would have her perform one additional trick to "show more sign of her obedience" by stepping on her cap at his command. The Widow and Bianca are appalled by this display of something Bianca hesitates to call "duty." To Lucentio's complaint that she has made him lose five hundred crowns, she replies, "The more fool you for laying on my duty," as indeed he is. The wish is father to the critical thought that Kate's early tantrums express an intrinsic honesty while Bianca's amiableness and dutifulness are proof of a simpering, scheming hypocrisy. Other evidence, I imagine, are her love of music and poetry and her attractiveness to many suitors. The final revelation of the hardness and latent shrewishness of her nature is presumably her refusal to return to the wedding table, where she has been baited by her brother-in-law on her wedding day while her bridegroom sat silent. If her anger at her husband's wager on her obedience is reprehensible, we must rejoice in Ophelia's submission to Polonius's dictates and idealize Helena's willingness to be humiliated by Bertram.

Where Petruchio is rude and determined to turn the wedding into a bear-baiting, Ferando is the soul of courtesy in the final scene of *A Shrew*. When Kate stamps on her cap at his bidding, he remarks that "this is a token of her true love to me." The word "obedience" does not roll off his tongue as it does off Petruchio's, and it is not used by the other husbands. The test, as Ferando describes it, is to see whose wife "shows her self most loving" to her husband. He does not speak as Petruchio does of "an awful rule and right supremacy"; he bids Kate explain to the "headstrong women / What duty wives do owe unto their husbands." Petruchio bids Kate explain to them "what duty they do owe their lords and husbands." In *A Shrew* Kate delivers a lecture on how God brought order out of chaos in creating the universe, and how woman, "the woe of man," brought disorder back in Adam's fall. Since they are responsible for that original sin, Kate says, women should obey, love, and keep their husbands, even by laying their hands beneath their husbands' feet if that will ease their walking. In *The Shrew* Kate offers no metaphysical justification for wifely obedience; instead she dwells on the natural superiority of men (who are spoken of as "prince," "lord," "king," "governor," "head," and "sovereign") to women, who are described as "muddy," "ill-seeming," "thick," "froward," "sullen," "peevish" and "sour" when they disobey their husbands, to whom they owe all. Kate also reminds the brides that they are "unable worms" with soft and weak bodies.

This is not the speech of a woman who has blossomed under her husband's tutelage and can confidently enjoy her femininity. Of course, some suggest that Kate speaks these lines with a knowing wink or smile to assure an audience that she does not mean what she says. No doubt the speech can be made comic by a wink or a sly manner of delivery—almost any speech can— but ironic subtlety is not Kate's distinguishing characteristic, and these lines are too earnest and weighted with conviction to be a clever gambit.[13] She means what she says; she takes pride, if not pleasure, in stooping to Petruchio's whistle, especially when she proves herself more valuable and praiseworthy than the other wives, who have the ease and confidence she lacks. She must take a demeaning view of her sex or be oppressed by the realization of her singularly demeaning marriage.

As many of its editors and critics point out, *The Shrew* is or can be quite attractive in performance. Its first half is energetic and filled with boistrous good humor. The early Petruchio is engaging in his outrageousness, especially when he first comes wooing the obstreperous Kate. The later Petruchio can also be made attractive by playing him as if he were Ferando rather than the character Shakespeare drew. Even then the coarseness and gratuitousness of his pedagogical methods may show through, but, as Leggatt observes, we can "enjoy Petruchio's brutality . . . because it is limited and conventionalized; and this rather than a notion of romantic love is the real source of our pleasure in the play."[14] Similarly the Kate of the last scenes can be made to seem a subtle humorer of an overbearing husband, though to create this impression an actress and director must agree together to subvert Shakespeare's text.

That one can humanize *The Shrew* in performance is beyond question: generations of actors have done so. The question is, however, whether critics should continue to "save" the play by casuistic interpretations that do not bear close scrutiny. Critical honesty requires, I suggest, that we recognize what is unpleasant in the play, because only then can we acknowledge that Shakespeare deliberately chose to make the taming story more unpleasant than it is in *A Shrew*. Sometime in 1593, it would seem, Shakespeare's company came into possession of two plays, *The Troublesome Reign of King John* and either the text of *A Shrew* or the play on which *A Shrew* was based. Asked to revamp both plays, Shakespeare did so, but apparently without enthusiasm, for neither *King John* nor *The Shrew* is a particularly inspired work. Indeed, his revisions created flaws of dramatic structure that do not exist in the source plays. Many critics have noted the muddle of dramatic action in the final scenes of *King John*.[15] Many have puzzled over the fact that Shakespeare elaborated the Induction that exists in *A Shrew*, but destroyed the symmetry of the dramatic frame by failing to return to the Sly plot at the close of *The Shrew*. He eliminated the crude anti-Catholicism of *The Troublesome Reign* in revamping it but took an opposite tack with the joke of wife-taming, which *A Shrew* makes palatable by depicting Kate as a virago and Ferando as a loving and considerate husband. Turning this conception inside out, Shakespeare makes Kate more sensitive and tormented and Petruchio an unregenerate boor. By doing so he invites an audience to acknowledge the nastiness of the farcical premise of most taming stories: namely, that a bit of rough treatment will make any woman more amiable and malleable. Since this is too uncomfortable a recognition for most audiences, Petruchio is sentimentalized on stage now as he may well have been in Shakespeare's time.

Later in his career Shakespeare, one imagines, accepted other assignments that were not completely to his liking. *The Merry Wives*, for example, strikes many critics as a potboiler written to fatten the company's coffers if not, as legend has it, to satisfy Elizabeth's desire to see Falstaff in love. But after seeing what Shakespeare had done with *The Troublesome Reign* and *A Shrew*, his company had the good sense not to ask him to refurbish another old play, because even if he consented to do so, he inevitably had the last word.

6

A Midsummer Night's Dream

If the only plays of Shakespeare that survived were the comedies written before *A Dream*, he would seem an interesting, gifted writer who failed to realize his potential as dramatist. The unfolding of his powers is evident in the early comedies, but with each artistic advance there is an apparent loss or setback, so that all the achievements are somewhat flawed if not uncertain. *Love's Labor's* reaches beyond the Plautine farcing of *Errors* but lacks satisfying dramatic form. *Two Gentlemen* adds psychological complexity and subtle irony to romantic characterization but loses itself in a meandering and ultimately self-parodying plot. *The Shrew* is competent and malicious hackwork.

When Shakespeare's apprenticeship in comedy ended is a matter of personal judgment. Some critics find the characterizations of *A Dream* sketchy, except of course for Bottom, and think its flights of lyric poetry are a bit self-indulgent. They do not find in it the maturity and substance of *The Merchant, Much Ado,* and *As You Like It.* Others suggest that it is too rarified in sensibility to belong to the mainstream of his work and was probably written for a special audience. Although the Quarto announces the play as one that "hath been sundry times publicly acted," they hypothesize that it was commissioned for performance at a great wedding. No doubt *A Dream* would be more appropriate as a nuptial entertainment than *Errors* with its strain of marital discord, or *Love's Labor's* with its unfortunate title, and would be far more appropriate for a nuptial than *The Shrew*. Still, it has shortcomings as a hymeneal celebration. Any bridegroom would be pleased to identify himself with the noble Theseus and could therefore ignore Demetrius and Lysander's early wrangling and unseemly treatment of their future brides. A bride would have to have more of a sense of humor, however, to see Hippolyta, the bouncing Amazon, or Hermia or Helena as her counterpart. Both bride and groom might stir uneasily at the bitter quarreling of Titania and Oberon, who plans a nasty revenge on his refractory spouse. Of the bride's father in the play, Egeus, the less said the better.

aristocratic wedding is an occasion for high-sounding conventionalities, for the idealized (and flattering) abstractions of a court pageant or masque. As a wedding play, *A Dream* is too quirky and perhaps even risky. If some noble person took umbrage at what seemed to be a satiric mock, Shakespeare's company could have lost its fee. Humorlessness is the better part of artistic valor in aristocratic entertainments. Even today a production of *A Dream* may prove to be a risky artistic venture. If a director is eager for laughs, Bottom and his colleagues become buffoons, and the comedy of love in the forest scenes descends to a slapstick farce performed by antic puppets. Indeed, it is more likely that *A Dream* will be vulgarized in performance than that it will prove too ethereal for popular audiences.

It is a mistake to stress the delicate imaginings of *A Dream* when its characterizations, plotting, and humor are robust, and its true charm can be appreciated only by those who have a taste for very bad poetry. Compared to the mysteries of Prospero's island, the magic of the forest of Athens is homely and mundane. Puck is part mischievous child, part practical joker; Peaseblossom and Mustard Seed are a common garden variety of fairies. Rather than a play for the esoteric few, *A Dream* is the very kind of play that Bottom and his companions spent their pennies to see, and Shakespeare keeps reminding us through their earnest attempts to wrestle with problems of stagecraft that they are part of the drama-loving populace that supported the public theaters. Indeed, the comedy of their rehearsal scenes cries out for performance on the bare sunlit stage of a public playhouse, in which settings are evoked primarily by language and can be instantaneously altered, expanded, and shrunk through a magic at least as artful as Oberon's.

What sets *A Dream* apart from the earlier comedies is not so much its richly sensuous and evocative poetry, though that is new to the comedies, as its complex and perfectly assured dramatic structure. It is as if the problems of comedic form that defied solution in *Love's Labor's* and *Two Gentlemen* no longer seem to exist, or are, of a sudden, erased by an artistic inspiration that transcends logical calculations. A lesser dramatist would have retreated from the romantic extravagance of *Two Gentlemen* to a simpler, more tightly constructed comic plotting. Shakespeare takes the opposite tack, and by weaving together three separate but intersecting strands of action achieves an apparently effortless, harmonious design that can bear comparison with the splendid double plotting of *1 Henry IV.* The earlier comedies expand the dimensions of Roman farce by mingling clowns and caricatures with romantic heroes and heroines. *A Dream* has the expansiveness of the later comedies that is created by the presence of multiple dramatic worlds; the interplay between the lovers, the fairies, and the rude mechanicals points toward the interplay between Venice and Belmont in *The Merchant*, Olivia's household and Orsino's in *Twelfth Night*.[1]

By all the conventional rules of artistic decorum, the three worlds of *A*

Dream cannot be part of the same dramatic universe. Theseus, mythic demigod and epic hero, should be battling minotaurs, not arbitrating a family dispute; the fleeing Athenian lovers should encounter Macedonian outlaws, Persian pirates, or Turks, not an English hobgoblin and the king of the fairies; and neither Theseus, nor the Athenian lovers should make the acquaintance of Bottom and his fellow artisans, who daydream of tragic art in their Cheapside shops and patronize the Theater, not the Theater of Dionysius. Beaumont will burlesque bourgeois taste for romance and melodrama in *The Knight of the Burning Pestle*. Shakespeare does not allow us to patronize any of the characters in *A Dream* even though much of the comic effect of the play depends upon the incongruity of the high-flown passions they self-consciously express, either in their own person or in the role of Pyramus, Thisbe, and Wall. For nothing is exaggerated, nothing in the responses and behavior of the characters is made to seem ridiculous. If the comedy of *A Dream* depended on the transformation of personality by magical enchantment, Shakespeare, not Quince, would be the mechanical playwright. The chief source of delight is the refusal of those who are enchanted to change their customary way of behaving or even admit that they are enchanted despite the curious lengthening of Bottom's ears and the instantaneous reversals of Demetrius and Lysander's passions. Although their circumstances radically change, they remain stubbornly the same, their feet firmly planted on the floor even when the floor becomes the ceiling.

Lacking confidence in the high comedy of the forest scenes, directors sometimes play them as slapstick farce. This approach reduces the enchantment of Demetrius and Lysander to a tiresome gag of B-movies—the push-button hypnotic trance. In such films the hero is at one moment his ordinary self; the next moment a telephone rings or a special word is spoken and the shy retiring bank clerk becomes an irresistible lothario; an incompetent athlete, a superstar. Oberon's magic may alter the object of the heroes' affections or change Bottom's physiognamy, but it does not alter their essential natures. Despite Oberon's ministrations and manipulations, these characters never become marionettes, and since they are always in their right minds, they have no difficulty in rationalizing the irrational. Demetrius and Lysander are no more astonished by their changed desires than the lords of Navarre are dismayed to learn that they prefer love to monastic discipline. They know, as Orsino does, that men are not as steadfast in affection as women and that their quest for the ideal may require the jilting of one woman for another as they see more clearly into the neoplatonic mystery of love. If Proteus and Romeo can change loves, why cannot Demetrius abandon Helena for Hermia, and rediscover Helena, and think that all the time he is ascending the ladder of love? More innocent than Proteus and Valentine in their attitude toward women and romantic rivalry, they are not ambivalent about love; they do not speak cynically of the susceptibility of

women to flattery or greed. Their rivalry is open and declared, not cunningly concealed and Machiavellian. Indeed, they treat one another in a
gentlemanly way even when they would settle their rivalry with swords.
They are ungentlemenly only to women, as Bertram will be in *All's Well* and
Posthumus will be in *Cymbeline*. Behind the absurdity of the heroes' behavior in the forest is the ironic truth of male egotism in affairs of love and
honor.

If the emphasis falls on the irrationality of love in *A Dream*, it does not
follow that Shakespeare is advancing the cause of sobriety or moderation.
What Theseus and Bottom say about reason and love is well said and
eminently reasonable, as reasonable as Benvolio's attempt to restore Romeo's
equanimity by proving to him that Rosaline is not the only fish in the sea. It
is dangerous to make a god of love and folly to surrender to the melancholy
of unrequited desire. The absoluteness of romantic passion can be tyrannical
and destructive. Mischance, an ancient feud, and the passions of friends and
foes all conspire against Romeo and Juliet. Ultimately, however, they are not
victims of circumstance; they choose to die because they will not live
without each other, because, as Donne would have it, they are "one another's
all," and unless they may live in each other's arms they have no wish to
breathe. What could be more senseless? Experience assures us that the
misery of unrequited love fades and that people love and marry again after
the deaths of beloved spouses. Yet the mystique of romantic passion insists
that in this vast world there is only one Isolde for a Tristan, only one Romeo
for a Juliet. Too sensible to credit such a view, Benvolio proves to Romeo
that there are women in Verona more beautiful and desirable than Rosaline.
He proves conclusively that Romeo's love melancholy can be cured, but his
sensible remedy leads only to Juliet and a deeper emotional commitment
that costs Romeo's life. If we are to set limits to the role of passion in our
lives, we must also be willing to set limits to the role of common sense and
reason because the ideal of love *is* absolute and unbending and defined as
such in marriage vows that pledge eternal devotion. It is easy to smile at the
irrationality of romantic yearnings, but there is something irrational also in
the loyalty of Shakespeare's heroines to those who betray them or prove
unworthy. At some point we must refuse to reason the need for love, refuse
to measure out the appropriate emotional responses of those in love, and
refuse to moralize the deaths of Romeo and Juliet, who are the victims of
other characters' vanities, follies, and timidities, not of their own passions.

Since Hermia and Helena are equally fair and alike in gentleness and a
capacity to love, there is no reason why Demetrius should abandon Helena
to pursue Hermia; but then Demetrius and Lysander are so alike, there is no
reason why Hermia detests the former and risks all to elope with the latter,
despite the sharp penalty threatened by Athenian law. Still Shakespeare does
not present the turmoil of the lovers as much ado about nothing, and he does

not make their choices seem arbitrary or capricious. For if romantic love is blind, it is less blind and irrational than the obstinate insistence of an Egeus (or a Capulet) on choosing his daughter's husband despite her anguished objections. If anything, Egeus's choice of Demetrius is more irrational than Hermia's choice of Lysander because Demetrius has sullied his reputation by jilting Helena. The tyranny of Cupid is nothing compared to the tyranny of the ancient custom that allows a father to dispose of a daughter as chattel and thereby turn wedding vows into legalistic shams.[2]

Since Hermia and Lysander thrill to the idea that they are star-crossed, we suspect that they will not suffer the tragic fates of the legendary lovers to whom they compare themselves. Like Bottom and Quince they have read tales like "Pyramus and Thisbe" and perhaps read *Dido, Queen of Carthage* (in translation), and they agree with the artisans that a bit of tragic calamity is the best beginning for a happy marriage. Although they bemoan their fates, they intend to live happily ever after. Unlike Romeo and Juliet, they have no need of a tragic chorus, because they gloss their own story in a high rhetorical vein:

> *Lysander.* Ay me! for aught that I could ever read,
> Could ever hear by tale or history,
> The course of true love never did run smooth;
> But either it was different in blood—
> *Her.* O cross! Too high to be enthrall'd to [low].
> *Lys.* Or else misgraffed in respect of years—
> *Her.* O spite! too old to be engag'd to young.
> *Lys.* Or else it stood upon the choice of friends—
> *Her.* O hell, to choose love by another's eyes!
>
> (1.1. 132–40)

Lysander is not the worst of lyric poets; he can speak as eloquently of love's brevity as Romeo or Juliet because he shares their knowledge that love can be

> momentany as a sound,
> Swift as a shadow, short as any dream,
> Brief as the lightning in the collied night,
> That, in a spleen, unfolds both heaven and earth;
> And ere a man hath power to say "Behold!"
> The jaws of darkness do devour it up:
> So quick bright things come to confusion.
>
> (1.1. 143–49)

Hermia is no less romantic but far less imaginative; she can turn a heartfelt vow into a classroom recitation. When Lysander asks her to join him in fleeing the severe law of Athens, she pledges

> by Cupid's strongest bow,
> By his best arrow with the golden head,
> By the simplicity of Venus' doves,
> By that which knitteth souls and prospers loves,
> And by that fire which burn'd the Carthage queen,
> ....
> In that same place thou hast appointed me
> To-morrow truly will I meet with thee.
>
> (1.1. 169–78)

No lawyer could make the contract of love more literal and specific; this is the very boiler-plate of passionate commitment. Bottom and Quince are even more literal-minded in their approach to the staging of tragic passion, but their yearning for romantic angst is as genuine as Hermia's, as genuine as the yearning of ordinary Elizabethans for tales of exotic adventure and plays filled with sound and fury. Quince was not born to write poetic tragedy any more than Bottom was born to act in it. They are not Marlowes or Burbages any more than Hermia and Lysander are Isolde and Tristan, and their longing for the heroic is therefore the source of a new kind of verbal comedy that is neither witty like the wordplay of Berowne and Rosaline, nor pedantic like the wordplay of Holofernes and Nathaniel. Bottom and Quince do not stumble over words because they are ignorant or out to impress their comrades. They misuse terms and figures of speech because they are out of their depths as dramatists and dramaturges. They are earnest rather than pompous in dealing with the mysteries of aesthetic terminology, and they approach the task of presenting high tragedy with the solemnity that Hermia and Lysander bring to the adventure of elopement.

In romance a jilted maiden is wreathed in a delicate, wistful pathos. She is vulnerable like Ophelia, her cheeks are wan and tear-stained, and she sings a plaintive willow song. Mariana of *Measure for Measure* is the only heroine of the comedies to conform to this romantic archetype. Helena, like Julia, Hero, and Helena of *All's Well*, is far more sturdy. She is too stubborn to accept rejection and has too strong a sense of herself to wilt before Demetrius's scorn. Refusing to abandon hope of regaining his love, she dedicates all thought and action to that goal. Although she dwells continually on her unhappy state, she is not self-pitying and she does not want to be pitied by others. She talks to herself about her situation the way tennis players talk to themselves when their game has slipped and they must regain concentration. She is not certain why she is losing but she knows she must not concede defeat, and she studies Hermia's success to see if she can pick up some useful hints. She is determined to understand what has happened, what cause in herself or Demetrius has made her the underdog. Ready to chase after Demetrius, she is too proud to beg for love and is inclined rather to accuse and scold him. She may be jealous of Hermia, who now has Demetrius's love, but she does not accuse her of stealing her fiancé. It is as if she long ago accepted the fact that Hermia was a bit more attractive and would always be the first one asked to dance. She does not wish that Hermia were less beautiful; she would simply like to be more fair. "Sickness is catching," she muses; "O, were favor so." She does not brood over her appearance, however, because she knows that through Athens she is thought as fair as Helena. Because jealousy is foreign to her nature and she is absorbed in her own problems, she does not seem to notice the feline pleasure Hermia takes in describing Demetrius's infatuation with her:

> *Her.* I frown upon him; yet he loves me still.
> *Hel.* O that your frowns would teach my smiles such skill!
> *Her.* I give him curses; yet he gives me love.
> *Hel.* O that my prayers could such affection move!
> *Her.* The more I hate, the more he follows me!
> *Hel.* The more I love, the more he hateth me.
> *Her.* His folly, Helena, is no fault of mine.
> *Hel.* None but your beauty; would that fault were mine!
>
> (1.1. 194–201)

If Helena were more calculating, she would keep silent about Hermia's elopement and be rid of her rival for good. But that would be to win the match by default; no, she must rush to tell Demetrius so as to have his thanks and the excuse to trail after him while he pursues the eloping lovers. Although she harps on her unhappy state, she does not enjoy it in any masochistic way, and she is quick to react to any imagined slight or mockery. Hermia expresses her prosaic nature in a detailed inventory of Cupid's armaments; Helena reveals her dogged approach to experience by subjecting the ancient myth of Cupid to modern scientific analysis in an attempt to determine why Demetrius dotes on Hermia. The answer, she concludes is that

> Things base and vile, holding no quantity,
> Love can transpose to form and dignity.
> Love looks not with the eyes but with the mind;
> And therefore is wing'd Cupid painted blind.
> Nor hath Love's mind of any judgment taste;
> Wings, and no eyes, figure unheedy haste.
>
> (1.1. 232–37)

So much for the mystery of love! Dan Cupid is clearly a public hazard on the road to marriage. She is equally adept at analyzing human psychology, with the aid of some deliciously flat-footed puns:

> . . . ere Demetrius look'd on Hermia's eyne,
> He hail'd down oaths that he was only mine;
> And when this hail some heat from Hermia felt,
> So he dissolv'd, and show'rs of oaths did melt.
>
> (1.1. 242–45)

Helena has a gift of metaphor that is fatal to the poetic imagination. When Demetrius complains because she is following him in the forest, she explains:

> You draw me, you hard-hearted adamant;
> But yet you draw not iron, for my heart
> Is true as steel.
>
> (2.2. 195–97)

Lysander and Hermia speak of the accidents that can befall true love; Helena assumes that nothing is accidental; for every effect, there is a cause, whether the effect be Demetrius's swerving or Hermia's beauty:

> Happy is Hermia, wheresoe'er she lies,
> For she hath blessed and attractive eyes.
> How came her eyes so bright? Not with salt tears;
> If so, my eyes are oft'ner wash'd than hers.
>
> (2.2. 90–93)

If favor is not catching, pedestrian wordplay seems to be. Exasperated by Helena's pursuit in the forest, Demetrius at last complains that he is "wode within this wood."

The matter-of-factness of the lovers is understandable; they are citizens of an Athens in which heroic adventures are no longer commonplace but belong to a mythic past that Theseus and Hippolyta have put behind them. The law that threatens Hermia should she disobey her father's wishes is a vestige of that mythic past, but one doubts that Egeus's paternal tyranny will have tragic consequences when there is a comic fussiness in the accusations he levels at Lysander:

> Thou, thou, Lysander, thou hast given her rhymes,
> And interchang'd love-tokens with my child;
> Thou hast by moonlight at her window sung
> With faining voice verses of faining love,
> And stol'n the impression of her fantasy
> With bracelets of thy hair, rings, gawds, conceits,
> Knacks, trifles, nosegays, sweetmeats.
>
> (1.1. 28–34)

Sweetmeats! Shall Hermia die the death or wither away in a convent because of Lysander's cunning sweetmeats? The conflict between love and statute seems to admit no reasonable compromise except Lysander's suggestion that Demetrius, who has Egeus's love, marry him.

Since Egeus's preference for Demetrius is as idiosyncratic as Hermia's preference for Lysander, the laws of Athens provide no solution to the seeming anarchy of passion; obedience to order and degree merely buttresses Egeus's obtuse willfulness. The mythic allusions in *A Dream* underline the terrifying force of sexual passion, which turned some gods into adulterous seducers and ravishers of innocence. The power of love to change the lives of mortals is the continuing mythic theme of Ovid's *Metamorphoses*. The wonder and fear that overwhelming passion evokes is recorded in the ancient legends of men and women enslaved by love potions and spells. Like Egeus, Brabantio is convinced that his daughter has been bewitched, and not long after we smile at Egeus's superstition, Oberon and Puck appear to make the fantasy of enchanted love a reality.

Despite Egeus's complaint, these moonlit enchantments are quite impossible in an Athens where Theseus, who ravished Perigenia and broke his faith with Aegles, Adriane, and Antiopa, is now a model of princely respectability. Properly raised, the maidens of Athens are chary of their reputations and expect their suitors to honor their virginal modesties. Although Lysander waxes amorous for a time, Hermia cools his ardor, and Demetrius's threat to ravish Helena is made out of exasperation, not lust. Primal natural passions do not make their claim in the dark forest because Athenian youth do not lie together under the greenwood tree or abandon themselves to desire in May or in midsummer.[3] The forest of Athens is not a trysting place; it is a retreat for nature walks among the woodland flowers, a place to dream of elves who war with bees and reremice and sleep in flowers and discarded snake skins. The dark underside of nature in *A Dream* is nothing more than the delicate world of the fairies, who embody our age-old fear of the shadowy night and derive their being from winter tales repeated around the fire. Oberon and Titania are well bred, benign, and tolerant in their view of mortals, even though the former allows Puck's practical jokes. Oberon, when crossed by his wife, can be as blustering as any husband or father and capable of plotting a nasty revenge, but he is a romantic at heart who is sympathetic to the lovelorn Helena and offended by Demetrius's abuse of her.

Since Oberon cannot settle his own marital problems, it is not surprising that his intervention creates additional difficulties for the lovers. His herbal remedies are all-powerful but they are misapplied because Puck sensibly decides that Lysander, who sleeps apart from Hermia, is the nasty lack-love he seeks. Oberon's charms can make a sleeper adore the first person he sees when he awakes. They cannot, however, change anything essential in either a mortal or a fairy's nature. Titania's tenderness for the long-eared Bottom is natural in a woman who dared her husband's royal anger for the sake of a changeling child and the memory of the mortal woman who bore him. Lovers and rivals before they entered the forest, Lysander and Demetrius continue as such when enchanted; the magical drops do not make them forget their earlier loves, and they are perfectly aware of their sudden alterations of affection. Unperplexed, they rejoice in their new loves and justify their giddiness with hackneyed sophistries. They must be unfaithful to their former loves to be true to themselves because they know now that they did not really love before. Until the drops were placed in their eyes they did not see clearly. Oberon's magic does not make them inexcusably rude to Hermia; their desire to prove their devotion to Helena prompts that un-chivalry, and the fever of competition makes them careless of all else, as they were in the opening scene, in which they insulted one another. Having ascended the neoplatonic ladder of love, they see clearly and rationally that all's fair in love and war and that the sensible thing to do is eliminate their rival in a duel. Ever the gentlemen, they are ready to protect Helena from Hermia's fingernails by brute force if necessary.

In itself, the joke of the love drops is limited and repetitious. Demetrius and Lysander imitate one another in their suddenly discovered eternal devotion to Helena, their facile rationalizations, and their romantic hyper-boles. The richest comedy of the forest scenes lies in the heroines' attempts to make sense of the heroes' bizarre behavior. The comic situation resembles that of *Errors* in that Oberon's enchantments create for the lovers the supposes that confuse the twin brothers, except that Demetrius and Lysander find nothing strange in their new circumstance; and, unlike Adriana and Luciana, Hermia and Helena know that something is terribly amiss and do their best to fathom the muddle. There are shrill accusations, false surmises, and whirling swords in the Athenian forest as in the streets of Ephesus, but we delight now in Hermia and Helena's psychological responses rather than in Shakespeare's ingenious manipulation of his farcical situation. The more conventionally feminine of the heroines, Hermia will not let Lysander sleep near her in the forest. He suggests that one turf serve as pillow for them both: "One heart, one bed, two bosoms, one troth." "Nay, good Lysander," she replies, "For my sake, my dear, / Lie further off yet, do not lie so near." When she awakes to find Lysander gone and Demetrius present, she leaps to melodramatic conclusions, a tendency in those who have read too many tragical tales. If Demetrius has slain Lysander for her love, she says,

> Being o'er shoes in blood, plunge in the deep,
> And kill me too.

> (3.2. 48–49)

Where Hermia is ready to believe the worst of the well-shod Demetrius, Helena is not willing to accept the astonishing reality of Lysander's and Demetrius's sudden passion for her. She has grown accustomed to her underdog role with all the moral advantages it allows, and she is too sensible to believe that passions instantaneously alter; there must be a reason for the heroes' sudden attraction to her even as there had to be a reason for Demetrius's desertion of her for Hermia. When Lysander awakes to declare that reason leads him to her eyes, she wonders why she was born to this "keen mockery," why he flouts her female "insufficiency," why a lady "of one man refused, / Should of another therefore be abused." A loyal friend, she does not find Lysander's passion a sweet recompense for her rejection by Demetrius; instead she is appalled by his untruth to Hermia. When Demetrius leaps up to deify her with Marlovian hyperboles and invidious comparisons, she is convinced of their derision because she knows when men "superpraise [her] parts." The last piece of the puzzle slips into place for Helena when Hermia appears and is spurned by Lysander as one he hates. Now she knows that she is the victim of one of the cruel jokes school children play on one another. They have whispered in a corner and ganged up to make her miserable. It pains her to recall the days when she and Hermia were as one in all they felt and did.

> . . . with our needles created both one flower,
> Both on one sampler, sitting on one cushion,
> Both warbling of one song, both in one key,
> As if our hands, our sides, voices, and minds,
> Had been incorporate.

> (3.2. 204–8)

These innocent days are ended; sexual maturity has expelled them from the Eden of their girlhood into an adult world of rivalries, insecurities, and pain. Helena feelingly complains that her dear friend has set Lysander to praise her eyes and face and set Demetrius to call her "goddess, nymph, divine and rare, / Precious and celestial" so that they may wink and smirk at her when her back is turned. What could be more diabolical? To prove the truth of their affections, Demetrius and Lysander are ready to slay one another. Incredulous, Hermia asks what change is this in Lysander, her sweet love. "Thy love? Out tawny Tartar, out," the chivalric Lysander exclaims, "Out, loathed medicine! O hated potion, hence!" Now Hermia sees the light. She cannot blame her beloved Lysander for mistreating her. The fault must be Helena's, the "thief of love" who came by night and stole Lysander's heart. This accusation is the last straw for the aggrieved Helena, who turns on Hermia with "impatient answers" torn from her gentle tongue: "Fie, fie! You counterfeit, you puppet, you!" These unguarded words give away

Helena's cunning game to Hermia, who realizes that her rival has won Lysander by the Machiavellian trick of comparing their heights.

> And are you grown so high in his esteem,
> Because I am so dwarfish and so low?
> How low am I, thou painted maypole? Speak!
> How low am I? I am not yet so low
> But that my nails can reach until thine eyes.
>
> (3.2. 294–98)

At last Helena begins to enjoy her enviable position; turning shy, defenseless maiden, she implores Lysander and Demetrius to protect her from this vixen who is dangerous though "something lower than myself," fierce in nature though "little." As the argument continues, Hermia's stature dwindles until she is hardly visible in the undergrowth. "Get you gone, you dwarf," Lysander urges,

> You minimus, of hind'ring knot-grass made;
> You bead, you acorn!
>
> (3.2. 328–29)

The joke of Hermia's littleness was no doubt inspired in part by the actors in Shakespeare's company, one appreciably shorter than the other, who played women's roles. The comic quarrel does not depend, however, upon a real difference in height between actors because here as elsewhere in *A Dream* words magically affect the size and appearance of things. In English and Celtic folklore, fairies, elves, and goblins are not much smaller in stature than humans; they are perhaps childlike in manner but not diminutives. In *A Dream* the fairies are tiny creatures, a patent impossibility because they are played by actors of average height who speak of themselves as dwarfed by cowslips. Yet the drastic illusion holds because believing is seeing, and because on stage one need not nibble a mushroom to shrink in stature; Hermia dwindles to a mere bead once Helena and Lysander begin to slang her.

To say that a few words suffice to indicate setting, time, or season of year on Shakespeare's stage is not to say that audiences imagine rosy-fingered dawns when characters describe them, any more than readers of poetry "see" its "visual imagery." In the opening scene of *Hamlet*, the sentries say that they are cold and frightened keeping watch at midnight on the battlements of Elsinore, even as they challenge one another on a bare, sunlit stage. The power of dramatic illusion does not depend upon the ability of poetic language to persuade an audience that light is dark; it requires only that the characters be convinced of the reality of their dramatic circumstances and communicate that conviction through dialogue and stage business. If they do not recognize someone in disguise, the disguise is impenetrable even though accomplished by the flimsiest of means. Because Bottom and his companions are unimaginative, it does not occur to them to bring in moonlight the way Shakespeare does, through poetic allusion. They are as earnest about their stagecraft as the lovers are about their passions and more literal-minded. If the play calls for a wall, they will bring a wall on stage, and perhaps they are right to do so because they do not possess a professional actor's ability to make an imaginary wall real by stage gesture and action. They are not so prosaic, however, as to aim at mundane realism; they know that symbolism is native to art and are ready to enlist members of the company to play Moonlight and Wall. Such people, one thinks, should not be allowed on stage, and yet the stage is their natural habitat because only in a Shakespearean comedy will one find a joiner like Snug, who wants the lion's part writ out because he is slow of study. Their rehearsal scenes are at once a travesty of theatrical production and a celebration of the versatility of the public playhouses. The would-be actors walk out on a bare platform stage and tell themselves and the audience that they are in a forest. For lack of a theater in which to rehearse, they will pretend that a woodland clearing is a stage, and they will also pretend that the imaginary shrub Quince points out will serve as a tiring house from which to enter. Compared to these instantaneous metamorphoses, Oberon's spells are very limited in effect.

We need not eke out the imperfections of the rehearsal scenes with our thoughts because the dramatic situations are absolutely convincing in performance and any use of scenery would only blur the gentle humor of Shakespeare's comments on dramatic illusion. If Quince says that a stage is a forest and a greensward a stage, who will argue with him? If an actor says that he is small enough to sleep in a snakeskin, who will object that he is five feet six inches tall and perhaps a bit paunchy?[4] It is Bottom's unshakable sense of the reality of his experience that equips him to enter into the fancifulness of Titania's world. Introduced to someone called Cobweb, he makes appropriate small talk. He does not wonder at his hairy ears and face and at his ungulate appetites; whatever is, is right. He does not worry over the Queen of the Fairies' sudden adoration as Helena wrestles with Lysander and Demetrius's yearning for her. He knows there is no accounting for the heart's desires, and he is too polite to question a lady's motives or refuse her attentions. His ease and graciousness in fairyland confirm the virtue of an innocent if prosaic sensibility. Although scholars sometimes assume that the best audience for Shakespeare would be learned and urbane auditors like themselves, Shakespeare would, I suspect, have rejoiced in audiences that could respond to stage illusion with something like Bottom's unspoiled simplicity.

Where Demetrius and Lysander are at times nasty to Hermia and Helena,

Bottom and his colleagues are deeply concerned not to offend the ladies in their audience. The heroes strike chivalric postures, but Bottom is instinctively chivalric toward women: modest, tactful, thankful for small favors, he would not think of taking advantage of Titania's infatuation. She would shower him with luxuries; he would be happy with some oats, hay, and dried peas, and someone to scratch his hairy face. Inevitably he is friendly rather than amorous, for he is the kind of bachelor on whom all communities depend, one who is enthusiastic, energetic, knowledgeable, and free of evenings. The politician's gift of friendly solicitude that he demonstrates with Mustard Seed guarantees that he will sit some day on the county council and perhaps wear an alderman's robe.

Because of Bottom's unvarying good nature, Oberon's plan to humiliate Titania produces only sweetness and light. On the other hand, his attempts to dissolve the love triangle in the forest leads to greater animosity and unhappiness. Puck's mistaken applications of the love drops may be easily rectified; the jealousies and rivalries of the lovers can not, however, be amenable to chemical therapy. For if they were, love would be a joke in *A Dream*, and the romantic heroes and heroines stick figures who are manipulated for an audience's amusement. If all is to end well, Demetrius must discover that he loves Helena still despite the lure of rivalry with Lysander for Hermia's hand. Titania must also be reconciled with Oberon rather than humiliated by him. The reconciliation with Titania that Oberon describes to Puck is not what the heart desires. He does not regret the revenge he took and he does not seem more sensitive to the motives that prompted her stubbornness. He tells Puck that after he had taunted her for loving a monster, she begged his patience and gave up the child. He did not have to grow more understanding because she was prepared to submit to his authority. If this encounter were staged, it might leave an unpleasant aftertaste, but it is reported to us as a conclusion to a marital dispute that ends, as so many do, without explicit resolutions of issues and with unspoken recognitions.

The resolution of the lovers' difficulties is similarly understated. When morning comes, the anxious terrors of the night end; broad daylight brings the reassurance of familiar sights and sounds. Where Puck had led Demetrius and Lysander on confused chases through the dark forest, now Theseus and Hippolyta enjoy the healthy athleticism of a morning hunt. Where Oberon had elaborated his metaphysical conceits of dew-drenched flowers, Theseus now grows rhapsodic over his dewlapped, crooked-kneed hounds, whose ears sweep the ground and whose baying voices thrill his Amazonian bride more than any singing to a lute. She may not know what poetry or music is, but she knows what she likes. The lovers awake to find themselves changed by their experience in the woods; all else remains the same. Athens' law still gives Egeus the right to dispose of his daughter as he wills, and now his hand is strengthened by her unlawful flight with Lysander. He would have the law on Lysander's head and he would choose Demetrius as his son-in-law, but Demetrius announces that his love of Hermia has melted, dissolved away, and is remembered as "an idle gaud, / Which in my childhood I did dote upon." Now he has eyes again only for Helena. To prevent Egeus from any more sputtering, Theseus, who once let Demetrius's breath of faith to Helena slip his mind, corrects this oversight by allowing the lovers to choose their mates. In Athens, as in many other polities, the law is the law except when it is convenient for authorities to let slip a statute or two. If Theseus can suddenly reverse his edicts, Lysander can as suddenly return to Hermia once the love drops are removed from his eyes. Demetrius's change of heart is more ambiguous because it seems to be effected by Oberon's magic, and that is too facile. An audience must feel that Demetrius has come to realize the superficiality of his attraction to Hermia and the depth of his love of Helena. The thrill of rivalry with Lysander has been thoroughly chastened by a bad night in the forest, one which revealed that Lysander too could play the fool as a rivalrous suitor. Hermia, who was somewhat smug at the outset, has experienced the pain of rejection that Helena knew, and Helena's confidence in her attractiveness has been restored. All accusations, recriminations, and posturings ended in the peacefulness of sleep, the same sleep that claims Bottom as he lies in Titania's arms, his ears garlanded with flowers. The lovers do not remember what happened the night before, but the audience does and is prepared to accept the resolution that follows.

Unlike the sentimentalist, who believes that every grasping slumlord can be moved to generosity by a crippled child, Shakespeare offers his audience no sudden, miraculous uplifting of moral character—or none that is not subject to devastating irony. The lovers of *A Dream* need not suffer a sea-change (or forest-change) because Lysander's forthright confession of his elopement is admirable; Demetrius's honest perplexity about his renewed love for Helena is equally admirable and convincing, especially after all the blusterings and casuistries of the preceding night. The heroines need not say very much when they awake, because their affections never wavered. Since they do not remember their jealous quarrelings, they need not be reconciled to one another. It is as if the unspoken tensions of the love triangles, once acted out, have become as distant as the memory of an unhappy dream.

With the lovers happily paired off, nothing remains to be settled except the choice of dramatic entertainment for the wedding feast. "Pyramus and Thisbe" seems an impossible entry until the others are described: " 'The battle with the Centaurs, to be sung / By an Athenian eunuch to the harp,' " and " 'The riot of the tipsy Bacchanals, / Tearing the Thracian singer in their rage.' " It is amusing that Theseus, who steps forth as an expert on art and love, finds nothing indecorous in the subject matter of these nuptial entertainments; he rejects them as old hat, too familiar to be staged at another wedding. He has a firmer grasp on the question of artistic decorum than do the rude mechanicals, who feared to bring a lion on stage, but perhaps their respect for the power of illusion is closer to the mark than is Theseus's urbane skepticism about the lovers' brush with fantasy. What he says about lunatics and lovers is well said; he takes his stand against poetry in memorable verse. His dismissal of antique fables is a sly Shakespearean touch given the fact that he and Hippolyta owe their very existence to classical mythology.[5] The desire to make sense of the world is native to our humanity; we are instinctively curious and unnerved by the illogical and unpredictable. Like Theseus, we would brush away the cobwebs of superstition and take a scientific approach to experience. Thus Helena sees the bizarre behavior of Demetrius and Lysander as a heartless attempt to humiliate her, and Bottom interprets his comrade's fear of his ass's head as an attempt to make an ass of him. His days of heroic adventure behind him, Theseus is not ready to credit tales of minotaurs or magical enchantments, for he knows how deceptive shadows can be in moonlight. His explanations make very good sense, but they are, in this instance, completely erroneous. He is so intent on scientific reasoning that he ignores the scientific evidence supporting the lovers' stories, which is palpable enough even for Hippolyta to grasp: namely, that the story of the night each separately tells "grows to something of great constancy."[6] It may well be that the lovers have dreamed all that they dimly remember, but the dreams that we all share are intrinsic to our common experience as humans.

The final authority on epistemological questions is Bottom, not Theseus. His was the most remarkable adventure, and unlike the others he remembers what happened to him with some clarity. He does not question whether he wakes or sleeps; he knows what is real and what is unreal and will not be persuaded that his wonderful experience was a fantasy induced by indigestion or sleeping on damp ground. He also knows the cash value of bottomless dreams. Like Autolycus, and Stephano and Trinculo after him, he has entrepreneurial schemes to satisfy the popular yearning for the fabulous; he will have his share of fairy gold in the receipts from a puppet show and the sale of broadside ballads based on his dream. His gifts as impressario are confirmed by the production of "Pyramus and Thisbe," which also provides a definitive answer to the question of what play is best for a wedding feast. Undoubtedly the ideal choice is a romantic tragedy written and performed by earnest incompetents. The tedious brief comedy is a cathartic experience for playwrights as well as lovers, because it exorcises both the fear of tragic misunderstandings and the dramatist's recurring nightmare that his plays will be staged by actors who cannot even recite his lines correctly. The result is very decorous, however, for in muddling their speeches, the actors are true to Shakespeare's artistic intention. Indeed, their incompetence is triumphant because only by misreading every one of his lines is the Prologue able to achieve his ingenious, unforgettable rhymes. When Jonson transforms the legend of Hero and Leander into an obscene puppet motion at the close of *Bartholomew Fair,* he shows his contempt for his actors as well as his audience. When Quince's lines prove unwittingly obscene, they testify to his innocence as poet and playwright. Compared to the baiting of the actors in the Pageant of Worthies by the lords of Navarre, the comments on the play by Demetrius, Lysander, and Theseus are good-natured sport. Moreover, these players are not easily put out of their parts, for they have supreme confidence in their play, and Bottom, a patient dramaturge, explains the rationale of the company's artistic choices. While the men show off their satiric wit, Hermia and Helena are courteously silent. The humorless Hippolyta is a bit bored by most of the play but moved by Bottom's tragic apostrophe, which Theseus also admires, "This passion, and the death of a friend, would go near to make a man look sad."

The last words of the play belong to the fairies, whom Theseus assures us do not exist. Since Elizabethan wedding masques appeal to classical deities to bless the marital unions, it follows that English fairies will give the benediction to Athenian brides and grooms. The hope is that the children born of the marriages will be as lively and mischievous as Puck; the fear is that they may be defective, marred by blots of nature or marks prodigious, harelips and disfiguring moles.[7] The dread possibility also exists that one of the women will die in childbirth as did the mother of Titania's changeling boy. Earlier in the play Oberon's spells gave Bottom a monstrous shape; now his spells are a defense against the birth deformities that make midwives cross themselves and whisper of witchcraft. Night can be a time, Theseus observes, when shadows confuse and terrify; it can also be a time when lovers go astray, or as in "Pyramus and Thisbe," when tragic misapprehensions take their toll. As *A Dream* concludes, however, night is a time when lovers enjoy the happy consummation their true affections deserve.

Although Oberon presides over the concluding scene of *A Dream,* Bottom is the chief fashioner of its harmony. He is the best of all possible weavers, a craftsman who intertwines the separate threads of the play by being equally at home among his usual companions, among the fairies, and in the ducal palace of Athens. His good nature is the emotional ballast of the plot and a continuing assurance that all will end well. His most immediate descendants are Dogberry and Verges, the non-pareil guardians of law and order in Messina. More distant relations are Bassanio, Benedick, Adam, the good Lafew, Pisanio, and Camillo, whose kindly natures never change and whose decency and loyalty sustain the belief that despite violent passion and reckless deeds, love and laughter will finally prevail.

The Merchant of Venice

Like most Shakespearean comedies, *Errors, Love's Labor's*, and *Two Gentlemen* do not achieve their dramatic resolutions until very near the end of their concluding scenes. *The Merchant* and *A Dream* have a somewhat different dramatic structure. Their climactic moments of conflict occur in their fourth and third acts respectively, and all antagonism and discord are resolved before their fifth acts begin. In both plays the last act is a long graceful coda in which the triumph of love is celebrated by a dramatic entertainment or charade, with witty gibes and affectionate teasings, with music and poetry.

Few endings in the comedies are as relaxed and as playful as that of *The Merchant*. The dialogue is charming; the heroes and heroines are attractive and appealing. Every obstacle that lay in the paths of the lovers has been removed, and as further proof that fate smiles, the news comes that Antonio's ships have come safely to port so that once again he is a prosperous merchant of Venice. Since other comedies end in less cheerful and harmonious ways, it may seem ungrateful to question the resolution of *The Merchant*, but the delight of its last scene depends, not on a transformation of discord into harmony, but rather on a denial that any price has been paid for the happiness of those who gather on the steps of Portia's mansion. This denial makes their gaiety seem somewhat amnesiac, for they have no thought of Shylock; they do not mention his name, though they speak of the rich Jew from whom Jessica "stole," who has become the unwilling benefactor of his daughter and son-in-law. It is as if Shylock the man had never existed, had never fathered Jessica, and had never cried out to Antonio and Salerio and Solanio about the indignities they heaped upon him. The heroes and heroines have come through the crisis of Shylock's murderous hatred unscathed and unaltered—and there's the rub, because those who have watched in the audience have been moved and perhaps disturbed by the nature of the victory that the last scene celebrates, and their memory of Shylock and the courtroom scene is still immediate and vivid. The joy of the final scene might be more satisfying if it were tinged with regret or if it included one touch of sorrow. But to wish for this complexity of tone is to wish that Shakespeare's characters were different in nature—or is it to wish that Shakespeare did not share the blindered attitudes of the Venetians to the alien Jew?

To some *The Merchant* is a reminder that Shakespeare was necessarily a man of his age, one who accepted its fundamental biases because it would never have occurred to him to question them. E. E. Stoll has no doubt that Shakespeare conceived of Shylock as a buffoon and comic villain because Jews were condemned and anathematized by Church doctrine, accused through the centuries of inhuman crimes, portrayed as bloodthirsty in legend and folktale, and despised throughout Christian society.[1] As an alien minority they were barely tolerated in the best of times and made the targets of official extortions, recurrent pogroms, and occasional wholesale massacres. The sorry history of Jew hatred does not, however, support Stoll's claim that Shylock is to be equated with conventional stereotypes of Jewish villainy. The villainous Jew can be found in novellas like *Il Pecorone*, but he is remarkably absent from the great literature of the Renaissance, and especially from the great literature of Renaissance England. He does not appear in any of the extant comedies or tragedies of Kyd, Greene, Dekker, Chapman, Jonson, Tourneur, Webster, Middleton, and Ford. The only villainous Jew portrayed in Elizabethan drama before Shylock is Marlowe's Barabas, and Barabas serves for much of *The Jew of Malta* as a stalking horse for Marlowe's scathing satire on Christian greed and hypocrisy before he achieves a degraded grandeur as a murderous Machiavel. The only other dramatic portrait of a Jew that precedes Shylock appears in Wilson's *Three Ladies of London* (1583), and there the Jew is not a snarling monster but rather noble and forgiving. In other words, Shylock is not one of many similar anti-Semitic dramatic portraits that can be explained by reference to Elizabethan prejudice against Jews. He exists, it would seem, because Barabas exists, because Shakespeare was inspired by *The Jew of Malta* to write his own play about a Jew and his daughter. If Shakespeare reduced the complexity of Marlowe's protagonist to a simple anti-Semitic caricature, he was almost unique among Elizabethans to use his art in this way.[2] Shall we believe that the dramatist who portrayed the black Othello as a noble heroic figure could not imagine a Jew as possessed of human feeling or deserving of understanding and sympathy? If this is so, we have mistook him all this while—his was not the most universal of minds.

The beginning of wisdom about *The Merchant* is a recognition that historical scholarship cannot establish what Shylock is or has to be and it cannot dictate our response to him.[3] The attempt to reduce Shylock to the bloodthirsty usurer of *Il Pecorone* is especially ironic in view of the astonishing transformation of source materials that takes place in *The Merchant*, which turns a cynical and somewhat sordid tale of Italianate cunning into a greatly poetic, romantic comedy; it also makes the despised money-lender a great dramatic figure, equal in importance to the romantic hero and heroine. Like many other novellas, *Il Pecorone* tells of intrigue, lust, and greed. Its hero, Giannetto (Bassanio) is a little soiled in the working; he lies to his benefactor to get money to obtain a rich wife, and when he finally outwits and marries her, he forgets for a time his benefactor's terrible plight. The Lady of Belmont is not a virginal maiden but rather a scheming, mercenary widow who offers to wed any man who can bed her, and by drugging the wine of her suitors wins the forfeit of their wealth. If the Lady of Belmont can turn into Portia, and Gianetto into the gentle Bassanio, it is conceivable that the Jewish money-lender may also become a nobler figure than he is in Shakespeare's source.

Errors, as we have seen, also significantly alters the tone of its source, *Menaechmi*, by eliminating its cynical assumptions and values and by making its characters more attractive and sympathetic. But the dramatic world of *Errors* closely approximates the bourgeois milieu of *Menaechmi*, whereas the dramatic world (or worlds) of *The Merchant* bears no resemblance to the tawdry novella world of *Il Pecorone*. For Shakespeare creates in Belmont and Venice a sense of splendor that is unique in the comedies, an imaginative realization of the magnificence of Renaissance Italy without any trace of Italianate corruption. To Belmont come the greatest princes of the world, for Portia is a rich and beautiful prize that inspires mythic comparisons. She is the golden fleece for which argonauts risk their chance of future happiness in marriage. She is another Virginia, a newfound land that offers the spendthrift gallant a second chance to recoup his estate. Feminine, delicate, graced with music and poetry, Belmont is the ideal setting for a romantic quest but Portia is not to be won by sighing protestations, aubades, and love poems. Who would win her must make hazard of himself, accept the fairytale challenge of the three caskets, and prove his worthiness in a trial of mind and heart that is redolent of many legendary testings of the purity and dedication of questing heroes.

Superficially Belmont is opposed as well as juxtaposed to Venice, a world in which men compete for profit and commercial advantage, in which ordinarily they risk only their capital—and their seamen's lives—in hope of the fabulous wealth to be gained by trade with Africa and Asia. Yet money and contract are as significant forces in Belmont as in Venice because Portia is immensely rich and the terms set down for winning her are as specific as those in any commercial transaction, even to stipulation of the forfeit that will be exacted should the wooer fail to achieve his objective. The law that protects the sanctity of commercial contracts in Venice also protects the right of Portia's deceased father to determine by will the way that his ducats and his daughter may be obtained. Conversely, Venice is not merely a trading center like the busy ports of Holland and Germany. She is a great maritime republic whose influence extended throughout the known world, whose argosies returned with silks and spices and treasures bartered for, or ransacked from, the fabled cities of the Mediterranean. The queen of the Adriatic, Venice was celebrated for its music and painting, its exquisite glasswares, splendid palaces, and churches.[4]

The dialogue of *The Merchant* makes clear the opulence of Venice, whose merchants are aristocratic in manner as well as means. The chaffering of the marketplace is heard only in the scenes with Shylock; otherwise the streets of Venice are the places where friends meet to talk and pass the time, to give and accept invitations to dinner and festive evenings. Great merchants like Antonio do not spend anxious hours in counting houses, for their risks are spread over many enterprises and a single loss cannot disable their estates. With such security, Antonio can indulge his generous instincts and be gracious to those less fortunate. He can look tolerantly on Bassanio's prodigality, which has made him as much Antonio's dependent as his bosom friend. Such wealth also breeds a kind of ennui, for Antonio lacks a challenge or goal to excite his interest. He has no taste for extravagant expenditure and he does not speak of his commercial successes with the pleasure Shylock takes in describing his cunning "thrift." It would be a mistake, however, to exaggerate Antonio's sadness or to take seriously Gratiano's boisterous rebuke of Antonio's "lifelessness"—"why should a man whose blood is warm within, / Sit like his grandsire, cut in alabaster?" Although life seems to have passed Antonio by, he does not regret bygone days or lost friends; it is unlikely that he ever heard the chimes at midnight. He takes a modest pride in his sobriety, even as he apologizes for it. By choice or by accident he is older than his companions; and by calling attention to his sadness, he invites and enjoys their somewhat envious solicitude and ragging. His affection for Bassanio, however, is not consciously selfish, and he takes a genuine if vicarious pleasure in advancing his younger friend's prospects.

Some who think that Shylock is a nasty caricature of a Jew are ready to compensate for Shakespeare's anti-Semitism by turning Antonio into a closet homosexual whose love of Bassanio is greedy and possessive.[5] Others, too polite to inquire into Antonio's sexual preferences, nevertheless speak of Antonio and Portia as rivals for Bassanio's love, although Antonio presses Bassanio to accept his aid in the quest of Portia's hand in marriage. Surely an Antonio who wished to monopolize Bassanio's affections could find an excuse not to provide money for the venture in Belmont, given the fact that all his wealth was engaged at present and he had to borrow money to lend it to Bassanio. Without a moment's hesitation, however, he sends Bassanio off to obtain the loan and insists on taking the loan from Shylock over Bassanio's objection. To all but Shylock, Antonio is the noblest of men, one who does not brag of his wealth or lecture others on the need for thrift. A pompous man would not have accepted Gratiano's raillery with such good humor. When Gratiano advises him not to fish "with this melancholy bait / For this fool gudgeon, this opinion," Antonio responds with smiling humor; he will grow a talker for this gear.

Antonio's love of Bassanio hints of qualities in the latter that may not be immediately apparent, although from the beginning Bassanio stands apart from the other Venetians who surround Antonio. Awed by Antonio's wealth, Salerio and Solanio would like to have Antonio's gallies and the anxieties about their safety they humorously ascribe to him; they would like to worry about tempests when they cool their tea with a breath or fear jagged rocks when they go to church and look at stone monuments. Bassanio is not, like them, excited by the thought of such great wealth. He has a gift for friendship, not only with the sober Antonio but also with the madcap Gratiano, who is ready to gibe at any pretense or cant. He likes Gratiano even though he knows his limitations. After hearing Gratiano's advice to Antonio not to be a stuffed shirt, Bassanio sums up his friend's wisdom: he speaks "an infinite deal of nothing." These are not the words of a shallow prodigal or one incompetent to manage his own life. Indeed, no one suggests that Bassanio is spendthrift in his tastes or extravagant in his entertainments. He bears not the slightest resemblance to the gaming, wenching, decayed gentlemen who appear in the Jacobean comedies of Shakespeare's contemporaries.

If we listen carefully to Bassanio, we will appreciate those virtues that win the love and regard of Antonio and Portia. He is soft-natured rather than improvident; tender-hearted, not irresponsible; and more indulgent of others than himself. Although he has no money, he takes Gobbo into his service because Gobbo wishes to leave Shylock's employ, and although he knows that Gratiano's brashness may jeopardize his venture in Belmont, he will not deny Gratiano's request to accompany him. He is not good at keeping money, either his own or his wife's. He wishes to give the three thousand ducats that were meant for Shylock to the young judge who saved Antonio, even though the judge desires no fee. Having no head for business, he has nothing to show for the monies he borrowed before from Antonio, and it is clear that he will always need generous friends if he does not marry an heiress. This is not to say, however, that the need for money oppresses Bassanio or that he brands himself a fortune hunter. He is not inspired to woo Portia as Petruchio is inspired to woo Kate, by talk of her dowry. Like Claudio and Benedick in *Much Ado*, he has a sensible interest in his future wife's estate, but he speaks less of Portia's wealth than Sebastian speaks of Olivia's gifts in *Twelfth Night*. Calculations of profit and loss are not Bassanio's forte; his appeal to Antonio for additional funds is almost child-like in its naïveté and in its shame-faced hesitancies. His parable of arrows lost and found is innocent enough, but not germane to the case and far more appropriate to a schoolboy than a Venetian nobleman. The money he spent will not be found again; it does not lie like an arrow in the underbrush waiting for the keen-eyed archer to find it. If his present venture follows the path of his earlier ones, his failure is assured. Although eager to present himself as a practical man, Bassanio unfolds a business prospectus for Antonio that is a tale out of Mother Goose, one that would draw laughter from any impartial entrepreneur. He does not disclose all the risks of this venture, for though it is true that Portia looked at him in a way that tokened her affection, she is not able to follow her heart. Everything depends on Bassanio's ability to solve the riddle of the caskets. Yet he is honest enough in detailing the odds against him. He speaks of the suitors who flock to Belmont from every nation, and he confesses that he has only a presentiment that he will succeed where many others have failed. His little homilies and indirections are not clumsy attempts at evasion; they reveal how painful it is to ask for more money when he has been unable to repay previous loans.

Antonio is annoyed that Bassanio does not immediately ask for the money he needs because that hesitancy makes some small question of Antonio's generosity. He does not sympathize with—or understand—Bassanio's need to "wind about his love with circumstance"; nor does he realize that his readiness to allow Bassanio to make "waste of all I have" must pain his unsuccessful friend. Such generosity is as insensitive as it is noble, for while he is insulted by Bassanio's hesitancy, he will not allow Bassanio any vestige of manly pride. Moments like these leave no doubt that it is better to give than to receive, and it is much easier to be able to give than to have to receive. Later in the play Antonio will discover how burdensome the debt of gratitude can be; here he is too accustomed to his role as benefactor to appreciate Bassanio's feelings, and because of that role Bassanio cannot be his equal in friendship, for the older man has the power money bestows while the younger man must accept his generosity knowing that he will probably be unable to repay what is loaned to him. Jessica can take what she needs (or wants) from Shylock without hesitation or shame at stealing from her father. Bassanio finds the gift of love burdensome even when freely offered because he would have the sense of worth that is denied the dependent.[6]

The power that Antonio's wealth gives him over his younger friends is matched by the power that Portia's father exerts over her life through the instrument of his will, which stipulates how she can be won. Like Antonio, Portia is very rich, and, so she says, weary of this great world. Nerissa has heard these sighing complaints before and rebukes them with gentle humor and sound philosophy even as Gratiano, her future husband, rebuked Antonio's melancholy. Portia's reflections on life reveal that she is as witty and perceptive as the heroines of *Love's Labor's*, but more obviously romantic in temperament; although she has, like them, a keen eye for the follies of men, she gives her heart ardently and completely to the man who deserves her love. Her pleasure in her femininity appears in her plaintive reference to her "little body" and she enjoys her role as the beauteous heiress whom all desire at the same time that she complains that she cannot choose whom she will marry. A few pious sentences from Nerissa about her father's virtue are sufficient to curb these rebellious thoughts, even though Portia has just before observed that good sentences are ineffectual when the will rebels. Her situation is that of the fairy-tale heroine who languishes in a tower and can be released only by a lover's courage and ingenuity—a sleeping beauty who can be awakened by a lover's kiss. As such, she should have long golden hair and a passive disposition. But she is not helpless or docile; even before she defeats Shylock, she is clearly a match for any man in insight and shrewdness.

The characterization of Portia is a triumph of artistic inspiration over ordinary logic, for how can she be both the princess in the tower and the confident, adventurous clever wench of folklore who defeats a cunning ogre? Only an unconventional woman could dominate the masculine arena of the law court, but only a conventional dutiful woman would submit to her father's will and not bend an article of it to assure her own happiness. Whereas the heroine in *Il Pecorone* is all of a piece, a cunning contriver in Belmont and in Venice, Portia is rich in seeming contrarieties, a heroine who is eager to assume a traditional role as adoring wife, and yet one who is confident of her ability to defeat Shylock when all others have failed. Despite the fairy-tale aura of the caskets, her situation is not radically different from that of Silvia or other heroines whose choice of husband is subject to a father's will and to the proprieties that dictate the nature of maidenly behavior. She waits to be wooed as women have always waited because modesty and caution forbid her to be too forward. Like any well-bred gentlewoman, Portia's freedom is circumscribed by her position in society. She must marry well, even if that means marrying some dolt with a title and money; she cannot follow her heart unless she is willing to sacrifice the opinion of the world.

One cannot imagine Beatrice waiting patiently in Belmont for a Benedick to arrive while a dozen dismal suitors try their luck at winning her. One doubts also that she would have allowed a great inheritance to quell her independent spirit. On the other hand, one cannot imagine Beatrice, for all her bristling independence, venturing forth as Portia does to rescue Antonio, for in a moment of crisis she turns to Benedick to champion Hero's cause and complains that she is not a man. Portia does not chafe at her circumstances, because even as she scrupulously obeys the dictates of her father's will, she seems to command her fate and does not seem to dread the possibility of being won by some lucky boor. She views her current suitors with cool amusement and describes with mocking satire their chasings after fashion, their rudenesses, and lack of breeding. She is relieved that the Frenchman, Englishman, Scot, German, and Neopolitan have left without risking the choice of the caskets, but her pulse quickens at Nerissa's praise of Bassanio and she hesitates only a moment before admitting her interest in him.

Portia enters the play immediately after Bassanio's glowing description of her. Shylock, who is to be her adversary, enters unannounced, as it were; there is not the slightest anticipation that Bassanio's need for money will involve him with a hated Jewish moneylender. If Shylock is immediately identified as a Jew by his clothing and manner of speech, he is not immediately typed as a cunning villain. Bassanio is not afraid of Shylock and nothing he says intimates that out of necessity he is dealing with a blood-sucking usurer. He walks on stage with someone who is obviously unlike the other Venetians in dress and mien, not with a villain who, sotto voce, gloats over the prospect of yet another victim. If anything, Shylock seems more concerned about the safety of his capital than the prospect of a handsome return. His slow, repetitious consideration of the terms of the proposed loan is the familiar hesitation of a businessman who does not want to seem too eager to close a deal. Where a confidence man would pretend an affable indifference to the terms to allay his victim's suspicions, Shylock is all caution, pedantic in his enumeration of the risk involved, even to the explanation of what he means by land rats and water rats. He exaggerates nothing in hope of greater usury. He readily admits that Antonio, whom he detests, is a "good man"—that is, financially sound. He knows precisely what ventures Antonio is presently engaged in, and, after consideration, he acknowledges that they do not imperil his worth: "I think," he concedes, "I may take his bond." This does not sound like a man who is ready to risk all to be revenged but rather one who has no taste for the risks that Antonio ordinarily assumes. He would not squander his ventures abroad, and he cannot, as a hated alien, afford the luxury of denying loans, even to his enemies.

Of course, Shylock is not all business. His pauses, seeming forgetfulness, and repetitions prolong the pleasurable moment when a Christian must wait upon his answer, and the moment is doubly pleasurable because Bassanio is so eager, so anxious for the loan, ready even to invite Shylock to talk with Antonio over dinner, an invitation that Shylock feels he can scornfully refuse. The luxury of contempt is not one he can usually afford; what he can assert is his right to make up his own mind. When Bassanio assures Shylock that he can take Antonio's bond, Shylock replies, "I will be assured I may. / And that I may be assured, I will bethink me." If Shylock's careful consideration of the bond and his readiness to express his repugnance at Christian ways ("I will not eat with you, drink with you, nor pray with you") are supposed to identify him as an unscrupulous but artful dissimulator, they do not succeed; and one must wonder why Shakespeare does not remove any doubt of Shylock's wickedness in the asides Shylock utters. The worst

Shylock reveals about himself is that he hates Antonio bitterly and, if he could, he would "feed fat the ancient grudge" he bears him. That Shylock even now hungers to tear the flesh from Antonio's breast is dubious. His figure of speech is a conventional expression of hatred similar to Beatrice's desire to eat Claudio's heart in the marketplace. To see the half-mad Shylock of the courtroom scene in the Shylock who discusses terms with Bassanio is as mistaken as to see the Iago who senselessly murders his wife at the close of *Othello* in the petty cheat and confidence man who brags of his duplicity to Roderigo in the opening scene of the play. Iago's progress from swindling to murderous conspiracies is paralleled by Shylock's progress from a proud, successful businessman to the defiant outcast who whets his knife on the sole of his shoe, indifferent to everything but the satisfaction of his blood-lust. We can say that, like Iago's, Shylock's descent into villainy actualizes what is latent in his nature so long as we keep in mind that the same can be said of Macbeth when he murders Duncan and of Hamlet when he murders Polonius.

Because Portia is utterly convincing as a character, so too is the fairy tale of the caskets that hold the key to her future. Because Antonio and Shylock are completely convincing as characters, they persuade us that intelligent, prac-tical men can agree to the horror of the "merry bond," which stipulates a forfeit of human flesh if the loan is not repaid. The agreement would present no problems if Antonio were ignorant of Shylock's hatred or if he were desperate for funds and had no choice but to accept whatever terms Shylock demands. But no, Antonio is not hard-pressed; he borrows only because he wishes to underwrite Bassanio's venture in Belmont, and he agrees to the bond with full knowledge of Shylock's hatred—indeed, only moments after he and Shylock have openly expressed their loathing of one another. That enmity is one of the more fascinating puzzles of the play because Shylock is not an obvious bloodsucker; he does not resemble the grasping usurers of the Jacobean stage who brag of their nefarious extortions, who foist off worthless commodities on foolish heirs and trick them into signing away their estates.[7] What rate of interest Shylock usually charges is never revealed, and we never learn what rate he intended to charge Bassanio because just when he is at the point of naming the rate, he launches instead into a recital of the wrongs and abuses he has endured from Antonio.

Is that not bizarre behavior for a diabolical villain? Does one lay a cunning snare for an enemy by reminding him of the reasons one has to loathe him? Not a fawning hypocrite who pretends friendship and love, Shylock has learned the necessity of cringing before Venetians, as he does in his first words to Antonio, but he would rather point out the contradictions and cruelty of Antonio's behavior than close a loan at advantageous terms. He could, in fact, have concluded the terms with Bassanio, contingent on Antonio's signature, but he wants to speak to Antonio before he makes the loan, knowing of course that Antonio would prefer to say nothing to him in these circumstances. If Antonio were a voice for moderation and reasonableness in commercial transactions, we could judge from his loathing how exorbitant Shylock is in his money-lending. But Antonio is not revolted by exorbitant rates; he objects to the charging of any interest on loans, even though in Venice as elsewhere in Renaissance Europe, borrowing money at interest was a customary business practice, which was tolerated though not officially "allowed" in Shakespeare's England.[8] Antonio's revulsion against interest is an extreme form of idealism, one which the Catholic church could expound but which had no meaning in the burgeoning commercial world of Elizabethan England, where venture capital was an economic necessity and public playhouses were constructed with funds obtained in the form of interest-bearing loans.[9]

Antonio's condemnation of interest is not echoed by any other Venetian and does not appear to be customary or universal. He is able to champion an outworn ideal because he is wealthy enough to be generous, and he practices his generosity within a small circle of Venetian friends and acquaintances. Now he stands on very slippery ground; wanting to be generous to Bassanio and morally superior to Shylock, he finds it unbearable to have to chaffer with the moneylender he despises. He salves his conscience, however, by announcing that he would not lend or borrow money for interest in his own behalf; "yet to supply the ripe wants of my friend, / I'll break a custom." Since he has no compelling reason to violate his sacred principle, he must convince himself that he is not stooping to an abhorred practice. The solution is to make Bassanio his "damned soul," even though it was Antonio who unhesitatingly decided to borrow the money Bassanio needed. His selflessness declared, he feels justified in continuing to revile Shylock. Indeed, precisely because his moral situation is slippery, he must be unbending in his scorn. He is the kind of idealist who demonstrates the purity of his conviction by his uncompromising contempt for those who believe otherwise. His high-mindedness and his championing of a universal moral principle free him from any need for civility to Shylock, and yet one cannot imagine him making interest-free loans to foreigners or aliens; his "universal" principle assumes a world of Venetians and Christians, a world without Jews or Turks.

Enjoying Antonio's discomfort, Shylock prolongs the negotiations; brushing Bassanio aside, he forces Antonio to deal with him face to face, one successful businessman to another. His pride in his success blinds him to the ugliness of defending sharp practice by citing the story of Jacob. He does not speak as one who wants kinder treatment from Venetians; indeed, he can hardly hope to educate Antonio, who rated him, called him misbeliever and cut-throat dog, spat on his beard and his Jewish gabardine, and kicked at him as "you spurn a stranger cur / Over your threshold." He has been allowed his place on the Rialto because he is needed and because he has accepted his humiliations as a good Jew (or a good nigger) should, without ever attempting to talk back, much less strike back. Now he would lift his head and talk plainly to these Christians, who make use of him or abuse him as their occasion warrants:

> . . . moneys is your suit.
> What should I say to you? Should I not say,
> "Hath a dog money? Is it possible
> A cur can lend three thousand ducats?" Or
> Shall I bend low and in a bondman's key,
> With bated breath, and whisp'ring humbleness,
> Say this:
> "Fair sir, you spet on me on Wednesday last,
> You spurn'd me such a day, another time
> You call'd me dog; and for these courtesies
> I'll lend you thus much moneys"?
>
> (1.3. 119–29)

That Shylock has not exaggerated is made clear by Antonio's furious response:

> I am as like to call thee so again,
> To spet on thee again, to spurn thee too.
>
> (1.3. 130–31)

It is bad enough that Antonio has come to the Jew to borrow money at interest. It is intolerable to him that Shylock should expose the false assumption that supports his high principle. That is to say, how can the generosity of friendship be accepted as a norm of commercial dealings when all men are not friends and when Antonio, like the other Venetians, is incapable of treating Shylock like a fellow human being? Since he cannot ask Shylock to lend money gratis as to a friend, his only alternative is to ask Shylock to "lend it rather to thine enemy, / Who if he break, thou mayst with better face / Exact the penalty." What a mind this is! Antonio cannot admit the possibility that lending money is a business transaction, not an act of friendship, and therefore should earn a reasonable profit for the lender. But he can turn his idealism inside out to justify his present actions: if interest-free loans are the appropriate arrangement between friends, then loans at interest are an appropriate arrangement between enemies. Who could ask for a more high-minded conclusion?

Shylock, of course, is not morally superior to Antonio. The abuse he has endured has not made him patient or compassionate. His awareness of the hypocrisy of Christians does not prevent him from using his religion to justify a personal vendetta: "Cursed be my tribe," he whispers, "If I forgive him." He fawningly rejects Antonio's suggestion that they deal with one another as enemies. He would be friends, he says; he would have Antonio's love, forget past insults, and lend him money without interest. Shylock's manner is cunning and hypocritical; his motive, however, is far from clear. He cannot hope that Antonio will break the merry bond because the sum in question is trifling in comparison with Antonio's wealth. Only a fool would dream of catching Antonio on the hip in this transaction, though the dream must give Shylock greedy satisfaction. He can also enjoy the fact that Antonio responds as if the offer of friendship were genuine, even though the terms of the forfeit express a sickening hatred. If Antonio were more principled—or more sensitive—he would refuse Shylock's offer; he agrees to it, however, because it allows him to take the Jew's money and keep his idealism unsullied. It also allows him to tell himself that his steadfast adherence to principle has improved the Jew's character. Not fearing the possibility of forfeiture, he says that the Jew grows kind while Shylock rolls his eyes at the suspiciousness of Christians, whose bad dealings teach them to doubt the motives of others.

At this moment Bassanio's nobility asserts itself. Although he needs the money and has more compelling reason than Antonio to deceive himself about this merry bond, he would not have Antonio seal to it for him. He likes not "fair terms and a villain's mind," but Antonio pushes aside his fears with assurances about his ability to repay the loan. When Shylock exits, Antonio remarks to Bassanio that "The Hebrew will turn Christian; he grows kind," a statement that borders on the fatuous and could be made only by one whose high principle is insulated from reality. He can patronize Shylock knowing that his hatred is impotent; the loan will be repaid, and if it were not, the despised Jew would not dare to take his savage forfeit.

Unless we believe that Shylock knows in advance what Antonio is going to think and say, we cannot believe that the merry bond is a calculated strategem, for it is Antonio who first suggests that the loan be signed to as an act of hatred between enemies. Shylock, who takes pride in his business acumen, never gloats over his success in this matter or congratulates himself on deceiving those Christians. In his next appearance, he makes no reference to the "ensnaring" of Antonio either in dialogue or soliloquy. He speaks to Jessica only of his scorn for Christian prodigality and idle amusements. Alone with his daughter, Shylock reveals a claustrophobic contempt and suspicion of the Christian world in which he lives. His soul is not great with evil desires, it is petty in its aspirations and satisfactions. By instinct he is joyless and acquisitive, and both traits have been exacerbated by his outcast role in Venetian society. He is capable of at most a grudging affection for Launcelot Gobbo, who is leaving his household to enter Bassanio's service. "The patch," he confesses, "is kind enough, but a huge feeder / Snail slow in profit." Gobbo knows that such responses do not bespeak a fiendish mind. When he debates with himself whether to leave Shylock, he calls his master "a kind of devil," nay, "the very devil incarnation," yet his conscience, he says, tells him to stay with Shylock while the fiend tempts him to go. Either Gobbo is all confusion or there is a suggestion that loyalty to a Jew has some meaning. The unhappy Jessica also contemplates leaving her father to marry Lorenzo; she is both ashamed to be her father's daughter and ashamed to be disloyal in thought and deed, but her struggle of conscience is, if anything, more shallow than Gobbo's.

Jessica's elopement by torchlight into a Venetian carnival is not a quintessentially romantic adventure, for she is not a Julia or a Hermia who hazards all for love. She helps herself to her father's money and jewels to finance a honeymoon with Lorenzo, and she is as casual in spending Shylock's money as she is lighthearted in taking it. Portia's situation parallels Jessica's; her response to it is totally different. She keeps faith with the terms of her father's will and she makes certain that those who try the riddle of the caskets understand precisely what they stand to lose and win. Her welcome to Morocco and Arragon is correct if not cordial. Like Venice, Belmont opens its gates to visitors from every nation and Portia treats all with official courtesy. All have the same opportunity to win her, but they are far from equal in her judgment. She assures the Prince of Morocco that despite his dark complexion he stands "as fair / As any comer I have looked on yet / For my affection." This is tactful and politic (he may, after all, guess rightly) but not quite sincere, for she had earlier said to Nerissa, "If he have the condition of a saint and the complexion of a devil, I had rather he should shrive me than wive me," a casual joke of course, but the kind that only those with fair complexions make. When Morocco fails the test of the caskets and departs, Portia sighs with relief,

> A gentle riddance. Draw the curtains, go.
> Let all of his complexion choose me so.
>
> (2.7. 78–79)

This is not a Desdemona who could find a Moor's visage in his mind; she is very much a product of her society, as she will demonstrate in her treatment of the defeated Shylock. Before Bassanio arrives, she regards all her suitors as foreigners who can be described with the usual canards about their national characteristics.

Complexions are also at issue in the choice of the caskets: one of bright gold, another of gleaming silver, and the third of sullen lead. To choose rightly is to win a beauteous heiress; to choose wrongly is to forfeit one's chance to marry anyone. Since the task requires an ability to solve the riddles of the inscriptions and to assay the silent messages of the caskets, no fool need apply. On the other hand, if the choosing were merely a test of intelligence or worldly shrewdness, the fairy-tale quest would lose its romantic aura. To win Portia, a suitor must have the right motive as well as an ability to see through false appearances; he must love her for herself and understand the intrinsic connection between loving and hazarding.

Morocco and Arragon choose sensibly and wrongly according to their individual bents and unwitting needs. It is almost inevitable that Morocco choose the gold casket because, despite Portia's assurances, he knows the way Europeans look on dark-skinned races and cannot admit the possibility that he is inferior to them. In greeting Portia he proclaimed the worth of his blood and courage and announced that he would not change his hue except to "steal" her thoughts. Yet when he mulls over the inscription on the silver casket, "Who chooseth me shall get as much as he deserves," he wonders if his desert "may not extend so far as to the lady." He immediately dismisses this thought as "a weak disabling" of himself but he has neither the wit nor the self-confidence to make an unconventional choice. It is necessary for him to identify himself with all the world and therefore choose "what many men desire." His reward is a death's-head and a scornful message about false seemings and foolish judgments that befits his shallow calculation that nothing less than gold could be worthy of this "angel" Portia. He does not convict himself of greed; he is too ordinary, however, to transcend the crass values expressed in his meditation on the decorum of noble tombs and the appropriate coinage for Portia's semblance.

Arragon comes closer to solving the riddle of the caskets. He knows that gold, which promises what many men desire, is often a snare, for the many are often a fool multitude that judge by outward appearances. His reflections are impressive in their way, and his choice of silver a logical enough deduction from his premises. Since he will not "jump with common spirits," and since it is hubristic to aim above one's deserts, he chooses the silver casket, but not before he delivers a shrewd commentary on the inequities of a world in which true merit is often ignored while title and wealth are often "derived corruptly." Does Arragon deserve a portrait of a blinking idiot and a sneering bit of doggerel about foolish judgments? If it is folly to hope that one will be rewarded according to one's deserts, it is folly also to hope for justice on earth. Arragon lacks imagination, not shrewdness. He is blind to the hint of the lead casket that love involves a hazarding of self as well as a gaining of desire. He chooses very sensibly and, therefore, not well. Even so, Portia's response seems unfeeling: "O, these deliberate fools, when they do choose, / They have the wisdom by their wit to lose." The way that clever men outsmart themselves amuses her here, as it will again in the trial scene and afterward.

Arragon's defeat sets the stage for Bassanio's arrival and testing, which comes even as Antonio's losses and Shylock's frenzy at Jessica's elopement are preparing the way for the horror of the forfeit in Venice. Ill fortune can bring a successful merchant to his knees; it is less probable, however, that the improvident Bassanio, whose other ventures failed, will be able to solve the baffling riddle of the caskets. Even Portia, who loves and cherishes Bassanio before he proves his worthiness in the trial of the caskets, is fearful that he may choose wrongly, and that fear shakes her customary poise. Her willingness to declare her love before he chooses is a lovely touch of incaution that testifies to the depth of her feeling. When she speaks of her desire to keep him a month or two in Belmont before he risks the test, her lines are as hesitant and her thought as indirect as Bassanio's when he had to ask Antonio for money:

> There's something tells me (but it is not love)
> I would not lose you, and you know yourself,
> Hate counsels not in such a quality.
> But lest you should not understand me well—
> And yet a maiden hath no tongue but thought—
> I would detain you here some month or two
> Before you venture for me.
>
> (3.2. 4–10)

Despite her fears, she will not give in to the temptation to teach him how to choose, though some have found a cunning hint of the solution to the riddles in the lyrics of the song that is sung while he ponders his choice.[10] But if she is going to be false, she would be a fool to risk losing Bassanio by using so indirect a hint. Where Jessica says it is a heinous sin to be ashamed of her father and elopes with crammed pockets, Portia will be a faithful daughter whatever the consequence. She must have confidence in Bassanio's wisdom as well as her father's because if he cannot by himself solve the riddle, he is not worthy to be her husband. As Bassanio pauses before the caskets, she tries to allay her fears by mock-heroic imaginings. He is her Alcides about to slay the sea monster; she is Hesione saved from death. She will have music sound while he chooses so that he may swanlike die, "fading in music," if he loses. If successful, he will be greeted with flourishes like a new-crowned monarch and with the dulcet music that awakens a bridegroom on his wedding day. Love quickens what is best and brightest in Portia's spirit; for the first time she is not in command of the situation and having frankly confessed her love and vulnerability, she tempers her anxiety with humorous self-irony.

What was before a contest of wits between Portia's father and her suitors becomes now a meeting of true minds. "If you love me," she says to Bassanio, "you will find me out." To find her requires innocence as well as worldly wisdom, a sense of the ideal in love that is unspoiled by knowledge of the tawdriness of most of the prizes of the world. Since Portia imagines herself a virgin sacrifice, Bassanio must rise to heights of mythic heroism: he must be like Oedipus before the Sphinx or Alexander facing the Gordian knot. His ability to match Portia's wordplay about treason and confession augurs well of their future together and of his ability to succeed where Morocco and Arragon have failed. He approaches his task with a wariness that at first seems limited to commonplace prudence. He will not be taken in by false appearances because he knows that corrupt pleas, religious errors, vice, and cowardice can be masked by pleasing shows. As he continues to assess the choices, however, prudence gives way to poetic insight. The thought of a woman's false hair—golden locks taken from a corpse—connects human vanity and meretricious beauty to the lesson of the death's-head. There is no thought of himself, not a single "I," in Bassanio's lines until his mind is made up, then he swiftly rejects "gaudy gold, / Hard food for Midas," and silver "pale and common drudge / 'Tween man and man." Intuition rather than reason guides his choice of "meager lead," whose "paleness moves [him] more than eloquence." Fearing lightness, that which is easily acquired, he chooses the "threatening" heaviness, the sadness of lead, on which he hazards all. The ability to see beneath appearances that made Bassanio recoil from Shylock's merry bond is here confirmed. He is wise enough to doubt all but love itself, which is not mocked by time and death as are the prizes for which other men hazard all.

Opening the casket, Bassanio is dazzled by the beauty of Portia's image, yet not so dazzled that he forgets that this prize is itself an appearance cunningly contrived. The scroll bids him claim his lady with a loving kiss, as Morocco or Arragon would have done if either had succeeded. Before he did not calculate what he deserved; now he will not claim his bride unless she offers herself, and so he turns to Portia to give and to receive; he will not think that she is his unless she ratifies his victory. Thus at the moment that supposedly reduces Portia to the victor's prize, Bassanio releases her from bondage to her father's will and allows her freely to choose her husband. The other romantic comedies end when the obstacles to love have been overcome or are dissolved. Here love triumphs without the customary rituals and trials of wooing, and yet Portia's and Bassanio's speeches are the fullest realization in the comedies of the ideal of romantic love. The Petrarchan conceits that fell so easily from the lips of Proteus, Valentine, Lysander, and Demetrius echo briefly in Bassanio's admiration for Portia's portrait; then they gave way to the lovely simplicity of their mutual vows.

Only a skilled actress can convince us that the poised, witty Portia of the first scenes is the anxious, vulnerable, ardent bride-to-be of the casket scene who speaks of herself as an unpracticed maiden, happy in her innocence and ability to learn, and who commits herself to be schooled by "her lord, her governor, her king." If this surrender of self is an artful pretense, it is a gratuitous one, however, because Bassanio does not solicit it with manner or words. He does not play Petruchio in a way that would tempt her to play at being the Kate of the last scene of *The Shrew.* Rather than conceiving of himself as Portia's lord, he describes her loving words to him after he has chosen the right casket as "some oration fairly spoke / By a beloved prince." Portia does not speak like Kate; she speaks like Juliet of the immeasurable bounty of her love, and being more worldly than Juliet she attempts to express that yearning in arithmetical figures:

> I would not be ambitious in my wish
> To wish myself much better, yet for you
> I would be trebled twenty times myself,
> A thousand times more fair, ten thousand times more rich,
> That only to stand high in your account,
> I might in virtues, beauties, livings, friends,
> Exceed account.
>
> (3.2. 151–57)

The joy of the occasion, which increases when Nerissa and Gratiano tell of their love and desire to marry, is brief, for Jessica, Lorenzo, and Salerio enter with news of Antonio's peril. If any doubt of Bassanio's nobility remained, it is erased by his response to Antonio's letter. He makes no attempt at self-justification; he does not tell how he recoiled from Shylock's proposal of the merry bond and told Antonio not to seal to it. He needed the money and he allowed Antonio to brush aside his fears. He confesses that when he told Portia he had nothing, he spoke falsely because in truth he "was worse than nothing"; he was the penniless man who allowed his dearest friend to engage himself to a mere enemy to feed his means. Portia is as generous as Bassanio is honest. She would have Shylock paid double or triple the sum owed to him; more important, she immediately chooses to subordinate her rights and desires as Bassanio's bride to his obligation to Antonio. She would have him leave for Venice before they have enjoyed their wedding night, for she knows that he could not lie by her side with a quiet soul while Antonio is in mortal danger. On the surface, at least, Antonio's letter is more generous still because it makes no claim on Bassanio; although he faces a terrible death, Antonio would not have Bassanio return to Venice if it were inconvenient.

"Sweet Bassanio, my ships have all miscarried, my creditors grow cruel, my estate is very low, my bond to the Jew is forfeit; and since in paying it, it is impossible I should live, all debts are clear'd between you and I, if I might but see you at my death. Notwithstanding, use your pleasure; if your love do not persuade you to come, let not my letter."

(3.2. 315–22)

Can Antonio imagine that Bassanio will refuse the pathetic appeal implicit in his words? The very thought that Bassanio might prefer to "use [his] pleasure" is mean-spirited. Antonio was annoyed when Bassanio hesitated to ask for more money because that hesitation seemed to question Antonio's willingness to give all. Yet he does not see the insult implicit in the suggestion that Bassanio might be too busy to visit him in his time of extremity. This is a man who slenderly knows himself and will not see that his extreme of self-abnegation must lacerate Bassanio's already tormented conscience.[11]

Shylock, of course, is infinitely more repellent in his gloating over Antonio's plight. He will not heed any appeal for mercy, he says, because he has sworn an oath in heaven to have his bond, and of course religious vows take precedence over earthly considerations. Shylock's pleasure in having his enemy in his power is understandable. It is richly satisfying to cast away his fawning manner and openly express his contempt for the Christian even as he makes Antonio's insults the excuse for his inhumanity: "Thou call'dst me dog before thou hadst a cause, / But since I am a dog, beware my fangs." What is astonishing is the surprise of the Venetians at Shylock's fury, for Solanio and Salerio continue to bait him in the street and jeer at his misery even after learning of Antonio's losses. They brag to him of their role in Jessica's elopement and find his sorrow and anger at her "rebellion" a subject for coarse joking. When Shylock ominously warns, "Let Antonio look to his bond," they cannot believe that he will demand the terrible forfeit. It is not that they grant him any shred of human feeling; they simply cannot imagine that the hated outcast, the comic butt, will strike back at those who torment him. How could the buffoon who cried out in the streets for justice, for his ducats and his daughter without a sense of shame, be dangerous? The Christians laughed when he spoke of Jessica as his "own flesh and blood." They stole from him a child who was his collop, his flesh; should he not now tear away a pound of flesh from the bankrupt Antonio? It is ironic that Shylock's memorable assertion of his humanity should come at the very moment that an inhuman purpose is becoming fixed in his mind, but this irony does not lessen the force of Shylock's outcry. By now he is beyond caring about the Venetians' opinion, beyond wanting their recognition of him as a fellow human. He has tried to live with them, swallowed their insults, and put on a false geniality when the occasion demanded, but no longer. Now he will be himself with them—or rather he will be a new, terrible self—the very incarnation of the inhuman Jew of anti-Semitic legend. His is the hopeless self-destructive rage that burns down ghettos and that justifies a society's contemptuous view of its niggers. Having written off his daughter as an irretrievable loss, Shylock thinks only of the money she stole that he may yet recover. Thus he is made frantic by reports of the sums Jessica has already squandered:

A diamond gone, cost me two thousand ducats in Frankford! The curse never fell on our nation till now, I never felt it till now. Two thousand ducats in that, and other precious, precious jewels. I would my daughter were dead at my foot, and the jewels in her ear! Would she were hears'd at my foot, and the ducats in her coffin!

(3.1. 83–90)

This is Job turned burlesque comedian, wringing his hands over *his* turquoise that he had of Leah. He consoles himself with the fantasy that with Antonio gone, he can "make what merchandise I will" in Venice. But even if this outcome were possible—and it is not—the thought of profit is not uppermost in Shylock's mind, for he will not take nine thousand ducats for a pound of Antonio's flesh.

When Solanio and Salerio jeered at Shylock's misery, he claimed that he learned from Christians how to revenge a wrong. In the courtroom, however, he does not claim that the injuries done to him entitle him to mutilate and kill Antonio. He claims only that his bond is legal and cannot be abrogated. At least half-aware that his bloodlust is inhuman, he does not argue that his cause is good or just or even rational; instead he insists on the privilege of his "humor" as if his desire for Antonio's lifeblood were comparable to the harmless eccentricities and phobias of other men, some of whom cannot abide cats or pigs or bagpipes:

> So can I give no reason, nor I will not,
> More than a lodg'd hate and a certain loathing
> I bear Antonio. . . .

(4.1. 59–61)

Earlier he would not listen to Antonio because he would not be made "a soft and dull-eyed fool, / To shake the head, relent, and sigh." By the trial scene, however, he can listen to any appeal unmoved; he is even amused by the impotent rage of the Venetians. He answers Bassanio patiently, without vituperation; he responds to Gratiano's stream of invectives with smirking indifference. He affably counsels this "good youth" to repair his wit lest it fall to cureless ruin.

> Till thou canst rail the seal from off my bond,
> Thou but offend'st thy lungs to speak so loud.

(4.1. 139–40)

If Portia had known Shylock she might have been less confident of success when she set out in disguise for Venice, but then she does not assume that she alone will be able to save Antonio's life. She does not hasten to confront

Shylock and thereby perform the task that rightly belongs to Bassanio. She enters the courtroom only after the others have failed to change Shylock's mind or find a way to prevent his murderous purpose. She necessarily wears a disguise to plead in a court of law, which is open only to men, and she is content to leave the court in disguise once she has accomplished her purpose. Portia's disguise, like her talk of a religious pilgrimage, is a convention of romantic fabling, not a confirmation of a devious nature. She is nowhere more attractive than in her response to the threat to Antonio's life. She immediately gauges Bassanio's devotion to Antonio, and she knows he would be shattered by grief and remorse if Antonio were to die. Knowing that Antonio's plight must take precedent over her rights she does not pretend to be self-sacrificing, as Antonio does. It is for Bassanio's sake and for their future happiness that she sends him off, and she goes too because in rescuing Antonio, she rescues Bassanio from a life of regret. Splendidly composed in this crisis, she gives her household over to Lorenzo and gives specific instructions to Balthazar, her messenger to Doctor Bellario. When Lorenzo praises her selflessness in sending Bassanio to Venice, she replies that since Antonio must be very like Bassanio to be his "bosom lover," she is doing little enough to purchase "the semblance of my soul / From out the state of hellish cruelty!" Although this is modest enough, Portia catches the tincture of self-flattery in her explanation and adds, "This comes too near the praising of myself." Where Julia blushed at the thought of wearing a cod-piece, Portia looks forward to pretending to be a man, knowing that many cowards and braggards make the same pretense. Her host of suitors have taught her much about the foibles of men and she will use that knowledge when she confronts Shylock.

Portia's dialogue with Nerissa about their trip to Venice, and Shylock's clashes with the Duke, Bassanio, and Gratiano prepare the way for a climatic battle of wits between them. Some would find a clash of principles as well as personalities in the courtroom scene. Shylock they see as an embodiment of Hebraic legalism and Portia as a spokesman for the New Dispensation of Christian mercy.[12] This allegorical interpretation would be more convincing if Shylock, like Angelo in *Measure for Measure*, argued the necessity of strictness in the application of the law. What Shylock claims is only the right to "humor" his hatred of Antonio by taking the forfeit that his bond and Venetian law allow. The theological overtones and Morality echoes of Angelo's debate with Isabella are lacking in Portia's clash with Shylock because Antonio is not, like Claudio, a sinner who has broken the moral and divine law and must die if his offense is not forgiven. Antonio faces a horrible death because the law of contracts in Venice (and all the world) takes precedence over humane sentiments. As Antonio knows, the law is the law, and its course cannot be denied by the Duke, even if the law permits one man to have a lien on another man's flesh. As Shylock points out, what difference is there between having the right to a pound of human flesh and owning a man outright, as the Venetians own their slaves?

Allegorical interpretations of *Measure for Measure* are reductive because they erase the drama of human personality and motive in the memorable scenes between Isabella and Angelo. Allegorical interpretations of the trial scene in *The Merchant* are distorting because Portia does not have a profound belief in the ethic of mercy any more than Shylock has a profound belief in the sanctity of law. Imbued with spiritual ardor the novice Isabella would have Angelo reach up toward the mercifulness of God, whose grace saved erring man from the just wages of his sins. Portia is too comfortable in her worldliness and too great a respecter of legalities to make impassioned pleas for mercy or to question the validity of human judgments. She believes in the sanctity of contracts even when, as in the case of her father's will, they restrict her own freedom. Just as she specified the conditions under which she may be won, she spelled out to Bassanio the contract of love that is symbolized by the gift of her ring, one that is based on customary notions of equity and speaks of the penalties that will be exacted if the agreement is broken. Of course she does not live by strict measurement of rights and wrongs. With strangers like Morocco and Arragon she is coolly impartial in behavior; with those whom she knows and loves she is unstinting in her generosity. Her appeal to Shylock for mercy is eloquent, but measured rather than impassioned in tone. She knows she cannot ask the Jew to follow the example of Christ; she can only remind him that mercy is an attribute of God and becomes the kings of this world better than their crowns. When he brushes aside the appeal, she asks him to be merciful only once again.

Her manner suggests that despite the terrible circumstances she enjoys her encounter with Shylock, another deliberate fool who is found to defeat himself with shallow wit. Thus while she holds the trump card—her knowledge of Venetian law—she is willing to humor Shylock and disarm him by allowing him to think that she fully supports his claim to Antonio's flesh. Bassanio would have her wrest the law in this instance, and "to do a great right, do a little wrong," but she is above such casuistries, which allow many an error to "rush into the state." From the beginning she grants the legality of Shylock's position, examines the bond and finds it forfeit, and bids Antonio prepare his bosom for Shylock's knife. Her style is brisk and efficient, her only concerns practical ones: Is there a balance to weigh the flesh? Is there a surgeon to stop Antonio's wounds lest he bleed to death? Her manner is so convincing that when at the last moment she abruptly turns Shylock's legalism against him, he is too astonished to speak, much less think of a counter to her somewhat fantastic argument. By delaying the blow until the very last moment, she not only stuns Shylock but also erases all doubt that he intended to kill Antonio. Shylock's hypocritical legalism is sickening: he will pay for no surgeon because he does not find that minimal decency stipulated in the bond. Antonio is nobler in his resignation, and also somewhat lifeless. He speaks of death as sparing him from the lingering misery of an impoverished age, and he is again unctuously selfless in his farewell to Bassanio:

> Give me your hand, Bassanio; fare you well.
> Grieve not that I am fall'n to this for you;
> . . . .
> Repent but you that you shall lose your friend,
> And he repents not that he pays your debt.
>
> (4.1. 265–79)

In his eagerness to salve Bassanio's conscience Antonio subtly revises the past. When he brushed aside Bassanio's objections to the merry bond, he said, "Why fear not, man; I will not forfeit it." He did not assume that Bassanio would repay the loan although Bassanio was to receive the money from Shylock. He would not have Bassanio mourn for him, only suffer a lifetime of agonizing remorse.

Portia's judgment that Shylock cannot take less than a pound of Antonio's flesh or spill one drop of his blood is absurdly literalistic but exactly what Shylock's hypocritical legalism deserves: he is deterred from taking his inhuman forfeiture by the fear of losing his own life. He told Solanio and Salerio that if they prick a Jew he bleeds; now he must tremble lest in cutting Christian flesh it bleed. Yet at the joyful moment when Shylock is confounded and Antonio saved, the tone of the scene begins to change as Portia's manner with Shylock changes. Is there a reason to warn him not to shed "one drop of Christian blood"? Would Jewish or Turkish blood be less precious in the eyes of the law? The mention of *Christian blood* would not be significant if the phrase did not evoke ancient tales of ritual slaughter of Christian by Jews. Following Portia's lead, Gratiano begins to bait the confused Shylock with his own words as Salerio and Salanio had baited him about Jessica's elopement. When Portia cites the law that is directed against aliens who seek the life of a Venetian citizen, it becomes clear that Venetian justice is not blind; it makes distinctions between those who are Venetians and those who are not.

The only mercy Gratiano offers Shylock is the freedom to hang himself. Others are more kind. The Duke pardons his life before he asks it and suggests that contrition will reduce the state's share of the wealth Shylock must forfeit to a fine. Antonio would allow Shylock to keep half his wealth, and he promises to use the other half in his business only until Shylock dies, when it will be deeded to Jessica. But Portia, who eloquently spoke for mercy to Shylock, shows no pity to her fallen adversary. She does not allow Shylock to take his principal in lieu of the forfeit although Antonio and

Bassanio do not object. When the Duke speaks of reducing confiscation to a fine, she warns him not to overstep his authority. He can speak, she says, "for the state, not for Antonio." After Antonio has proposed to give his share of Shylock's wealth to Jessica and Lorenzo, provided that Shylock turn Christian and leave all he owns at his death to his daughter, Portia asks, "Are you contented, Jew? What dost thou say?" Without another word to Shylock she orders the clerk to draw up a deed of gift. Far nobler than the Lady of Belmont in *Il Pecorone,* Portia is also far more vindictive to her defeated foe. In *Il Pecorone* the Jew, thwarted of his evil purpose, tears up the bond and leaves the court. Portia could allow Shylock to do this, but instead she insists that he face the full penalties of Venetian law. If Antonio, who faced Shylock's knife, can be compassionate, why must Portia now stand for the severity of the law? Of course, Antonio's mercy is itself legalistic. Perhaps he and the others believe that a coerced baptism will save Shylock's immortal soul—that it will be better for him to die a sham Christian than a "heathen" Jew. No doubt some in Shakespeare's audiences grew moist-eyed at the prospect of Shylock's forced conversion, but many others, both Protestant and Catholic, must have shared their queen's conviction that it is tyrannical to enforce religious conscience. The Marian persecutions were not that distant and forced conversions were part of the horror of the Spanish Inquisition. Although Elizabethan laws against overt Catholic worship were severe, and Puritan zealots were harshly dealt with, Elizabeth, with good reason, was reluctant to open windows into her subjects' souls or to pry into their private convictions, for bloody religious conflicts were tearing apart France and Germany and the shock of the Saint Bartholomew's Day massacre of Huguenots was still a vivid memory.

The forced conversion of Shylock is all the more interesting because religion does not seem to be a powerful force in Venice. Antonio and his friends do not seem more devout as Christians than Shylock is as a Jew. He uses his Jewishness as an excuse for personal vindictiveness; they carry their religious convictions so lightly that we scarcely know they exist. Their speeches are graced with the conventional pieties of those who live comfortably in this world and do not worry very much about their eternal destinies. Solanio can joke about the stones of a church making a merchant fear that his ships may founder on a rocky shoal. Portia shrewdly observes that "it is a good divine that follows his own instructions." When she tells Lorenzo that she and Nerissa are leaving for a monastery where they will "live in prayer and contemplation" until their husbands return from Venice, we smile even before we know her true purpose because we cannot imagine her giving her days and nights over to pious meditations. She speaks of shriving only in a jest about Morocco's dark complexion, and she would not be scandalized by Gobbo's jokes about religion. He tells Jessica that she will be damned for being a Jew's daughter. She protests that she will be saved by her Christian husband, but Gobbo points out that many conversions to Christianity will have an injurious effect on the Venetian economy by raising the price of hogs and that will dampen the zeal to convert the Jews. Declaring her father's house is hell, Jessica will turn Christian, not because she believes in the Savior but because she loves Lorenzo and hates her life with Shylock.

Not accustomed to agonizing over spiritual matters, the Venetians will not agonize over Shylock's immortal soul or state of grace; his Christianity may be sham, but it is enough that they have conferred a spiritual benefit on him by opening up the possibility of redemption. Portia can have no regrets about her treatment of Shylock because she knows him only as the monster of the courtroom. She did not witness Antonio's abuse of him; she was not present when Salerio and Solanio jeered at his misery. If Shylock spoke again at the trial of the indignities Antonio heaped on him, or if he gave in the courtroom the speech about the humanity of Jews he made to Solanio and Salerio, we would judge Portia's behavior differently. Whether she would be more compassionate to Shylock if she shared an audience's knowledge of his mistreatment by Venetians, one cannot say. Bassanio, Antonio, and the Duke do not murmur at Portia's insistence that he be punished, and others find Shylock's misery merely ludicrous. Once she has dealt with Shylock, Portia is as generous as before with those of her circle. She refuses Bassanio's offer of three thousand ducats and accepts Antonio's gratitude with lovely humility:

> He is well paid that is well satisfied,
> And I, delivering you, am satisfied,
> And therein do account myself well paid.
> My mind was never yet more mercenary.
> I pray you know me when we meet again;
> I wish you well, and so I take my leave.
>
> (4.1. 415–20)

Would that Antonio were capable of this unostentatious generosity.

The gentle Bassanio begs forgiveness for attempting to pay the young judge and asks Portia to take some personal remembrance as a tribute, not a fee. Since he expressed his willingness during the trial to sacrifice his wife as well as himself to save Antonio, Portia can, in good conscience, test his loyalty to the bond they swore together in Belmont. Casually she asks for Antonio's gloves and then for Bassanio's ring, a commonplace request in an age when rings were given as tokens of affection and gratitude. Having set no limit to his efforts to save Antonio, Bassanio is too embarrassed now to confess that he did not quite mean what he said. Unable to say that the ring is too precious to be parted with, he declares that it is too trifling a gift. When Portia persists he squirms, hedges, and finally explains why he cannot part with the ring. She should be delighted by his response and let the matter go, but the challenge of obtaining the ring intrigues her, and she makes one last inspired assault on Bassanio's convictions:

> And if your wife be not a mad woman,
> And know how well I have deserv'd this ring,
> She would not hold out enemy for ever
> For giving it to me.
>
> (4.1. 445–48)

Those who dislike Portia speak of her cunning attempt to manipulate and dominate Bassanio by tempting him to break his vow. But if domination were her goal, she had only to remove her disguise to make Bassanio feel overwhelmingly obligated to her. What is at issue over the ring is the same question of generosity and indebtedness that arose when Bassanio discussed his need of money with Antonio in the first scene of the play. Bassanio, who has accepted the generosity of Antonio and Portia, is also able to accept the generosity of the young judge even though he is uncomfortable and somewhat ashamed. Antonio, who wondered why Bassanio could not easily accept repeated gifts of money, is unable to accept the generosity of the young judge because he is accustomed to giving, not receiving, and he finds the acceptance of generosity too burdensome. If he were more sensitive to the feelings of others, he would respect Bassanio's fidelity to his vow, but then if he were more sensitive to the feelings of others, he would not have spat on Shylock's beard. It takes more generosity of spirit than Antonio possesses to accept a gift outright. Even though Portia has already exited, Antonio appeals to Bassanio to part with his ring, and Bassanio cannot again say no.

The comedy of the ring episode brings the trial scene to a happy conclusion and provides an emotional transition from the rancor of the courtroom to the peacefulness of Belmont, to which the heroes and heroines will soon return. Because of Portia's witty handling of the chagrined Bassanio, Jessica does not walk out on stage immediately after Shylock has been crushed to join Lorenzo in a charming love duet. They enter after Portia has received Bassanio's ring and after she and Nerissa have planned their comic revenge on their luckless husbands. Ignorant of the bitterness and vituperations of the trial, Jessica and Lorenzo enjoy the beauty of the night and add to it the beauty of their poetry. Although somewhat shallow and unscrupulous, at least about taking Shylock's money, they are capable of fine sentiments and tender feelings. Perhaps when Jessica sold her father's treasured ring for a monkey, she did not know the ring was a gift from her dead mother; perhaps she could not believe her father could be attached to a gift from his dead wife, though she knew well enough his love of her. In any event, her charming duet with Lorenzo does not alter our sense of their limitations because untroubled by pangs of conscience, they joke about Jessica stealing from the wealthy Jew with her unthrift love. Lorenzo's memorable description of the heavens and the music of the spheres expresses a refinement of sensibility, not a spirituality of attitude. He describes the "floor of heaven" as if it had been fitted by Venetian craftsmen, "thick inlaid with patens of bright gold." He speaks of angels singing "to the young-eyed cherubins," as if he were describing a beautiful fresco. In the best of possible worlds, the irresponsible and improvident will be dull as clods. In Shakespeare's dramatic world as in ours, shallow, improvident and self-absorbed persons can be charming conversationalists, connoisseurs of fine wine, and lovers of art.

To appreciate Jessica and Lorenzo's charm is not to say that they deserve Shylock's money because they have an appreciation for fine things while he is miserly and incapable of enjoying his money. If this argument holds, we must agree with the reasoning of Victorian factory owners, who justified paying starvation wages on the ground that workers would probably squander additional wages on gin. When Nerissa tells of the "special deed of gift" that Shylock signed leaving all his possessions to Lorenzo and Jessica, Lorenzo exclaims, "Fair ladies, you drop manna in the way / Of starved people." The age of miracles has apparently not ended so far as Venetians are concerned, for God still watches over his chosen people. It might be difficult for Portia to prove in a court of law that Shylock plotted against Antonio's life by offering a loan under terms that Antonio called kind and "Christian" and willingly sealed to, but in any event Shylock's hatred of Antonio has ensured Jessica's material prosperity, and that is the kind of providence that matters to Lorenzo.

All the news in the final scene of *The Merchant* is joyful. Jessica and Lorenzo are provided for; Antonio learns that his ships have come safely to port. Portia and Nerissa, Bassanio and Gratiano are safely home and can enjoy their belated wedding night. The only bar to future happiness is the failure of Bassanio and Gratiano to keep their marriage rings, a failure in which their wives are implicated. Since no wrangling or discord between the lovers occurred before their betrothals, some affectionate teasing and mock accusations are not out of place. Having taught Shylock the dangers of a hypocritical literalism in the trial scene, Portia now pretends to be more literal-minded than Shylock in identifying her truth to Bassanio with his possession of her ring. Whoever owns the ring, she declares, is her husband and has the right to possess her. With Nerissa, she refuses to believe any preposterous tales about rings given to a young judge and his clerk. Bassanio swears that if Portia understood why he surrendered her ring, she would not be angry. She replies that no man would be so unreasonable as to want the ring after Bassanio had explained its sacred meaning. Perhaps she means what she says, because men can reason the need to keep or part with wedding rings but women will not acknowledge a debt greater than the vow of marriage. Or at least, one cannot imagine Portia surrendering her wedding ring to relieve a friend of a sense of obligation.

Ideally, love does not traffic with wills and estates; ideally it is unmindful of wealth or the color of a skin or religious preference. In Venice and Belmont, however, love cannot be blind to such considerations, and contracts of marriage, like many other contracts, necessarily deal with the ownership of property and dowries as well as the obligations of love and fidelity. This does not mean, however, that the sanctity of wedding vows is mocked by crass considerations. Behind Portia's pretended literalism is a belief in the literalness and absoluteness of wedding vows, which do not admit of sentimental gestures, sensible compromises, and accommodations to circumstance. Love is not love that alters when it alteration finds, and therefore Bassanio had no right to part with Portia's ring nor Portia the right to use his "infidelity" as the excuse for her own bending. *The Merchant* does not pose the higher law of love against the quid pro quo of worldly bonds because the bond of love is in itself transcendent, a world-without-end bargain that is an act of faith in another. Once again Antonio offers to be bound for Bassanio's sake. Portia relents, and with the threat of infidelity exorcised, all ends well for the lovers and their dear friend.

Dissatisfied with that conclusion, Sir Laurence Olivier ended a fine television production of *The Merchant* with a close-up of a pensive Jessica reading over Shylock's deed of gift to her and Lorenzo, as if she were troubled at the last by her father's fate and even a bit regretful of her abandonment of him. This note of sadness was moving in its way but false to the character of Jessica and to the mood of the final scene. It did not clarify Shakespeare's artistic intention or improve upon it. It was a sentimental gesture that Olivier felt obliged to make because religious bigotry still plagues the world four hundred years after the composition of *The Merchant.* There is no reason to sentimentalize Jessica when thousands of immigrant children have, like her, felt estranged from parents whose foreign speech and ways seemed embarrassing and stultifying. In the past century thousands of American children have fled their old-world parents to become part of the American present and future. The "problem" of the final scene is not rooted in Shakespeare's failure to see Jessica, Lorenzo, and the others as we see them. The problem lies in our unwillingness or inability to accept the portraits Shakespeare draws of both the Jew and his Christian enemies. We want Portia and Antonio and Jessica to be more understanding of Shylock because they have so many attractive qualities. Or we want to be more certain that Shakespeare was aware of their limitations even though our sense of their limitations is created by the changes Shakespeare made in his source materials. It bothers us that having raised a cynical tale of intrigue and sordid motive to the level of great poetic drama, Shakespeare does not grace the ending of *The Merchant* with noble insight and recognitions. But such recognitions would hardly be appropriate when the climactic agon of the play pits Portia's cleverness against Shylock's, rather than the ethic of love and generosity against an inhuman legalism. After Gratiano's Jew-baiting, Portia's unrelenting attitude to Shylock, and the "mercy" of an enforced conversion, any final realization of Shylock's tortured humanity by the Venetians would be a last-minute revision of their characters. If the ending of *The Merchant* troubles, it does so because it is absolutely true to the preceding action, even though it is not "as we would like it."

Those who believe that Shylock was supposed to be a buffoon, a killjoy, and a ritual scapegoat whose expulsion makes possible the happy ending suggest that Shakespeare erred in making Shylock too human and sympathetic a figure. If the humanity of Shylock is an artistic error or miscalculation, however, it is one that Shakespeare was peculiarly prone to, for not long after *The Merchant* he was to make the same error again in the final scene of *2 Henry IV*, in which Henry rejects Falstaff; and not long after that, he was to repeat this very miscalculation in the unpleasant humiliation of Malvolio by Feste and Toby. Is it reasonable to assume that Shakespeare made the same significant artistic error three times? Or does the error lie in critics' attempts to reduce his complex art to simplistic ritual patterns that presume a denial of human sympathy to this character or that?[13]

The cheerfulness of the final scene of *The Merchant* is very like the cheerfulness of the final scene of *Henry V*, in which the dread anxiety that preceded the battle of Agincourt, the moral issues raised by the English soldiers around the campfire, and the slaughter of the French are wiped completely from the King's mind. Brushing aside Burgundy's pleas for an end to the devastation of France, Henry demands recognition of his "just" rights because the mercy he urged on his adversaries has no claim on him, and his only interest is to woo Katherine for his bride. The victory he has won has not enlarged his sympathies any more than Portia's victory has enlarged hers. Although Henry speaks of the French nobility as his brothers, his emotional attachments are limited to the happy few, the English band of brothers who stood together against great odds, indeed, whose devotion to one another was inspired by the threat of the foreign enemy. In a similar way the devotion of the characters to each other in *The Merchant* is inspired by the threat of the alien Shylock, and their identification with one another depends in part on an awareness of their difference from the many outsiders who are drawn to Venice and Belmont. Their insular world is limited to those of similar taste and breeding who look like them, dress like them, and pray like them. If that insularity breeds narrowness and arrogance, it also makes possible the solidarity of the group, its traditional civilities, and capacity for altruism. For centuries, after all, the little republic of Venice had defended its freedom and independence and extended its power and influence because it took pride in its unique heritage and place among the states of the world. Similar ideals of civic virtue inspired the American colonists, the happy few who stood against the power of Britain and founded a nation based on the principle that all men are created equal, but who reserved to themselves the right to keep slaves—that is, to own human flesh—provided the flesh was dark-complected and duly purchased. The mercy Antonio offers to Shylock is a solution to the problem of despised and feared minorities, but one doubts that baptism will make Shylock Christian and Venetian enough to be welcomed at Belmont, even if like Jessica, he grows ashamed of ever having been a Jew.

8

Much Ado About Nothing

If *Much Ado* is not the most genial of the comedies, it is perhaps the most satisfying in form and substance. It is warm as well as witty, and compassionate in its view of human frailties and limitations. Its chief characters, Beatrice and Benedick, are the most attractive pair of lovers in the comedies—the only ones perhaps who are equally matched in intelligence, humor, and humanity. Except for the morose Don John, the other characters are engaging enough to win an audience's affection. None is as coarse as Gratiano or as ignorant of self as Antonio or as shallow as Jessica. Because all are capable of kindness and some measure of nobility, the community of Messina can be forgiving of rashness. It does not close ranks against an outcast but rather tolerates the turncoat Don John in its midst, and it welcomes back at the close a Claudio who has mistreated Hero but who deserves a second chance at happiness and acceptance among those who gather in Leonato's household. At the same time *Much Ado* is as unsparing as *The Merchant* in its revelation of the obtuseness and cruelty with which the self-righteous can act. Its "trial" scene is uglier in its way than the one in *The Merchant* because it results in the condemnation of the innocent Hero and discloses something about conventional attitudes that we would prefer never to have known.

The rage in this scene is stunning because the early scenes of *Much Ado* are almost untouched by rancor or discord. Their easy informality and relaxed atmosphere are unique in the comedies, which more often than not open with a strain of antagonism or sorrow: a severe law threatens an old man's life, a would be suitor is held back by a lack of funds, a father would coerce his daughter into a loveless match. In contrast, the first scenes of *Much Ado* promise nothing but homecoming celebrations, good conversations, and perhaps a marriage or two. A war has ended and the victorious general and his officers are about to return to cordial reunions in Messina. The only threat to public tranquillity is the malcontented Don John, who was defeated in the war and now scowls and mutters of revenge. He is too grumpy, however, to seem very dangerous and he is known to be untrustworthy. The only plots that seem destined to succeed are those that are inspired by friendship and love, and they will unite rather than divide the citizens of Messina.

Although the slandering of Hero is a page out of romantic melodrama and her marriage as a veiled bride to Claudio is a page out of fairy tales, *Much Ado* has been called the most realistic of the comedies because it comes closest to mimicking the give and take of casual conversations and the daily routine of life in Leonato's household.[1] Here a love match can be arranged without the intervention of goblins, without a choice of caskets, and without the renunciation of monastic vows. The spontaneity of these scenes is both artful and paradoxical, however, because on the one hand the illusion is created that the audience is eavesdropping on conversations that were never planned or rehearsed; on the other hand, these seemingly improvised moments are ingeniously patterned by symmetries and repetitions so that as we eavesdrop on the characters, they eavesdrop and spy on one another—sometimes accidentally, sometimes intentionally, sometimes lovingly, sometimes maliciously. There is not only much ado about "noting," but also in this most realistic of comic plots, the acceptance of improbable fictions as undeniable truths by characters who are more sensible, skeptical, and wary of self-delusion than almost any others in the comedies. This is possible only because the twin orchard scenes in which Benedick and Beatrice are hoodwinked are at once gloriously exaggerated and utterly convincing as revelations of their emotional and psychological natures.

One comes away from a performance of *Much Ado* with a vivid recollection of Beatrice and Benedick, who dominate much of the play, and with fainter impressions of Hero and Claudio, who have less interesting and colorful personalities but are the central figures in the drama of slandered innocence and false accusation that is the main plot of *Much Ado*. While it is inevitable that Beatrice and Benedick should engross the attention of audiences, it is unfortunate that critics sometimes suggest that the unhappy love of Hero and Claudio is merely a utilitarian scaffolding for the witty badinage and prickly courtship of Beatrice and Benedick. If this is so, the plotting of *Much Ado* is somewhat peculiar and even a bit fumbling because Shakespeare, who transformed the base metal of *Il Pecorone* into the gold of *The Merchant*, failed to place the most interesting and important characters at the center of his dramatic fable. Can we assume, moreover, that Shakespeare merely used the story of Hero and Claudio as dramatic scaffolding when he restages this drama of betrayed innocence and mistaken revenge in *Othello*, again in *Cymbeline*, and once more in *The Winter's Tale*? Those who think Claudio and Hero do not really matter may also find that they are shallow and conventional because, unlike Beatrice and Benedick, they fall in love quickly and easily. But if to love at first sight is to love too easily, God help Romeo and Juliet, Rosalind and Orlando, and Ferdinand and Miranda.[2]

The problem of responding to Hero and Claudio is similar to the problem of responding to Bassanio, who seems so much blander and less interesting than Portia and Shylock or even Gratiano. Just as Antonio and Portia's love of Bassanio demands that we recognize his quiet virtues, Beatrice's devotion to Hero and Benedick's affection for Claudio deny the possibility that they are superficial or ordinary. Shakespeare could have made the relationship of Beatrice and Hero as one-sided as that between Antonio and Bassanio by depicting the stronger Beatrice as the protector of her more timid cousin. But there is not the slightest intimation that Beatrice is used to guarding Hero against the blows of life or that Hero requires such protection. It is sometimes suggested that if Hero were more like Beatrice she would not be incapable of defending herself when accused by Claudio, but Beatrice is there when Hero is brutally denounced and like Hero she is too stunned to rebut the false accusations. Critics also suggest that if Desdemona were more like Emilia she would not be so easily victimized by Othello, but they forget that Emilia is unable to defend Desdemona's honesty and life; indeed, she is unable to protect herself against her abusive husband, who murders her when finally she insists upon speaking out. In the four plays that deal with sexual jealousy the emphasis falls, not on the heroines' lack of courage, but on the vulnerability of the heroes to vicious insinuations and prurient fantasies.

A character like Mariana in *Measure for Measure* can be little more than the jilted maiden of romantic fables who remains loyal to the man who rejected her. We do not know why Mariana continues to love the mean-spirited Angelo, and pleads for his life when he shows not the slightest sign of affection for her or remorse for his mistreatment of her. Because Mariana is a minor character, it is enough if an audience pities her forlorn existence. Because she is a central figure in the dramatic action of *Much Ado*, Hero's emotional responses are crucial to the resolution of the play. Her acceptance of Claudio as husband is as important to the denouement of *Much Ado* as Imogen's forgiveness of Posthumus and Hermione's forgiveness of Leontes are important to the denouements of *Cymbeline* and *The Winter's Tale.* The first scenes of the play, however, do not lead us to believe that Hero will play a significant role. She speaks just one line in the first scene and not a word to Claudio, although they must be very aware of each other's presence. Indeed, she does not speak to Claudio on stage until Don Pedro announces that she has agreed to be Claudio's wife. Is this not the quintessence of docility: a shy, unspoken girl who obeys her father in listening to Don Pedro's suit and who accepts Don Pedro's proxy wooing for Claudio without a word to her future husband? But Hero and Claudio have no love scene together, not because she is too timid and retiring, but because he is too uncertain and hesitant to woo for himself, and she would never take the romantic initiative. Unlike her cousin Beatrice, she is content for the most part to remain in the background of a conversation, to listen rather than speak. Although not a talker like Beatrice, she can speak out when the occasion demands speaking out; and when she does, she shows her self-confidence and keen perception of others. With a visor to hide behind, she matches wits with Don Pedro at the ball in a way that suggests a readiness to follow her own inclinations in love, not her father's commands. Although primed by her father to encourage Don Pedro's courtship, she does not flutter her eyelids or turn coy at his approach:

> *Don Pedro.* Lady, will you walk about with your friend?
> *Hero.*   So you walk softly, and look sweetly, and say nothing, I am
>   yours for the walk, and especially when I walk away.
> *Don Pedro.* With me in your company?
> *Hero.*   I may say so when I please.
> *Don Pedro.* And when please you to say so?
> *Hero.*   When I like your favor, for God defend the lute should be
>   like the case!
>
> (2.1. 86–95)

These are not the responses of a shrinking violet; Hero does not lack wit but her sallies are gentler-edged than Beatrice's, more likely to elicit an smile than a tart reply.

Hero's qualities are more fully revealed in the orchard scene that is intended to bring Beatrice and Benedick together. Hero takes the leading role in the charade that Beatrice overhears, and demonstrates her understanding of her cousin and her willingness to risk Beatrice's anger by speaking plainly of her vanity. Her description of Beatrice's behavior is penetrating and just, and somewhat sharp in its rebuke:

> . . . nature never fram'd a woman's heart
> Of prouder stuff than that of Beatrice.
> Disdain and scorn ride sparking in her eyes,
> Misprising what they look on, and her wit
> Values itself so highly that to her
> All matter else seems weak. . . .
> . . . .
>   . . . I never yet saw man,
> How wise, how noble, young, how rarely featur'd,
> But she would spell him backward. . . .
> . . . .
> So turns she every man the wrong side out,

And never gives to simple truth and virtue that
Which simpleness and merit purchaseth.

(3.1. 48–70)

Shocked by Claudio's brutal denunciation on her wedding day, she is unable to defend herself; she can only simply and directly declare her innocence, and that is not enough to convince even her father. But it would not matter what she said because Claudio and Don Pedro have already made up their minds about her guilt and are prepared to believe nothing except a confession of lewdness. After the denunciation scene, she does not appear again on stage until the final scene, in which she enters as Claudio's veiled "second" bride. When she reveals herself to him, she speaks just a few telling lines:

. . . when I liv'd, I was your other wife,
And when you lov'd, you were my other husband.

(5.4. 60–61)

Should there be more anger or recrimination? Should she demand an abject apology from Claudio before she accepts him again as her husband? The answer depends upon our view of Claudio, and more largely on the way in which the moral and emotional drama of Hero's betrayal is unfolded by Shakespeare so that a happy ending is not only possible but the only appropriate conclusion. At no time in the play is Claudio contemptible or mean-spirited.[3] When he denounces Hero he is fully convinced that he has been terribly wronged and has the right to denounce her in public. If he is a gullible fool too easily duped by Borachio and Don John, so too is the noble Don Pedro, who is completely taken in by Borachio's contrivance and *volunteers* to join Claudio in exposing Hero on her wedding day.

Claudio enters the play a hero celebrated for his gallantry, who has earned the paternal affection of his general Don Pedro. Finding himself drawn to Hero, he discreetly inquires about her prospects, showing the same sensible concern about marrying well that Benedick does when he decides in soliloquy that the woman whom he will marry shall be rich—"that's certain." Claudio's questions are not those of a fortune hunter but of a young man uncertain of his judgment of women, and it is his lack of confidence that will make him vulnerable to Don John's insinuations as well as intensify his rage at being duped by an innocent-seeming wanton. Before he declares his love of Hero, he asks Benedick if he has noticed Hero and if she is "not a modest young lady." Despite Benedick's gibes, he persists in asking for his opinion of Hero. Don Pedro is delighted to hear of Claudio's affection for Hero. "Amen," he says, "If you love her, for the lady is very well worthy." Even this commendation does not assure Claudio. "You speak this," he says, "to fetch me in, my lord." Claudio's need for assurance seems perfectly genuine; if he does not fear the commitment that love demands, he fears being made a fool by love, and he therefore qualifies almost every statement he makes about Hero. "In mine eyes," he says, "she is the sweetest lady that I ever looked on"—"that I love her, I feel." That "I feel" speaks volumes of his inexperience in love and fear of misjudging his own emotions as well as Hero's nature. Although he asks Don Pedro's aid and advice, he does not use his commander to gain an heiress. It is Don Pedro's idea to act as Claudio's proxy and to speak to Hero and Leonato on Claudio's behalf.

Annoyed by Claudio's defection from the ranks of smug bachelorhood, Benedick goes out of his way to rag him. When Claudio asks his opinion of Hero, he jokingly replies, "Would you buy her, that you inquire after her?" This blunt-edged joke is not inspired by any crassness on Claudio's part. It displays the wit of one who by custom is "a professed tyrant" to women and who is both amused and irritated by Claudio's interest in Leonato's daughter. Convinced that Don Pedro woos Hero for himself at the masked ball, Claudio tries to hide his misery by saying, "I wish him joy of her." Benedick replies, "Why, that's spoken like an honest drovier. So they sell bullock." This wrenching of Claudio's words is not amiable or meant to be; it is spoken when Benedick is still smarting from an unpleasant encounter with Beatrice. After being ridiculed and insulted by Lady Disdain, he is ready to enjoy Claudio's misery and add to it. Claudio is a perfect target for such wisecracks because he has no aplomb as a suitor and it took an effort of will to speak of his feelings to others. He tells Don Pedro that before the war, he looked on Hero "with a soldier's eye, / That lik'd, but had a rougher task in hand / Than to drive liking to the name of love" (1.1. 298–300). A fear of surrendering to emotion is implicit in his need to "drive" (that is, deepen) liking to the name of love and makes him susceptible to the nasty insinuation that Don Pedro woos Hero for himself. But he is not more gullible in this respect that Benedick, who reached the same conclusion about Don Pedro's behavior without Don John's slanderous remarks.

When he is convinced of the seriousness of Claudio's interest in Hero, Benedick is generous in his praise of her. Because he has no romantic illusions or anxieties, he is capable of seeing women clearly and can appreciate their qualities. He enjoys most of his encounters with Beatrice and is very conscious of her attractiveness, but he also enjoys the freedom of his bachelorhood and, less sentimental than some critics, he does not mistake Beatrice's barbed remarks for Cupid's arrows. He knows the difference between tenderness disguised as witty banter and a cutting remark that is intended to draw a little blood. Some critics assure us that Beatrice and Benedick are in love with one another from the start and need only the slightest pretext to abandon their pose of independence and confess their true affections. But one can as justly say that the French Princess is in love with Navarre from the beginning of *Love's Labor's* and needs only the excuse of her sudden departure to discard her pose of satiric mockery. The close parallels between the masking-dancing-wooing scenes of *Much Ado* and *Love's Labor's* leave little doubt that Shakespeare was thinking of his earlier comedy as he wrote *Much Ado*, especially since he uses an eavesdropping scene in both plays as an occasion in which love is openly declared, and in both plays apparent scoffers betray their true affections by the writing of love poems. Beatrice is more like the French Princess than any other romantic heroines; she takes pleasure in her role of Lady Disdain and she abandons it only with great reluctance. Indeed, it is because Beatrice almost sacrifices her love of Benedick to her rage at Claudio that their meeting of minds and hearts in the final scene is so deeply satisfying.[4]

Although Benedick speaks several times of Beatrice's beauty, it is only after Claudio turns lover that he begins to think about marriage and to wonder how long his good sense will protect him from the irrationality of passion and the dullness of married life. He will make a fine husband because he is warm-hearted, gentle, and can laugh at himself; yet he is not, like Romeo or most of the heroes of the romantic comedies, born to sigh and eager to embrace the adventure of love. He could, one suspects, live as happily without a wife as with one, provided that he had enough bachelor friends and occasional invitations to dinner from his married ones. Beatrice is a kindred soul with a sharper satiric tongue. She likes men and she is well aware of Benedick's attractiveness; but she prides herself on her independence and self-sufficiency. Although her society assumes that she must marry to have a place in the scheme of things, she has no need of a man to protect her and she cannot imagine treating any man as her lord and master.

If Beatrice secretly desires Benedick's love, she keeps that desire well hidden and it does not prevent her from making him the butt of stinging remarks. Questioning the messenger about the returning heroes, she makes repeated sneers about "Signior Mountanto's" incompetence as a soldier and swears to eat all the enemies he has slain. Her joking about Benedick's good service at the officers' mess is amusing enough, but she will not admit that her mockery of his valor is a jest, and she refuses to credit the messenger's report of his bravery. Her impatience to have at Benedick is such that she rudely breaks in on the conversation the men are engaged in and gratuitously insults him: "I wonder that you will still be talking, Signior Benedick; nobody marks you." Refusing to play the demure maiden, she will trade jests, even off-color ones, with men to call attention to her unconventionality, yet even as she rejects the gentility and propriety that are second nature to Hero, she takes advantage of her femaleness to make the kind of remarks to Benedick that would be intolerable from a man. Thus she has her cake and eats it too; she is a free spirit, emancipated from the conventions of a male-dominated society, who depends on the chivalry of men to license her sarcastic sallies. Her quick wit instinctively looks for a target, but she is not a willing target of other people's jests. She has a thin skin and will not laughingly accept from Benedick the kind of remark that she makes at his expense. She does not feel oppressed by the conventions of her society, and she does not feel superior to her more conventional cousin. She does not urge Hero to rebel against her father's dictates; she would have her insist only that the suitor her father approves be "a handsome fellow." No railer against marriage as Benedick is, she delights in Hero's betrothal and prompts Claudio to seal it with a kiss. Although she pretends to sigh over her impending spinsterhood, she is not eager for a wooer and finds it hard to imagine herself as a wife. A beardless youth, she remarks, would not do for her because he would be too easily mastered; a Petruchio would appall her. Her idea of heaven is not a rose-covered honeymoon cottage for two, but an eternity spent trading quips with bachelors. Like Benedick she is too gregarious and too fond of good conversation to yearn for the intimacy of marriage.

Don John, not Beatrice, is the malcontent of the play, a creature so tart that his very appearance gives her heartburn. A perpetual scowler, he has a bastard's natural sinistral bent and relishes his role as killjoy, the very death's-head at the feasts of Messina. He tells himself that he would like to play Marlowe's Barabas and poison the whole city; but he is an uninspired villain who requires his henchman's aid to play Iago to Claudio's Othello. Since his treachery is known, he does not make a serious effort to appear a good fellow, and though on parole, he does not pretend to be repentant. His first attempt at creating mischief by slander fails when Don Pedro proves to be a loyal friend of Claudio. His success in defaming Hero depends upon the ingenious "ocular proof" of her wantonness that Borachio conceives and executes. Hardly a masterful poisoner of minds, he is a vain misanthrope, pedantic in thought and speech, who is addicted to slightly comic euphuisms. Advised by Conrade to accept his lot with patience, he announces his credo of sullen "honesty":

> I cannot hide what I am: I must be sad when I have cause, and smile at no man's jests; eat when I have stomach, and wait for no man's leisure; sleep when I am drowsy, and tend on no man's business; laugh when I am merry, and claw no man in his humor.
>
> (1.3. 13–18)

While other residents of Messina are warmly interested in the welfare and happiness of their friends and relations, Don John is interested only in his sour ruminations; like Jonson's Morose, he has no taste for anyone else's conversation but is infatuated with his own Lylyan turn of phrase:

I had rather be a canker in a hedge than a rose in [Don Pedro's] grace, and it better fits my blood to be disdain'd of all than to fashion a carriage to rob love from any. In this (though I cannot be said to be a flattering honest man), it must not be denied but I am a plain-dealing villain.

(1.3. 27–32)

He proudly describes himself as an ill-tempered dog who is trusted only with a muzzle "and enfranchised with a clog; therefore I have decreed not to sing in my cage." Although his metaphors are somewhat mixed, his intentions are clear: "If I had my mouth," he continues, "I would . . ." He would what? shout? rail? No, he would "bite." He is no snarling cur; he is the tyrant of the nursery school, the kind of spoiled sulky child who terrorizes babysitters. He makes a peacock display of his malcontent but will not let his followers have a share in it; it is, he remarks, for his use alone. Even so his small band of trusty knaves swear to assist him in his wickedness "to the death."

The touch of absurdity in Don John's speech and manner anticipates that his success as a conspirator will be short-lived. He plays a small role in the denunciation scene and never appears again on stage. His ability to destroy for a time Claudio and Hero's happiness does not testify to his evil genius but rather to the vulnerability of Claudio and Don Pedro to lies that touch their sense of honor and self. Since Shakespeare has the artistry to stage the twin orchard scenes in which Beatrice and Benedick are duped, he could no doubt have staged a window scene that would be convincing to an already anxious Claudio and Don Pedro. (Iago stage-manages a similar moment with Cassio for Othello to spy on.) But an audience does not need proof of Borachio's ingenuity because it understands why Claudio and Don Pedro are able to think the worst of the innocent Hero. Although they know that Don John is not to be trusted, they cannot reject out of hand his sneering insinuations of Hero's looseness, for he dares them to see for themselves, a dare that engages their manhood. Uncertain before of his judgment of women and tormented now, Claudio listens to Don John and asks, "May this be so?" The older, steadier Don Pedro replies, "I will not think it," as if he were unwilling to contemplate the possibility of her lewdness but not convinced of her chastity. They *have* to agree to witness Hero's lasciviousness because it would seem cowardly to refuse; in other words, it would take more courage and confidence in their own judgment than either possesses to laugh at Don John. They are not the only ones in the play who lose their good sense when their egos are threatened. Angered by Benedick's denigration of her wit at the masked ball, Beatrice describes him as a mere buffoon:

Why, he is the Prince's jester, a very dull fool; only his gift is in devising impossible slanders. None but libertines delight in him, and the commendation is not in his wit, but in his villainy, for he both pleases men and angers them, and then they laugh at him and beat him. I am sure he is in the fleet; I would he had boarded me.

(2.1. 137–43)

This portrait is not witty; it is grossly unfair and insulting. Beatrice does not speak her mind about Benedick; she strikes back because her self-esteem has been wounded.

If Claudio and Don Pedro are to be despised for believing what they think they see, what shall be said of the sensible, skeptical Beatrice and Benedick, who without ocular proof accept the most outrageous and transparent fictions about each other? Scholars who do not appreciate Iago's brilliance as a deceiver and manipulator of others hypothesize an Elizabethan dramatic convention to explain his corruption of Othello, but their appeal to convention does not explain how *Othello* is able to move audiences who have never heard of Elizabethan dramatic conventions. What we witness in the orchard scenes is not ingenious hoodwinking or absurd credulities or complaisant self-deception. Common sense dictates that Beatrice and Benedick cannot swallow the preposterous stories they hear about each other's secret passion, and yet they do not turn to the audience with a knowing wink and pretend to believe what they have overheard because they have always desired to confess their hidden love for each other. They listen carefully, weigh what they have heard, and credit it because those who "gull" them know them intimately.

In the first orchard scene, Benedick enters musing over the way love has transmogrified Claudio. He wonders if love can convert him from a talkative scoffer to a silent idolatrous oyster. With Claudio running a fever, he is no longer certain of his immunity to love's infection, and, preparing for the worst, he mulls over the choice of a wife. He does not desire the moon—she need only be rich, wise, virtuous, fair, noble, and *mild*—not one of Beatrice's chief qualities. She must also be a fine conversationalist and an excellent musician. This shopping list of female excellencies does not bespeak a longing for romantic ecstasy but rather a desire for the enduring companionship of a happy marriage. Siding with the Owl rather than the Cuckoo, Benedick imagines long winter evenings before the fire, not the excitement of Maytime trysts. His friends begin their angling casually and obliquely, first setting the mood with the music he loves but here pretends to find tiresome. They do not appeal to his vanity in having won the heart of a glorious woman who may die of her unrequited passion; they appeal to his decency, which will not allow him to be responsible for another's suffering. Shall his failure to love cause Beatrice to commit some desperate act upon herself? Must she languish in undisclosed misery because she fears to express her love lest he sneer? What makes the scene irresistible is the earnest description of Beatrice's sleepless nights spent pacing her chamber and writing Benedick's name over and over again on papers that she then rips to shreds: "Then down upon her knees she falls, weeps, sobs, beats her heart, tears her hair, prays, curses: 'O sweet Benedick.' God give me patience!" (2.3. 146–49). Benedick should suspect a device because two of the speakers are Claudio and Don Pedro, who swore not long ago that he would someday see Benedick a lover. The other, however, is Leonato, and Benedick will not stoop to suspect the motives of a reverend, white-bearded householder.

When the playacting is over, Benedick does not step out of hiding to declare that he has always loved Beatrice and is happy now to admit it. What he reveals is his sensitivity to the charge of unkindness:

> Love me? why, it must be requited. I hear how I am censur'd; they say I will bear myself proudly, if I perceive the love come from her; they say too that she will rather die than give any sign of affection. I did never think to marry. I must not seem proud; happy are they that hear their detractions, and can put them to mending.
>
> (2.3. 224–30)

Agreeing that the lady is fair, virtuous, and wise but for loving him, he decides that he "will be horribly in love with her"—a stunning penance. He knows that any sign of love will make him a target of gibes because he was so long a scoffer, but he is undismayed, for he knows that he remains true to his individuality and idiosyncratic bent. Although he now joins the mainstream of those who love, he sees himself as marching to his own drum. Benedick's appreciation for the comedy of his situation is endearing. He believes most of what he says and at the same time is as zany in his rationalizations as Launce is in his complaints about his incontinent hound. Although friends may jeer, he is determined to follow his "humor" and to prove that his aboutface is forward march: "When I said I would die a bachelor, I did not think I should live till I were married." Able now to perceive the loving affection that lurks in Beatrice's sallies, he can espy marks of love in her brusquest responses, whereas Claudio will soon be able to see only signs of luxury in Hero's blushes.

Benedick takes an active role in his orchard scene; he opens and closes it with lengthy soliloquies and he comments in asides on the speeches of his friends. In the second orchard scene, Beatrice silently eavesdrops until Hero and Ursula exit, and her response consists of just sixteen lines of formal, rhymed verse. Thus the emphasis falls, not on Beatrice's responses to the charade she witnesses, but on the rehearsed conversation between Hero and Ursula. They do not invent a tale of Benedick's love-lorn suffering; they speak of defects of character in Beatrice that trouble those who love her best. Where Benedick's friends play on his generous sympathy, Hero dwells on the pride and disdain that prevent Beatrice from loving Benedick or even acknowledging his virtues. Where Benedick responds to his friend's hyperboles with a whimsical determination to be horribly in love, Beatrice is too pained by the frank recital of her faults to joke about herself:

> What fire is in mine ears? Can this be true?
> Stand I condemn'd for pride and scorn so much?
> Contempt, farewell, and maiden pride, adieu!
> No glory lives behind the back of such.
>
> (3.1. 107–10)

Benedick will become a comic casuist to save a sweet lady's life; Beatrice is dismayed by Hero and Ursula's criticism of her arrogance. It is especially painful that they condemn the clever ripostes that she thinks are her chief ornament. Unlike Benedick, she does not welcome the role of lover or give herself wholeheartedly to it. He jokes when he says that he will be horribly in love; she is absolutely serious when she says that she will requite him, "Taming [her] wild heart to [his] loving hand." Her words suggest that it will take a conscious effort on her part to stoop to any man's embrace. Her commitment, moreover, is somewhat conditional; *if* he loves, she says, her kindness will encourage him to win her for his wife. She will not drop her handkerchief when next he walks by, but at least she will not tell him again that she takes as much pleasure in seeing him "as you may take upon a knife's point and choke a daw withal."

Immediately after the second orchard scene, Don John invites Claudio and Don Pedro to witness an exhibition of Hero's lewdness, and in the very next scene, the Watch apprehends Borachio and Conrade. Thus the crime is discovered almost as soon as it is committed and before the denunciation of Hero at the altar. Yet the denunciation takes place and is watched by an audience which knows that before long the truth of Hero's innocence will be known by all. Earlier scenes juxtaposed the vicious deception of Claudio and Don Pedro against the loving deceptions of Benedick and Beatrice. Now the merciless denunciation of Hero is juxtaposed against the incompetent but very polite and scrupulous interrogation of Borachio and Conrade by Dogberry. Unlike Bottom, who convinces us that he has the energy and ambition to be a successful weaver, Dogberry and Verges seem rather odd pillars of the community. They may own property and pay taxes; they may even have suffered commercial losses, but if they succeeded in any kind of business it was despite a magnificent inability to concentrate on the matter at hand. With the aid of Verges, Dogberry raises maundering to the level of art and is apparently unable to put together two sentences without savaging the king's

English. His command of proverbial sayings and pointless ejaculations does not breed confidence in his acuity, but it does signify his tolerant acceptance of things as they are—of human frailties and infirmities. His truisms celebrate the patient forebearances and petty compromises that make civility possible. Afraid that Verges, who is far more capable of direct communication than he is, will seem simple to Leonato, Dogberry explains:

> A good old man, sir, he will be talking; as they say, "When the age is in, the wit is out." God help us, it is a world to see! Well said, i' faith, neighbor Verges. Well, God's a good man; and two men ride of a horse, one must ride behind.
>
> (3.5. 33–37)

An original like Bottom, Dogberry is a mixture of ignorance and sagacity, self-importance and unself-consciousness. Where others in the play are busy noting, espying, eavesdropping, and interfering in the lives of friends and enemies, Dogberry and Verges take a Jeffersonian approach to the problem of keeping the peace; they believe that the least watch is the best watch. They know better than Borachio that it is wiser to sleep than to talk, and while their sworn duty is to safeguard the city, they are realistic about their limitations as an amateur constabulary. They would avoid the presence of rogues lest they be defiled—would that Claudio and Don Pedro were of the same mind! If they are lucky, they will have a quiet night; if it is raucous, they will not add to the noise and uproar by attempting to arrest drunks and vagroms. They are too shrewd to waste their time with anyone who does not recognize their authority. It is only by accident that they overhear Borachio gloating over his wicked success as they sit on the church bench waiting for their tour to end, but they are experienced watchmen who know how to sleep without having their weapons stolen, the true and ancient art of standing sentry.

It is a great pity that Dogberry does not come to the point and tell Leonato what the watch learned the night before, yet who would have him talk less, especially when he is concerned that Leonato be patient with Verges, whose wits are not as blunt as Dogberry would have them. Kindly himself, Dogberry inspires kindness in others. Although he is very busy preparing for his daughter's wedding, Leonato takes time to hear the constables, and after apologizing for not being able to join in the interrogation of Borachio, he bids them drink some wine before they leave his house. Inevitably the examination of Borachio and Conrade is a masterpiece of irrelevancies, interjections, and pointless digressions. It is also courteous and fair-minded, almost too much so. Dogberry would discover the better nature as well as the criminal acts of his prisoners. "Masters," he asks, "do you serve God?" "Yea, sir, we hope," they answer. "Write down that they hope to serve God," Dogberry tells the sexton. His inclination to take Borachio and Conrade's word for their innocence unnerves the sexton, and his bumbling manner exasperates Conrade, who calls him an ass. Although wounded by this insult, Dogberry speaks more in sorrow than in anger of this discourtesy:

> Does thou not suspect my place? Dost thou not suspect my years? O that he were here to write me down as ass! But, masters, remember that I am an ass; though it be not written down, yet forget not that I am an ass. No, thou villain, thou art full of piety, as shall be prov'd upon thee by good witness. I am a wise fellow, and which is more, an officer, and which is more, a householder, and which is more, as pretty a piece of flesh as any is in Messina, and one that knows the law, go to, and a rich fellow enough, go to, and a fellow that hath had losses, and one that hath two gowns, and every thing handsome about him.
>
> (4.2. 74–86)

Dogberry is never more appealing than in his earnest desire to be writ down an ass. Claudio's display of indignation in the preceding wedding scene is repellent, however. He too publicly declares that he was made an ass—that is, duped by the cunning whore of Messina whom he almost married. Dogberry expresses a heartfelt sense of wrong; Claudio's denunciation of Hero is self-righteous and premeditated, not a spontaneous outcry from the heart. As soon as he hears Don John's sneering accusation of Hero, he thinks of taking his revenge: "If I see anything to-night why I should not marry her, to-morrow in the congregation, where I should wed, there will I shame her" (3.2. 123–25). Galled by the possibility that he wooed a trollop for his noble friend, Don Pedro says he will join with Claudio in disgracing Hero if he sees proof of her lewdness. The outrage at being victimized is understandable; the manner of the denunciation is appalling. They never think of accusing Hero privately, and they give no warning that her wedding will become a public inquisition. Since they have no doubt of Hero's guilt, they need not scruple about their methods, for what they intend is not a trial but rather a public whipping, the appropriate punishment for a whore, especially one who dared pretend to be a modest virgin. With astonishing speed an adored woman becomes an object of scorn and abuse here as in *Othello*, and neither Claudio nor Othello questions whether he has the right to take a cruel revenge on the woman who wronged him because both assume that they are defending the cause of public morality, not soothing a tormented ego. It may not be quite fair to humiliate Leonato, whose only crime is a confidence in his daughter's virtue and a desire to have a brief wedding ceremony, but perhaps Leonato deserves a few lashes too, for if Hero is a common stale, Leonato may be unscrupulous enough to try to palm off what he knows is damaged goods as first-class merchandise.

Like many who lack spontaneity of feeling or are afraid of it, Claudio melodramatizes his outrage. When Leonato makes the innocent mistake of declaring that there is no impediment to the marriage known to Claudio, Claudio seizes on his words as if he has caught the old man red-handed: "O, what men dare do! What men may do! / What men daily do, not knowing what they do." This strained attempt at irony merely puzzles Benedick, who does not see the point: "How now? Interjections?" Claudio's desire to play the satiric scourge of villainy falls flat, and he approaches the ludicrous when he refuses to accept Hero as his wife:

> There, Leonato, take her back again.
> Give not this rotten orange to your friend.
>
> (4.1. 31–32)

Claudio's gift of phrase reduces his outrage to that of a shopper who finds that he has paid good money for spoiled fruit and wants the grocer pilloried.

Shameful as Claudio's behavior is, it does not condemn him as singularly brutal or insensitive. Every statement he makes is silently approved or actively seconded by Don Pedro, who, when asked to speak by Leonato, says:

> What should I speak?
> I stand dishonor'd, that have gone about
> To link my dear friend to a common stale.
>
> (4.1. 63–65)

Don Pedro and Claudio have seen the proof of Hero's lewdness. Leonato's belief in his daughter's innocence quickly disintegrates when she is accused by two noble gentlemen. He is not outraged by Claudio's attack on Hero, and he does not respond with angry denials and counteraccusations. His first thought is that Claudio wishes to reject Hero after having seduced her, a behavior not unknown to gentlemen. If so, Hero may well be damaged goods, but Claudio is the one who tampered with her and therefore he should marry her. This possibility does not alter Leonato's view of Claudio, whom he addresses as "dear my lord," because one expects men to be men. After all, it is a virgin's responsibility to deny her lover's importunities and her own sexual desires until her wedding night. In a reasonable conciliatory tone, Leonato tries to salvage the marriage as best he can. Hero, Beatrice, Benedick, and the Friar are too stunned to say very much. Nothing that could be said, however, would change Claudio and Don Pedro's minds. They do not give Hero a chance to defend herself; all they offer is an opportunity to confess her guilt. What man, they ask, did she speak with last night at her window? If she admits that she spoke with a man, she stamps herself a whore: if she denies she spoke with a man, she proves that she is a lying whore. Her denials settle the issue for Don Pedro: "Why, then are you no maiden." Unlike the interrogation of Borachio and Conrade, the trial of Hero is without civility, and yet it is what honorable men think appropriate to her treachery. This offense cuts deep; it insults a man's offer of love and makes him an object of contempt to other men, who might find his gullibility amusing but would feel justified in behaving exactly as he behaves. In this matter, men take their stand with other men against women.

If Hero had been seduced and abandoned, Leonato would feel compelled to seek satisfaction from Claudio. When it appears that she has deceived him as well as Claudio by being a cunning wanton, he abandons her because he feels the wound to his reputation as deeply as Claudio and Don Pedro do. Indeed, the blow to his honor erases all pity for Hero. When she faints, he wishes her dead, for he sees, as do her accusers, the very proof of her guilt in her maiden blush:

> Do not live, Hero, do not ope thine eyes;
> For did I think thou wouldst not quickly die,
> Thought I thy spirits were stronger than thy shames,
> Myself would, on the rearward of reproaches,
> Strike at thy life. . . .
> . . . .
> Why ever wast thou lovely in my eyes?
> Why had I not with charitable hand
> Took up a beggar's issue at my gates,
> Who smirched thus and mir'd with infamy,
> I might have said, "No part of it is mine;
> This shame derives itself from unknown loins"?
> But mine, and mine I lov'd, and mine I prais'd,
> And mine that I was proud on. . . .
>
> (4.1. 123–37)

Leonato's self-dramatization is similar to Claudio's; obsessed with his shame, he has no compassion for Hero, who just before had been his most prized possession—five times in the last four lines quoted above he speaks of her as "mine." Even when Benedick voices his disbelief and Beatrice explains that every night except the last one she was Hero's bedfellow, Leonato is unmoved. It stands to reason that Hero would lie about her lewdness, but "would the two princes lie?"

As he abuses his once-beloved daughter, Leonato blusters in the manner of Capulet browbeating Juliet when she refused to marry Paris. The echo of *Romeo and Juliet* grows more immediate as the Friar steps forth to play Friar Lawrence's role by offering a solution that involves the heroine's seeming death. Where the timid Lawrence evades his responsibility by refusing to

reveal Juliet's secret marriage to Romeo, the Friar in *Much Ado* is coura-
geous enough to take Hero's part. His is a welcome voice of sympathy and
reasonableness after so much emotional and rhetorical extravagance. He
points out what should be obvious to all, Hero's speechless anguish and
innocence. Leonato still mutters but the tide turns when Hero recovers and
swears her innocence. Benedick, who never doubted her, shrewdly guesses
at Don John's villainous part in all this, and Leonato, who just before was
ready to strike his guilty daughter down, is ready to revenge her, to which
end he pledges his blood, invention, means, friends, "strength of limb and
policy of mind" in a bragging Polonian speech. Once again the Friar must
intervene to bring Leonato back to reason. His cautious pragmatism opposes
any violent action, any challenge to conventional attitudes, even any public
defense of Hero's innocence. Such a course would probably not succeed and
only spread the scandal more widely. Since Claudio and Don Pedro's accusations have mortally wounded Hero's reputation, the Friar would counter the
false report of her lewdness with a false report of her death. Given the way of
the world, it does not really matter that Hero is chaste; the only hope now is
that Claudio, believing she is dead, will regret his actions and realize what he
has lost. In any event, Hero's death

> Will quench the wonder of her infamy.
> And if it sort not well, you may conceal her,
> As best befits her wounded reputation,
> In some reclusive and religious life,
> Out of all eyes, tongues, minds, and injuries.
>
> (4.1. 239–43)

Although the Friar does not accept Claudio's view of Hero, he implicitly
agrees with Claudio that she is damaged goods and unmarriageable unless
Claudio will have her.

Benedick thinks the Friar counsels well; Beatrice is not satisfied by this
solution, however. Enraged by Claudio's behavior, she wants the kind of
satisfaction one man can have of another in a duel. She weeps out of
frustration because she feels incapable of striking back:

> O that I were a man! What, bear her in hand until they come to take
> hands, and then with public accusation, uncover'd slander, unmitigated
> rancor—O God, that I were a man! I would eat his heart in the market-
> place.
>
> (4.1. 303–7)

Even here Beatrice is not a rebel who storms against the hypocrisies of her
society. She is enraged by men who are unmanly—that is, unchivalrous,
ungentle in their treatment of women. Instinctively, she seeks a man to

champion Hero's cause, one who will use his strength and valor to prove her cousin's innocence and punish those who have defamed her. Since Beatrice never pretended to scoff at romance, she does not seem to step out of character when she becomes the quintessential romantic of the play, one who wants a knight in shining armor to avenge her cousin's shame. When Benedick declares his love, she is so absorbed in her anger that she cannot think of him or of how she feels about him, although she half-confesses her love. Exhilarated by her declaration, Benedick would have her command some service of him; without hesitation, she tells him to kill Claudio and when he draws back in shock, she does not allow him to renege on his offer.

Her rage at Claudio is as blind and unreasoning as Claudio's treatment of hero. She ignores the fact that Benedick did not take Claudio's side and remained behind when Claudio and Don Pedro left, even though they are his closest friends. She does not see the terrible unfairness of her demand that Benedick kill Claudio to gain her love. Before this, the apprehension of Borachio by the Watch seemed to set limits on the tragic consequences of Don John's schemes; after Claudio's actions in the wedding scene, and after Beatrice's fury, one is no longer certain that all will be well. Very soon Hero's innocence will be proved, but the question will remain whether Claudio deserves to be forgiven because Beatrice insists he does not deserve to live, and she will not be satisfied until Benedick matches swords with him.

The change in the emotional weather of *Much Ado* from its first genial scenes to the furious passions of the wedding scene is astonishing. As in *The Merchant*, the outpouring of hate is counterbalanced by the triumph of love: the perversion of Hero's nuptial by the coming together of Beatrice and Benedick. But in *Much Ado* all will not be well when the villain is defeated because the ugliness of the wedding scene and its aftermath of bitterness must be dealt with before a happy ending is possible. Since Beatrice's reaction is as excessive as Claudio's, Shakespeare could have resolved the conflict by having one or the other retreat from his extreme position, but neither does. Claudio does not walk out on stage to regret his fury; Beatrice does not withdraw her demand that Benedick kill Claudio. When she next appears on stage, she does not speak of Claudio to Benedick, and need not speak of him, because Claudio, stunned by Borachio's confession of guilt, has already put himself into Leonato's hands and the denouement is at hand.

The happy ending of *The Merchant* demands that those who return to Belmont put out of mind all that happened in the Venetian courtroom. The denouement of *Much Ado* is more profoundly satisfying because nothing that is painful is forgotten; on the contrary, the resolution of anger and conflict comes through the reenactment of the wedding that had turned into a heartless denunciation of Hero, so that even as Hero and Claudio are reunited in love and marriage, all who are present at the ceremony and who watch in the audience must remember the pain of the aborted wedding. The

Friar predicted that all would be well when Claudio's heart softened toward the "dead" Hero, but Leonato, who assented to the Friar's plan, finds it humiliating to have to wait for a change of heart in the man who mistreated his daughter. Reliving the bitterness of the aborted wedding, he rejects his brother Antonio's counsels of patience because he finds no comfort in platitudinous consolations. Like Claudio, he takes pleasure in being aggrieved, and his sense of outrage is the greater when he imagines Hero as not only defamed but also robbed of life by vicious slander. Confusing fiction and fact, he tells Claudio that he has

> belied mine innocent child!
> Thy slander hath gone through and through her heart,
> And she lies buried with her ancestors—
> O, in a tomb where never scandal slept,
> Save this of hers, fram'd by thy villainy!
>
> (5.1. 67–71)

Having heard the false report of Hero's death, Claudio and Don Pedro do not want to speak to Leonato and Antonio. They are embarrassed and regretful, however, not stricken with remorse. In response to Leonato's accusations, Don Pedro replies:

> My heart is sorry for your daughter's death;
> But on my honor she was charg'd with nothing
> But what was true, and very full of proof.
>
> (5.1. 103–5)

Perhaps this reply is a bit facile, but Leonato's indignation is not entirely noble; he must know that these soldiers will have to bear his taunts and insults because they could not accept a challenge from an aging man. Before long, Antonio, the voice of patience, is swept up in Leonato's passion; he is ready to second his brother in a duel and, carried away on the tide of his invective, he shouts that Claudio and Don Pedro are

> Scambling, outfacing, fashion-monging boys,
> That lie and cog and flout, deprave and slander,
> Go anticly, and show outward hideousness.
>
> (5.1. 94–96)

At this point, it is Leonato's turn to restrain Antonio, who also speaks of Hero as "slandered to death by villains." If it is not quite fair for old men to challenge those who cannot defend their honor against them, there is nevertheless a rough justice in the denunciation of Claudio and Don Pedro, who denounced the helpless, defenseless Hero.

Once the heroes of Messina, Claudio and Don Pedro are now its outcasts. They rejoice in Benedick's entrance, thinking he will take their side and laugh with them about their aged adversaries. They cannot believe his pale-faced anger and readiness to draw his sword. He too accuses them of killing a sweet lady and promises that her death will fall heavy on Claudio. Thus the self-appointed preservers of public morality find themselves publicly denounced for a murder that never occurred. Their nadir comes when the Watch brings in Borachio, who remorsefully confesses all. Although stricken, Claudio and Don Pedro do not openly admit or perhaps even recognize how shamefully they treated Hero. They erred, they say, only in "mistaking." Claudio's speeches hint, nevertheless, of a deeper sense of guilt, because he offers himself as a sacrifice to Leonato's anger:

> Choose your revenge yourself,
> Impose me to what penance your invention
> Can lay upon my sin.
>
> (5.1. 272–74)

As Benedick put himself in Beatrice's hands by asking her to command some service of love, Claudio puts himself in Leonato's hands, bidding him impose a penance fit for his *sin*. Leonato's response is nobler than Beatrice's in that the only satisfaction he demands of the man he just before maligned and challenged is to marry his "niece," a maiden as fair as Hero was and heiress now to two family fortunes. This sudden reversal is not at all perplexing because Leonato's anger was strained and hyperbolic. He is by nature kindly, hospitable, and considerate of others, a leading householder who will invite the officers of the Watch to take a cup of wine. He may indulge his sense of wrong but he will not sacrifice his daughter's happiness to satisfy his personal honor. Thus the customary civilities of Messinian life exert their influence. Just as Claudio expresses his confidence in Leonato by putting himself in his accuser's hands, Leonato expresses his confidence in Claudio's nature by a willingness to accept him as Hero's husband despite all. Borachio also wants to do the right thing and make certain that Margaret is not blamed for her part in the deception at the window.

With the crisis past, Benedick has the opportunity to enjoy his role of lover. He can trade greasy jests with Margaret and try his hand at love poems. He can also wear his heart on his sleeve when he speaks to Beatrice. They do not dream of eternal Petrarchan bliss; they look forward to years of mutual affection and loving raillery. Benedick is his old self again, or rather he is his old self with a tincture of Dogberryan sagacity. His parting to Beatrice, who claims to feel ill, is "Serve God, love me, and mend." With the prospect of a lifetime with Beatrice before him, Benedick cannot pay much attention to the news that Don John's villainy has been uncovered. His universe, Donne would say, is contracted to his love of Beatrice. "I will live in thy heart," he tells her, "die in thy lap, and be buried in thy eyes."

Benedick's high-spirited amorousness contrasts with the solemn ritualism of Claudio and Don Pedro's pilgrimage to Hero's "tomb." The mourning scene is brief and the epitaph and song conventional because the true act of penance is to come on the morrow when Claudio will take as his wife a woman he is not allowed to see before the ceremony. This denouement will leave an unpleasant aftertaste if marriage seems to become a form of expiation or indeed of punishment, as it does in the last scene of *Measure for Measure*. Claudio, of course, believes that he is sacrificing his chance of happiness in marriage and expects the worst. Everyone else (except Don Pedro) knows that his marriage to a bride he is not allowed to see is, like the gulling of Beatrice and Benedick, a loving practical joke as well as a proper humbling for one who wrongfully rejected his first bride at the altar. If Claudio is to deserve a second chance at love and happiness, he must be able to trust, where before he was too ready to doubt; he must also keep his word however fearful he is of what his bride is like behind her veil. His situation is that of the folktale hero who, having sworn to marry the ancient hag who helped him, discovers on his wedding night that his bride is young and beautiful.

Claudio comes to the wedding grimly determined to marry even an Ethiope. When he tries to relieve his misery by some broad jokes about Benedick's impending fate as a cuckold, he is stung by remarks about his own bovine ancestry. When he asks which of the veiled ladies he must seize on, he is told he cannot see his bride's face until he has sworn to marry her. The testing of Claudio is only a ritual, however, because he has already been approved by Leonato. Like her father, Hero does not demand the satisfaction of humiliating Claudio as he humiliated her. She is content to make clear that she is not "another Hero." Claudio, she says, was her "other husband" when he loved her. Their reconciliation, like their falling in love, is expressed in silent looks and embraces, not in words. The lovers' dialogue belongs to Beatrice and Benedick, who express their mutual affection with mock dismay and teasing questions and answers. They will not admit that they love "more than reason" or other than "in friendly recompense," but they cannot deny the evidence of the sonnets they wrote about one another. Reluctantly Benedick agrees to marry because he pities Beatrice, and she will become his wife, she says, to save him from a reported consumption. Benedick is glad not to have to duel Claudio for Hero's sake; and Claudio is relieved that Benedick did not jilt Beatrice because he was ready to play her champion. Over Leonato's objections, Benedick decrees dancing before the weddings are solemnized, and he promises to devise brave punishments for the captured Don John. One doubts, however, that he will find the necessary thumbscrews and strappados in Messina.

In different ways *Much Ado* and *The Merchant* deal with the relationship between a society and those it makes its outcasts: a fallen woman, a disgraced hero, a money-lending Jew. The difference between Leonato and the Venetian Antonio is that between a man who treats all with simple courtesy and one who is convinced that he has the right to spit on Shylock's beard. While *Much Ado* reveals the obtuseness of conventional attitudes, it also reaffirms the preciousness of very ordinary virtues. When an assumption of moral superiority can lead to contempt for others and acts of cruelty, there is much to be said for unassuming decency, even when it is as bumbling as Dogberry's.

9

As You Like It

As You Like It is a more cheerful play than an abstract of its plot would seem to suggest. Its first scenes unfold a world apparently turned upside down; the reigning duke is a usurper who forced his older brother into exile, and Oliver tyrannizes over his younger brother Orlando, whom he has deprived of his inheritance, treats as a common herdsman, and would like to murder. The bonds of blood and kinship seem to have lost their cogency; loyalty and true service go unrewarded, the decent are driven into exile, and the aged are treated with contempt. But rather than a preliminary study for *King Lear, As You Like It* is a cheerful, indeed, sunny play. The third, fourth, and fifth acts are set in Arden, a never-never land free of anxiety and rich in laughter, song, and warmhearted sentiment. Even in the first two acts, which are set at court, the emphasis falls on Orlando's loving concern for Adam, not on Oliver's wickedness—on Celia and Rosalind's devotion to one another, not on her father's brooding malice. Although the wicked hold sway, they do not demoralize those they seek to oppress. No romantic is quite so innocent and purehearted as Orlando; no exile is so well adjusted to his banishment as Duke Senior. Many satiric observations are made in *As You Like It*, but none cut very deep. The soi-disant satirist and malcontent Jaques is much in demand as an afterdinner speaker; Rosalind and Touchstone are whimsical, yea-saying skeptics who affirm the values they seem to mock. Despite the absence of Dogberry and Verges, crime does not pay and there is never any doubt that all will end well. Indeed, *As You Like It* creates so strong an impression that decency is the norm of life that Shakespeare can be somewhat cavalier in the working out of his denouement, confident that no one will object to the means by which Oliver and Duke Frederick are reformed and redeemed.

Lodge's *Rosalynde* reaches a happy conclusion only after the wicked usurping duke is slain in battle. In Shakespeare's play, Celia's father, in pursuit of his disobedient daughter, is converted to a life of religious seclusion by a chance meeting with a holy man. This would strike an audience as

facile as well as fortuitous were it not that the duke is quite miserable in his
ill-gotten power, even as Oliver is more unhappy in his wealth and power
than Orlando is in his downtrodden state. He plots against his younger
brother, not because Orlando seriously threatens him but because he envies
the goodness in Orlando that wins so many hearts. After persuading the
mighty wrestler Charles to maim or kill Orlando, Oliver says of his brother:

> I hope I shall see an end of him; for my soul (yet I know not why) hates
> nothing more than he. Yet he's gentle, never school'd and yet learned, full
> of noble device, of all sorts enchantingly belove'd, and indeed so much in
> the heart of the world, and especially of my own people, who best know
> him, that I am altogether mispris'd.
>
> (1.1. 164–71)

Thus the Machiavellian intriguer is reduced to a malicious sibling rival who
wants to be loved but does not know how to give or receive affection. Duke
Frederick is also nagged by his unpopularity, by his knowledge that many
people loved his older brother and joined him in exile. He tells Celia that she
will be more admired when Rosalind is banished, but Celia only reinforces
his sense of isolation by fleeing with Rosalind. Unable to enjoy their money
and titles and envious of those they wrong, the villains of *As You Like It*
inevitably fall out with one another and must give up their high positions to
find happiness in a low content.[1] Since villainy is its own scourge, it is not
surprising that the angriest outburst in the play is directed against Jaques
rather than Duke Frederick or Oliver, and the vehemence of Duke Senior's
diatribe against Jaques' satiric pose suggests that the only unforgivable crime
is a lack of tolerance for the frailties of others. Those who are forever
dwelling on vices and sins, the Duke suggests, must have a special (and
perhaps personal) attraction to them.

After the flurry of events in the first two acts, the plot of *As You Like It*
loses its momentum and, indeed, its very direction in the forest of Arden.
When the exiles reach its borders, they leave all sense of crisis and urgency
far behind. Cut off from their usual round of activities they find themselves
on a perpetual holiday, and for want of other occupation devote their days to
aristocratic and pastoral recreations: philosophical reflections, music, hunting, courting, and the composition of love poetry. They enjoy venison
banquets under the trees even though Jaques moralizes the death of a stag
after eating his share and wiping the gravy from his lips. The only bar to the
fulfillment of love in the forest is Rosalind's reluctance to put off her disguise
as Ganymede; the only romantic complication is Phebe's mistaken passion
for Ganymede, a shallow, comic infatuation that does not inspire much
sympathy or raise any doubt that every Jack will have his Jill by the time the
play ends.

I do not mean to suggest that *As You Like It* wants plot or is too meandering to hold an audience's attention. I mean only that it persuades us of its coherence and unity even while it ignores the conventional canons of dramatic art. Its closest analogue is *2 Henry IV,* in which the forward progress of England's history is for a time suspended while the nation waits for an aged king to die and for rebellion to run its last lingering course. For the characters of *As You Like It,* exile is also a time of waiting, an interim period during which they play at pastorality while they wait for the opportunity to return to the court, which is their natural milieu.

Since action is nearly impossible in the forest of Arden, the exiles use their leisure to contemplate and reflect on life, love, sheepbreeding, the court, and the country. They wax aphoristic on a variety of subjects and are expansive if not solemn in thought. Duke Senior and Jaques were born sententious; Rosalind and Touchstone achieve sententiousness; and the others in Arden have sententiousness thrust upon them. While the sentences are often memorable, they cannot substitute for dramatic tension. Moments of relaxation in a play are delightful so long as they give way to a renewed intensity of dramatic action. If there is no apparent movement toward a climax or denouement, an audience will grow restless however delightful the dialogue is moment by moment. Much depends therefore on the response of the exiles in *As You Like It* to their enforced pastorality because the tension between character and setting must largely substitute for the more customary tension and conflict between character and character. If the exiles never adapt to Arden—if some of them never quite believe in Arden even when they are in its midst—then we know that eventually they must return to the city and the court from which they have never really departed in thought even though they sojourn in the forest.

Of course, only a Dr. Gradgrind would undertake to debunk the pastoral, which may deal with serious issues but never pretends to deal with the reality of nature and men's lives. The artificiality of the pastoral is essential to its appeal; from the earliest eclogues it expresses a sophisticated poet's nostalgia for a life of simplicity and innocence that he has never known and could not have long endured. English poets of the Renaissance made the pastoral a vehicle for their lyric impulse and delight in nature, and found it more congenial than the brooding psychological inwardness of Petrarch. Uninspired versifiers turned out pastoral dialogues by the yard; greater poets transformed the genre. Marlowe's famous lyric "Come live with me" is a study in cloisonné that gilds and enamels nature and inlays it with coral, pearls, and semiprecious stones. Ralegh replies to Marlowe's poem as if he were determined to shatter its illusion, but his antipastoral, "The Nymph's Reply to the Shepherd," is as idiosyncratic as Marlowe's lyric; indeed, it is as much as denial of the possibility of growth and maturation as the pastoral is a denial of the passing of time.[2] Ralegh's debunking of pastoralism need not be very earnest because his fellow Elizabethans had little inclination to abandon themselves to life in the countryside. Rich London merchants, eager for gentility and dynasty, were ready to buy up the estates of impecunious noblemen, but rural life did not have a seductive appeal for sophisticated Elizabethans. Rustication was a punishment imposed on courtiers who displeased Gloriana.

As the sixteenth century drew to a close, increasing commerce with the New World produced travelers' tales of Edenic unspoiled wilderness at a time when the ancient agrarianism of Europe was being superseded by a new mercantilism. Painters, poets, and philosophers celebrated the beauty of the Americas and the nobility of their native populations, but they did not rush to book passage either to Jamestown or Plymouth. They preferred to stay at home and dream of the Golden Age, when all men lived in harmony with nature and natural law. Shakespeare's characters are also dubious of rusticity. Valentine does not rejoice in his woodland life as head of an outlaw band; the lovers of *A Dream* find their woodland adventure unnerving, and mountain life seems rude to the characters in *Cymbeline* who are forced to endure it. Although Florizel dreams of spending his life with Perdita in a cottage, she knows that pastoral bliss is only a dream; true content lies in Leontes' court, to which all the characters in *The Winter's Tale* return. Even Prospero, who has no great desire to see Milan again, knows that he and Miranda must leave their island, which is as much prison as refuge to them. Although critics can idealize the pastoral experiences of Shakespeare's characters as renewing contacts with nature, that experience is often somewhat harrowing—they are wet and cold, their feet hurt, and they are at the mercy of goblins, monsters, outlaws, wind, waves, and boredom. Oliver and Celia are the only exiles who choose to remain in Arden at the close of *As You Like It*. Orlando, who has been deprived of education and forced to do menial farm labor, knows that feeding hogs and tending sheep is not the noblest work of man; only those who have never slept on a hillside can sentimentalize the life of the shepherd.[3]

Like other thoughtful Elizabethans, Shakespeare knew that the pastoral beckons when time weighs heavily upon us and the sophisticated world is too much with us. In Renaissance poetry, a green thought in a green shade is not an impulse from a vernal wood but an adventure of the mind, a turning away from crass pursuits and feverish competition toward the garden of the mind. A papiermâché sprig or two and a handful of painted leaves will suffice for the landscape of Arden because it has about as much to do with nature as a Fragonard painting. When, as in a recent BBC television production of the play, actors have to pick their way through real underbrush, the charm of Arden vanishes, and the Duke's banquet beneath melancholy boughs becomes as mundane as a family outing. Sword in hand, Orlando breaks in on the banquet ready to exchange blows for a handful of nuts and berries, or whatever mean fare the natives of Arden subsist on. When he and Adam are well fed on venison, he takes up the simple pursuits of the region and makes its trees bulletin boards for love poems.

Like all utopias, Arden has it limitations and its drawbacks. Corin's master is a penny-pincher; Audrey, the goatmaid, is slow of wit. The exiles do not rediscover innocence in the forest; they bring it with them together with well-filled purses, lutes, music books, and manuscript paper. Even then they find the unhurried pace of life in Arden something of a trial. Here ripeness is not necessarily all, for it may lead in the inevitable course of things to rottenness in men as well as fruit. Those bred at court do not adapt to forest ways; they adapt life in the forest to their courtly tastes. They prefer art songs to rustic hays and philosophical debates to basket weaving. Although the sentimental Duke Senior lectures on the sweet uses of adversity, he never tries to convince anyone that adversity is preferable to good fortune. The joy of life is not to be found in pastoral solitude, he notes, but in cities and towns. His fondest memories are not of trees and running brooks but of church bells and good men's feasts. The satirical Jaques similarly does not rejoice that he has escaped the corruptions of society, and he has too great a need of listeners to cherish the solitary stillness of nature. He belongs by the side of Duke and all those who live well and enjoy a sound scolding after a good meal, brandy, and cigars. The Jaques of the world have no feeling for nature; they thrive indoors and can be found on the lecture circuit and committees that deal with national issues and issue voluminous reports.

Actors who are fond of the sound of their voices make much of the role of Jaques, convinced that he is the soul of the play, a spokesman for Shakespeare's wisdom. They do not notice that Jaques is scarcely a match in conversation for anyone he meets in Arden. He enjoys Touchstone's reflections on time without understanding their sly humor. He thinks Touchstone a natural fool, but Touchstone plays the fool with a whimsicality that no coat of motley could give to Jaques. Where Touchstone is a true original, Jaques is all manner and the only one in the play who can make Orlando seem the soul of wit. When he tries to bait Orlando, he is puzzled by a suggestion that he go seek a fool in a stream because he knows that he will see nothing but his own reflection. His interest in others is as benign as it is shallow. He envies no one and is attached to no one. His set speech on the seven ages of man is an anatomy of human folly that delights without troubling the mind.[4] Its rubber-tipped arrows are directed at lovers, soldiers, venal judges, and pantalones, and only limitations of time preclude the usual jokes about doctors and clergymen. Jaques's description of the "whining schoolboy, with his satchel,"

> And shining morning face, creeping like snail
> Unwilling to school,

has an avuncular charm. Marriage and fatherhood, one imagines, never tempted Jaques. He is the neighborhood bachelor who enjoys chatting with children on the way home from school, so long as they do not linger or ask to be invited in.

The fastidiousness of Jaques makes all the more puzzling Duke Senior's attack on him as a libertine sick with all the sores and headed evils—a grossly venereal metaphor—which he would spew out into the world. Such an outburst would be appropriate to some of Marston and Jonson's satirists or to a character like Webster's Flamineo, but not to one as unphysical and unsensual as Jaques.[5] Perhaps the Duke must occasionally lash out at Jaques to justify the pleasure he takes in retaining him as an all-licensed malcontent who entertains his listeners with barbs meant to scourge the evils of society. After fuller acquaintance with Jaques, we understand the Duke's fondness for him, for the sentimentalist and satirist are not such an odd couple. The one labors to prove that this is the best of possible worlds; the other takes satisfaction in demonstrating that it could hardly be worse.

Where Jaques amuses his listeners when he thinks he is exposing their hypocrisies and shams, Touchstone knows that his satire is meant to entertain, and he also knows that his own zaniness is a richer subject for comedy than the silliness of others. He can be as earnest as the next man and protest the pandering of ewes to rams, but he has the advantage of knowing that his arguments are absurd and he will not fatigue his brain to settle the conflicting claims of court and country, nature and nurture. He has more wit than the clowns of the earlier comedies, but he lacks the shrewdness that will keep Speed in pocket money all of his life. Because he suspects that any woman willing to marry him cannot be overly bright, he does not mind Audrey's dullness. He also suspects that any woman willing to sleep with him would probably not shrink from having a few other "friends," but the prospect of horns does not horrify him. He will wear them if necessary with a difference.

Although Touchstone deflates ideals of romantic love by insisting that nymphs and swains are flesh and blood, he has none of Lucio's or Lavatch's smirking cynicism about women and sexual appetite. He jokes about horns, not about marriage. If Audrey were loose enough to submit to him, he probably would not marry her, yet he does not lament too much the bitter fate that made her both ugly and chaste. It is he, not Audrey, who proposes the marriage, for he would satisfy his nibbling desires in a lawful (well, almost lawful) bed.

Rosalind, the only one in the play who can match wits and whimsy with Touchstone, is much less tolerant of poseurs than he. Amused by Jaques, she nevertheless informs him that his melancholy is a tedious affectation. When she laughs at her passion for Orlando she does not make a joke of love; ardent and romantic by nature she is annoyed by Phebe and Silvius, who play at passion without verve or spontaneity because love can thrive on humor but finds no nourishment in arch attitudes and secondhand emotion. She enjoys a bout of wit but she does not, like Portia, take pleasure in matching her cleverness against others. Her wisdom is less practical than Portia's, and it is more likely to be zany in attitude than measured out in witty sentences. She is too wholehearted in her affections to wish to teach Orlando how to be a sensible lover. Her schooling of him is playfully extracurricular; she offers a short course in love and marriage that allows passion its rein but not its pretensions. When Orlando protests that he would have Rosalind as wife "for ever and a day," she advises him to "Say 'a day,' without the 'ever.'" Her ideal of marriage is one that keeps alive the playful excitement of courtship even as it transcends it. She doubts that pangs of love have ever proved fatal and, like Bottom and his colleagues, she exorcises the fear of romantic tragedy:

> The poor world is almost six thousand years old, and in all this time there was not any man died in his own person, *videlicet,* in a love-cause. Troilus had his brains dash'd out with a Grecian club, yet he did what he could to die before, and he is one of the patterns of love. . . . men have died from time to time, and worms have eaten them, but not for love.
>
> (4.1. 94–108)

Skeptical of the tragedy of love, Rosalind believes wholeheartedly in its comedy, and she intends to play her comic role so broadly that Orlando will never be certain of his wife's mood, although he will have no doubt of her devotion. The sensible Theseus patronizes the madness of love; Rosalind only pretends to try to cure it because she knows that the canker in the rose of love is not the exuberance of passion but the routine of marriage, in which the poetry of courtship turns into the dullest of prose.[6]

If Rosalind were as antiromantic as she is sometimes described, she would find Arden absurd; she is able to enjoy the pastoral holiday it affords because she is never arch or self-conscious or clever at someone else's expense. Sunny-natured and resilient, she is not forever on guard against the world. Although wise beyond her years, she can express her feelings with a childlike directness. Orlando's tardiness genuinely upsets her and she can sympathize with Silvius's unrequited love even though his outcries do not evince much suffering. Overcome by passion, he runs off stage, as he knows lovers should, shouting his cruel fair's name. An audience invariably laughs, only to discover that Silvius's anguish is not amusing to Rosalind, who also knows the sorrow of unfulfilled love: "Alas, poor shepherd! Searching of thy wound, I have by hard adventure found mine own."

Rosalind's melancholy is only momentary. Even after she falls in love with Orlando, she is happy enough to be with Celia, whether at court or in Arden, and she is not distressed by his absence or indeed by her separation from her father, to whom she reveals herself only in the last scene of the play. Orlando does not fill her thoughts until she meets him again in the forest and then her delight in the role of Ganymede keeps her from revealing herself to him. Loving in all her relationships, she does not, like Julia or Hermia, live for love, and her destiny is not to lose herself in marriage to Orlando but rather to widen his horizons by making him a proper husband.

At the beginning of the play, Orlando's naiveté does not matter because his sweet nature and chivalric manliness are attractive enough. With a wider experience of life and some schooling by Rosalind, he may develop a sense of humor and a more realistic view of things; but throughout the play he remains a Quixotic innocent, not quite able to cope with a world that does not conform to his heroic expectations. He is described by Adam as a latterday Sir Galahad, not only born centuries too late but destined to pay dearly for his knightly virtues:

> Why are you virtuous? Why do people love you?
> And wherefore are you gentle, strong, and valiant?
> . . . .
>   Your virtues, gentle master,
> Are sanctified and holy traitors to you.
>
>   (2.3. 5–13)

Robbed of his inheritance by Oliver, Orlando sets out to redeem his name and make his fortune by chivalric deeds. On the way to challenge the mighty Charles at wrestling, he meets Rosalind, who gives him a token to wear for her sake. She should also send him forth inspired by her confidence; instead she sighs, shakes her head, and hopes that she is mistaken in her estimate of his abilities. As in the old tales, the unknown challenger defeats the mighty champion and need only reveal his identity to receive the reward and recognition he deserves. When he speaks his name to Duke Frederick, however, he is told that he has the wrong father, one who was the Duke's enemy, and only the decency of Le Beau saves him from the usurper's wrath. He tries again to play the knight-errant in Arden by challenging the Duke's party to gain food for Adam, but succeeds only in being invited to dinner. Unable to find savages or dragons to overcome, Orlando turns love poet and proves less successful in this venture than in his knight-errantry. A man like this is a match for any villain and any lion, but he will need a loving wife to appreciate his virtues and to protect him from disillusion in a world that he will never fully understand.

In Lodge's story, the disguised heroine and her lover have one meeting in which they consciously assume the roles of nymph and swain. Shakespeare gives much more space to the masquerade and the role-playing in two lengthy scenes in which Ganymede invites Orlando to imagine that he is courting Rosalind when he speaks to her. Since the Elizabethan stage did not demand realism in disguise, Rosalind remains Rosalind for the audience whether she assumes the guise of Ganymede or plays Ganymede pretending to be Rosalind. Thus her pretenses do not invert or blur her sexual identity, especially when her role was taken by one of the actors in Shakespeare's company who was expert at playing female characters. If there is any risk of unpleasantness in the mock wooing scenes it lies in Orlando's inability to catch any of Ganymede's subtle hinting about her true nature. He is so carried away by Ganymede's impersonation of a woman that he asks her for a kiss. He is also less observant about Ganymede than is Oliver, who brings a bloody napkin from Orlando as a love token. When Ganymede faints, Oliver guesses that "his" passion is in earnest and almost seems to guess that "he" is a woman: "Be of good cheer, youth," he advises, "You a man! You lack a man's heart. . . . Well then, take a good heart and counterfeit to be a man." This is not to say that Orlando should be able to see through Rosalind's disguise any more than Orsino or Olivia should be able to see through Viola's, despite Viola's more urgent hinting about her identity. But Orsino can commune with Cesario and share with this "boy" his most intimate thoughts, while Orlando never progresses beyond a freshman's status in his schooling by Ganymede, who does most of the talking and all of the professing in their scenes together.

   Phebe also undertakes the education of her lover Silvius by sneering at his Petrarchan hyperboles while she enjoys all the literary rights and privileges of being the cruel fair of Elizabethan sonnets.

> Thou tell'st me there is murder in mine eye:
> 'Tis pretty, sure, and very probable,
> That eyes, that are the frail'st and softest things,
> Who shut their coward gates on atomies,
> Should be called tyrants, butchers, murtherers!
> Now I do frown on thee with all my heart,
> And if mine eyes can wound, now let them kill thee.
> Now counterfeit to swound; why, now fall down.
>
> (3.5. 10–17)

Silvius and Phebe assume the conventional roles that lovers have in the sonnets: he sighs and pleads and wallows in self-indulgent misery; she postures in deflating his romantic agony, playing the cruel fair while refusing to allow him to be the despairing victim of his mistress's disdain. Rosalind's disguise, which is also a cliché of romantic fabling, never strikes an audience as being a pose because her responses are always truthful even when she deceives and teases Orlando. Her lively interest in his emotional well-being is perfectly genuine, and since she does not love by the book, she can dissect the artificialities of romantic convention at the same time that she ardently affirms the meaning of romantic commitment.

Truth is the burden of Rosalind's message to the pastoral lovers. She advises Silvius to have his eye sight tested because it is myopic fools like him

> That make the world full of ill-favor'd children.
> 'Tis not her glass, but you that flatters her.
>
> (3.5. 53–54)

She would have Phebe appraise her own assets more realistically:

> But, mistress, know yourself, down on your knees,
> And thank heaven, fasting, for a good man's love;
> For I must tell you friendly in your ear,
> Sell when you can, you are not for all markets.
> Cry the man mercy, love him, take his offer.
>
> (3.5. 57–61)

Once Valentine's praises of Silvia made Proteus his rival. Now Rosalind's dispraise of Phebe inspires her passion. As the heroes of the comedies become more gentle—more like Bassanio and Benedick than Demetrius or Petruchio—heroines like Phebe and Olivia become aggressive in pursuing the "men" whose indifference or frankness seems overwhelmingly attractive. Ironically enough the only male character in *As You Like It* who is an aggressive rivalrous wooer is Touchstone, who is well aware of the ludicrousness of his determined pursuit of Audrey. A master of courtly bravado, Touchstone warns away his rival William in a style that is as precise and as martial as Don Armado's:

> . . . you clown, abandon—which is in the vulgar leave—the society—which in the boorish is company—of this female—which in the common is woman; which together is, abandon the society of this female, or, clown, thou perishest; or to thy better understanding, diest; or (to wit) I kill thee, make thee away, translate thy life into death, thy liberty into bondage. I will deal in poison with thee, or in bastinado, or in steel; I will bandy with thee in faction; I will o'errun thee with [policy]; I will kill thee a hundred and fifty ways.
>
> (5.1. 47–57)

This man could set the murderous Machiavel to school.

Although Touchstone can offer at times a barnyard view of love, his sense of bourgeois propriety is evident in his desire that Audrey have a ladylike bearing at her wedding. He will perforce marry a goatmaid but he has no intention of starting a career in animal husbandry. His natural place is the court, and like most of the exiles he is destined to return to it. Since nothing that happens in Arden can alter the situation at court, however, Shakespeare must take a hand in events. Yet the ending of the play seems neither contrived nor sentimental because the news of Duke Frederick's conversion to a religious life comes after the quadruple wedding ceremony that reunites all the exiles and ensures as much personal happiness as the different lovers of the play are capable of. The news also comes after Touchstone has reminded everyone of the unpleasant realities of court life to which they will soon return. That he is a courtier is beyond doubt because he has all the necessary credentials:

> I have trod a measure; I have flatt'red a lady; I have been politic with my friend, smooth with mine enemy, I have undone three tailors, I have had four quarrels, and like to have fought one.
>
> (5.4. 44–47)

By the time Touchstone has finished his explanation of the seven causes of quarrels and degrees of reply (Retort Courteous, Quip Modest, Reply Churlish, Reproof Valiant, and so on), pastoral dreams have given way to fantasies of aristocratic honor, in which courtly cowards may pass muster as heroes, and clever evasions, not cutlasses, are the weapons of choice.

Since there are no clocks in the forest, would-be duellers could not possibly make appointments to run each other through. Yet expectation and desire begin to create an urgent tempo in the pulses of the exiles as the play draws near its close. Touchstone is beset by nibbling desires; Orlando longs for Rosalind, and when he is an hour late for his schooling, it seems an eternity to her. The songs of act 5 also remind us that time passes and seasons change. Where "Under the greenwood tree" was an invitation to waste time in pastoral bliss, "It was a lover and his lass" is a celebration of rural life in farms and villages, where lovers tryst in fields of growing wheat and rye. They will court and marry in the spring, but before long they will be busy with the harvest and preparations for wintry days when icicles hang by the wall and the milk comes frozen home in the pails. Amiens' song anticipates the quadruple wedding celebration of the final scene, in which brides, grooms, friends, and relations gather under the boughs as if in the parish church. Music sounds as Hymen, *"god of every town"* (my emphasis), appears to remind us that if the ceremony took place at court, there would be a wedding masque enacted by mythological gods and goddesses, nymphs and nereids. Hymen does not trail clouds of supernatural glory; he is Rosalind's device for sorting out romantic entanglements, one which allows her to play the blushing bride and say nothing to Orlando of her earlier disguise. This discovery scene does not aim at the sublimity of the final scene of *The Winter's Tale,* but it has mystery enough to awe Orlando, who believes Ganymede's story that "he" was raised in the forest by an uncle who was a great magician.

As in *Much Ado*, the ritual of a wedding ceremony helps to shape the final sense of order and harmony in *As You Like It*. The muddle of unrequited love was ritually expressed by Phebe, Silvius, Orlando, and Rosalind in 5.2. The resolution of romantic muddle also takes a ritual form when Rosalind reveals herself and gives herself in turn to her father and Orlando. As presiding deity, Hymen passes judgment on each pair of lovers in turn, and Jaques pauses to offer his benedictions and add his formulaic predictions about the longevities of the various marriages. Phebe does not get what she thinks she wants, but she probably gets better than she deserves in Silvius. In any event, the sense of compromise in their nuptial as well as in Touchstone's alliance to Audrey keeps the resolution from seeming too pat. The world is not half so bad as satirists like Jaques describe it, nor half so good as sentimentalists like Duke Senior would have us believe. Not all marriages are made in heaven, despite the descent of Hymen, but the bonds of kinship and love, frayed in the opening scenes, are made whole again, and there is reason to hope for happiness in days to come. At this point, Jaques de Boys can materialize to inform everyone of the conversion to holiness of Duke Frederick because it does not matter precisely how the exiles are able to return to town and court, when that return is made to seem inevitable and right.

As You Like It is not more pessimistic about love or life than *Much Ado* or *The Merchant;* it does, however, remind us that not all difficulties can be erased by wit or good will. One can, like Orlando, shun the danger of ambition and still be punished for having the wrong name or the wrong father or the wrong brother. Because the race is not always to the swift, nor the prize to the deserving, men will continue to imagine Ardens and Americas, where innocence can be reborn and the world-weary find a second chance. In the earlier comedies the characters have to cope with the perplexing situations that Shakespeare creates through the presence of identical twins or the interference of a father. In the later comedies the impediments to love and happiness are more than complications of plot. They exist because the world is not "as we like it," because barriers of rank and class exist, and because envy and arrogance exact a price that brings Shakespeare's last romantic fables closer to the edge of tragedy.

10

Twelfth Night

Although there is no convincing evidence that *Twelfth Night* was written after *As You Like It*, we usually say that it was because *As You Like It* is not somber enough to be "the last of the romantic comedies." And once *Twelfth Night* is labeled "the last of the romantic comedies," it is easy to exaggerate its ironies and angularities and thereby persuade ourselves that it is a twilight work composed in the gathering darkness of Shakespeare's tragic period.[1] If one wishes a note of sadness to prevail, as in a recent BBC television production of *Twelfth Night*, one can through subdued lighting emphasize the lateness of the hour and the weariness of Sir Toby and Sir Andrew as they find their way to bed through unlit silent rooms. But this approach did not put modern stagecraft in the service of Shakespeare's imaginative vision; instead it made the play captive to a directorial conception that was further reinforced by casting Toby, Andrew, and Malvolio as somewhat fiftyish, and Feste as decidedly older than Olivia, Orsino, Viola, and Sebastian. When a difference of age in characters is important to a play, Shakespeare will underline it, as he does by making the Capulets and Montagues seem many years older than Juliet and Romeo. Nothing in the text of *Twelfth Night* suggests that any of the characters are middle-aged, and one doubts that a director would imagine Toby as fiftyish and a bit world-weary if critics did not continue to link his "saturnalian" indulgences to those of Falstaff. To give Malvolio gray hairs is to diminish Shakespeare's conception, for he is not one who feels that life is slipping by but rather one who has never known what it is to be young and yet is young enough to daydream of making love to the beautiful Olivia, as well as mastering her household.

A note of sadness, even of resignation, enters *Twelfth Night* with Viola, intertwines with Orsino's romantic, attitudinized melancholy, and recurs as both Olivia and Viola find themselves the victims of hopeless passions. But Viola is too cheerful to give in to self-pity and Olivia too determined to have Cesario to sink into gloom. *Twelfth Night* is noisy, energetic, colorful, and rich in contrasts, not lost in shadows. The intrigues in Olivia's household

offer plot material enough for several Roman farces, and these comic conspiracies intersect with the triangular passions of Olivia, Orsino, and Viola,
which only Sebastian can resolve. After the casualness of plot in *As You Like
It*, Shakespeare seems to enjoy the clockwork intricacies of the dramatic
action of *Twelfth Night*, which borrows the suppose of identical twins from
Errors and recreates with a difference its farcical climax of accusations and
recriminations that now suddenly ends with the discovery that Sebastian is
alive and Cesario his disguised sister. Yet *Twelfth Night* never seems busy in
the manner of Plautine comedy because, except for the scenes late in the play
in which Antonio and Sebastian become involved with members of Olivia's
household, the momentum of plot does not depend on accidental meetings
and the misunderstandings that arise from them. Here the complications of
plot grow out of the wonderfully various and idiosyncratic desires of its
characters, many of whom yearn—or want to think that they yearn—for
Olivia.

While it is inevitable that Viola should enchant audiences and engross the
attention of critics, it is unfortunate that Olivia is sometimes slighted in
discussions of *Twelfth Night* and reduced on stage to the cliché of a spoiled
heiress whose passion for Cesario is that of an older woman for a handsome
youth. Nothing in the play suggests that the two heroines are different in
age. Olivia speaks of Cesario's youth, not because she is older, but because
the delicacy of Viola's beardless face and voice set "him" apart from other
men as one who has kept the charm and beauty of boyhood into maturity.
Olivia's choice of her steward might suggest a matronly or priggish temperament except that no prig would tolerate Toby's drunken carousing or employ
a jester like Feste, who speaks freely and accurately about her pretensions.
She has a gravity befitting a young woman who is head of her own household and that gravity is accentuated by her garb of mourning, which is
intended to discourage Orsino's suit but excites his imagination and rightly
so, because what better evidence of a romantic nature can one imagine than
Olivia's extravagant gesture of seven years of mourning for a dead brother?
From the beginning, of course, Olivia's grief is suspect; indeed, there is a
touch of absurdity in Curio's description of her daily ritual of sorrow, in
which like a veiled cloistress she waters

> once a day her chamber round
> With eye-offending brine; all this to season
> A brother's dead love, which she would keep fresh
> And lasting in her sad remembrance.

> (1.1. 28–31)

The suggestion that her eyes are watering cans may be justifiable poetic
license but very soon these watering cans turn into pickling vats in which salt

tears keep her brother's memory fresh. While Orsino thrills to Olivia's ostentatious mourning, the audience knows that she is not sunk in grief because she enters with her veil up, busy about household affairs. She does not dwell on her brother's death, and neither Toby nor Feste is willing to take her funereal dedication seriously. Although she is content to hide herself from Orsino and other suitors, she is not indifferent to the outside world. She questions Malvolio about the messenger who refuses to depart from her gate and would know his personage and years. She is intrigued, not angered, by Cesario's witty insolence; she is not too austere or superior to match wits with a page, and takes real pleasure when she scores a palpable hit.

Twelfth Night is the only comedy that has two romantic heroines of equal stature, each fully developed as a dramatic personality and each as interesting in her own right as Shakespeare's other heroines. Olivia has Portia and Rosalind's forwardness in love but not their gaiety. Viola has their humor and sensitivity, but not their confidence and poise. Reticent if not actually timid, she rarely expresses her personal feelings to others except in oblique and riddling statements. Although she has more immediate cause to mourn a dead brother than Olivia, she does not grieve ostentatiously and speaks of her loss only to the sea captain who rescued her.

Unlike the earlier heroines, Viola is not adventurous by nature; she is very aware that she is alone and friendless in Illyria. Where Portia and Rosalind are sure of their ability to cope with new circumstances, she is conscious of her vulnerability and wary even of the kindness of the Captain:

> There is a fair behavior in thee, captain,
> And though that nature with a beauteous wall
> Doth oft close in pollution, yet of thee
> I will believe thou has a mind that suits
> With this thy fair and outward character.
>
> (1.2. 47–51)

Taking no delight in playing the swaggering gallant, she assumes a page's habit, not as a romantic lark, but as a practical necessity because she is not willing to face life as a friendless woman; indeed, though she thinks the Captain virtuous she offers to pay him bounteously for keeping the secret of her identity. Her first thought is to find a haven as one of Olivia's servants until the time is right to reveal who she is. Since employment there is unlikely, her wish is to pose as a eunuch and use her ability in music to obtain a place in Orsino's retinue. While her spirit is unclouded by suspicion, she will not allow herself to hope too much. When the Captain tries to comfort her by describing how Sebastian bound himself to a mast and seemed to survive the shipwreck, she thanks him and gives him gold "for saying so." She is the first of the heroines who finds herself completely dependent upon herself, and her instinct is to accept rather than challenge circumstances, even when, like Julia in *Two Gentlemen*, she is sent to woo another woman for the man she loves. If she did not feel compelled to hide her identity from the world, she could escape her predicament by revealing herself to Olivia or Orsino, but that is more than she will dare.

In love with Orsino, Viola seems at first determined to sabotage her embassy of love by an insolence that will irritate and anger Olivia. Her high-flown rhetoric is patently insincere, and her repeated questions are familiar and disrespectful:

> Most radiant, exquisite, and unmatchable beauty—I pray you tell me if this be the lady of the house, for I never saw her. I would be loath to cast away my speech; for besides that it is excellently well penn'd, I have taken great pains to con it. Good beauties, let me sustain no scorn; I am very comptible, even to the least sinister usage.
>
> (1.5. 170–76)

This brazenness is a curious pose for one who seemed timid before about venturing forth in the world. Irked, no doubt, by Olivia's haughtiness, she counters it with her own cheekiness. Olivia sneeringly asks if Viola is a comedian; she responds by a total inability to distinguish between the great lady and the members of her household staff. As the scene continues, however, it becomes more difficult to define Viola's motives, because her rudeness obviously does not have its intended effect: it intrigues rather than angers Olivia and it seems almost calculated to establish an intimacy that dissolves distinctions of rank. Annoyed by Olivia's supercilious remarks to Malvolio and Maria, she evens the odds against her by getting Olivia to send them away. When they are alone, the conversation becomes more personal, a contest of agile wits that proves not only that this great lady can unbend but that she has a mind as quick as Viola's and a spirit that is responsive to Viola's intelligence and humor, as it could never be to Orsino's overblown romanticism.

Olivia enjoys the encounter without any sense of condescension because it is soon obvious that Cesario is no ordinary servant but rather someone with the education, breeding, and flair of a gentleman. Where Phebe's passion is stirred by Ganymede's breezy rudeness, which is refreshingly unlike Silvius's cowed devotion, Olivia is attracted by the qualities of mind and imagination in Viola that any man or woman would cherish. She should be angered by Viola's request to see her face, which clearly oversteps the bounds of her embassy and her place as servant. Still, she unveils, confident of the effect that her beauty will have; "Is't not well done?" she asks. Viola, who would have preferred a plainer rival for Orsino, must admit Olivia's fairness. She

might rejoice that the beauty is flawed by vanity if she were not pained by
Olivia's indifference to Orsino. In rebuking Olivia's disdain, she can give
voice to the love that she must otherwise conceal from Orsino and the
world:

> I see you what you are, you are too proud;
> But if you were the devil, you are fair.
> My lord and master loves you. O, such love
> Could be but recompens'd, though you were crown'd
> The nonpareil of beauty.
>
> (1.5. 250–54)

Swept away by the thought of how she would express her love if she dared,
Viola imagines herself refusing to accept any denial of her suit. If she loved
Olivia, she says, she would

> Make me a willow cabin at your gate,
> And call upon my soul within the house;
> Write loyal cantons of contemned love
> And sing them loud even in the dead of night;
> Hallow your name to the reverberate hills,
> And make the babbling gossip of the air
> Cry out "Olivia!" O, you should not rest
> Between the elements of air and earth
> But you should pity me!
>
> (1.5. 268–76)

Like Rosalind, Viola can see the humor of romantic longing and still give
herself completely to it without any hedge of irony. Her ardent imagination
makes romantic clichés live again—in the noisiness of loquacious wooing
and in the silent pathos of unrequited love sitting like Patience on a monument smiling at grief.

The disdainful lady's passion for a cheeky servant is a nice irony, but not
one that invites an audience to enjoy Olivia's mistaken love. For she is not
really taken in by Cesario's false appearance—she does not moon over a
handsome appearance or become infatuated with a pretended masculinity.
She is not, like Phebe or Proteus or Demetrius, excited by the challenge of
winning the affection of one who professes only scorn for her suit. Her spirit
responds deeply to Viola's humor and passion, to her intelligence and
poetry.[2] Knowing that prudence and common sense forbid it, that she risks
humiliation and censure for this breach of propriety, she allows herself to fall
in love with a mere page. As impulsively as she showed her face, she sends
her ring to Cesario and willingly abandons herself to the adventure of love:

"What is your parentage?"
"Above my fortunes, yet my state is well:
I am a gentleman." I'll be sworn thou art;
Thy tongue, thy face, thy limbs, actions, and spirit
Do give the fivefold blazon. Not too fast! soft, soft!
Unless the master were the man. How now?
Even so quickly may one catch the plague?
Methinks I feel this youth's perfections
With an invisible and subtle stealth
To creep in at mine eyes. Well, let it be.

(1.5. 289–98)

Freudian critics suggest that Olivia, not ready for a mature emotional commitment, imagines herself in love with Cesario, whose beauty is feminine rather than masculine, and whom she could not possibly marry. But it is Orsino, not Olivia, who admires the delicate, almost female beauty of Cesario's lips, face, and voice; Olivia responds to Cesario's "manly" loyalty to Orsino. If she wished to avoid the challenge of sexual love, she had only to send Cesario away, remain behind her gates, and occasionally amuse herself by denying Orsino's half-hearted courtship. Olivia's attraction to Viola needs no subtle psychological explication, for most men and women in an audience would find Viola more attractive than the swooning Orsino. Moreover, there is nothing perverse or unpleasant in Olivia's attraction to Viola that needs to be explained away. She delights in those qualities in Viola that are not intrinsically masculine or feminine but transcend sexual identities. Although her passion becomes obsessive, love makes Olivia more spontaneous and sympathetic to the pangs of others. Before she loved she enjoyed her mastery over the men in her household. She was ready to order the Fool away and to tell Malvolio bluntly that he is too vain. At the close of the play she is touched by Malvolio's misery, having known a like humiliation.

Viola feels an immediate sympathy for this "poor lady" beguiled by a false appearance. She does not achieve Julia's communion with her rival Silvia, but like Julia she regards her rival as a kindred soul, a woman as soft and helpless as she:

How easy it is for the proper-false
In women's waxen hearts to set their forms!
Alas, [our] frailty is the cause, not we,
For such as we are made [of], such we be.
How will this fadge? My master loves her dearly,
And I (poor monster) fond as much on him;
And she (mistaken) seems to dote on me.
What will become of this? As I am man,
My state is desperate for my master's love,

As I am woman (now alas the day!),
What thriftless sighs shall poor Olivia breathe!
O time, thou must untangle this, not I,
It is too hard a knot for me t' untie.

(2.2. 29–41)

Viola's sense of the softness and frailty of women is very different from Kate's emphasis on the helpless, wormlike nature of women in *The Shrew*. It is almost a corollary of Orsino's romantic notion of the delicate roselike beauty of women, "whose fair flow'r, / Being once display'd, both fall that very hour," a view that Viola seconds in conversation with him. Her sense of personal vulnerability explains why she can take seriously Orsino's idealization of what is fragile and fleeting in feminine beauty and why she listens without ironic rejoinder to his lectures on the passions. She is not tempted to smile or patronize him when he opens his heart to her; on the contrary, at those moments they are one soul in bodies twain. He dreams of a woman who can love as profoundly as he; she touches his heart with a lovely fairy tale of a sister who, unwilling to declare her love, died of a broken heart.

If Shakespeare had followed the narrative line of Riche's tale of "Apolonius and Silla," which is a probable source for *Twelfth Night*, Olivia's love of Viola would be nothing more than a conventional complication of romantic fabling. In Riche's tale Julina/Olivia's passion for the disguised Silla/Viola is immediately transferred to her twin brother, Silvio, with whom she sleeps and by whom she becomes pregnant. Shakespeare, however, delays Olivia's meeting with Sebastian until the fourth act, and though their very brief encounter results in a hurried marriage, it is not a moment of tender communion or one in which Olivia, as it were, falls in love again with a Cesario who is attractive in a different way. Astonished by his good fortune, Sebastian plays a completely passive role; when he agrees, she hastens to arrange the wedding before he can change his mind. Thus the transference of Olivia's affection from Cesario to Sebastian must be accomplished in the denouement. At the same time Shakespeare carefully develops Orsino's love for Cesario in a way that anticipates his rapturous response to Viola once her identity is revealed. Content merely to send embassies of love to Olivia, Orsino shares his most intimate thoughts with Cesario, whose answering love assures us that there is more to Orsino than a tremulous sensibility. That assurance is necessary because Orsino is so absorbed in his own emotional states that one wonders if this seeming narcissist will ever be capable of loving a woman. While Romeo's love of Rosaline may be superficial, he is genuinely wounded by her rejection of his suit, whereas Orsino is unmoved by Olivia's repeated denials because she does not seem to exist for him except as a projection of his literary fantasy of love.

A virile actor can convince us that there is nothing limp-wristed about

Orsino, but it is not easy to convince an audience that he has the young manliness of Berowne, Bassanio, or Benedick. The problem is not that Orsino is too "poetic," or too ready to lose himself in romantic fancy because Romeo is no less "poetic" or self-absorbed in the first act of *Romeo and Juliet*. From the beginning, however, Romeo's speeches express a depth of feeling and responsiveness that is absent in the more sensible Benvolio and in Mercutio, whose cynicism about women and sex is coarse as well as jejune. Besides, Romeo must be vigorous and manly or he could not have Mercutio as a devoted companion. One cannot, however, imagine the humorless Orsino trading quips with Mercutio; his only confidant is Cesario, and their sole topic of conversation is the agony and ecstasy of romantic passion. If Rosalind loved Orsino, she would give him a crash course in the nature of love; Viola, who is content to hint obliquely of her femininity and love for Orsino, allows him to instruct her in the mysteries of love. She listens as he explains that

> no woman's sides
> Can bide the beating of so strong a passion
> As love doth give my heart; no woman's heart
> So big, to hold so much; they lack retention.
>
> (2.4. 93–96)

In turn, he listens intently to her tale of a lovelorn sister who

> never told her love,
> But let concealment like a worm i' th' bud
> Feed on her damask cheek; she pin'd in thought,
> And with a green and yellow melancholy
> She sate like Patience on a monument,
> Smiling at grief. . . .
>
> (2.4. 110–15)

If Orsino had a sense of humor he would smile at Viola's portrait of her fictitious sister. Because he is tenderhearted, however, he is moved by Viola's tale of a lovelorn maid even as he rejoices in Olivia's pretence of cloistered mourning for her dead brother.

Orsino's mooning adoration of Olivia may be the most telling Elizabethan comment on the self-absorption of Petrarch's self-dramatizing lover, who is content to worship from afar and ruminate over his emotional state. Like the lover who speaks in Petrarch's sonnets, Orsino is innocent at heart and has an artist's—or at least, an aesthete's—responsiveness to beauty. He savors the fragrance of music, "the sweet sound / That breathes upon a bank of violets, / Stealing and giving odor." He is not, like Sidney's Astophil, driven by sexual desire and he does not yearn for Olivia's sexual surrender. Ignorant of sensuality, he has apparently conned his knowledge of the physiology of love out of treatises on the passions; his study of the subject convinces him that the Olivia who seasons a brother's dead love with eye-offending brine will reach heights of passion when she gives her heart to a man:

> O, she that hath a heart of that fine frame
> To pay this debt of love but to a brother,
> How will she love when the rich golden shaft
> Hath kill'd the flock of all affections else
> That live in her; when liver, brain, and heart,
> These sovereign thrones, are all supplied and fill'd,
> Her sweet perfections, with one self king!
>
> (1.1. 32–38)

A bit of Ovid and a bit of faculty psychology—that's all Orsino knows of love and all he needs to know.

Lest there be any doubt of Orsino's maleness, Shakespeare provides two other suitors of Olivia who are clearly epicene in nature: Sir Andrew and Malvolio. Notwithstanding his enthusiasm for self-improvement, Andrew is a doltish caperer and a bit of a capon; ignorant even of how to talk to a woman, he is venereal, Toby suggests, only in his debilitated appearance. Malvolio's desire for Olivia is more real and it is also more genuinely sexual, even though he is all fussiness and prudery. Because he is vain and pedantic, he can be tricked into playing the ludicrous yellow-stockinged lover. Still his desire to marry Olivia is erotic as well as arriviste; he dreams of making love to her of an afternoon and imagines that her astonished responses to his amorous manner are an invitation to her bed.[3]

The arriviste Malvolio and the narcissistic Orsino are not the only egotists in love in *Twelfth Night*. Although humbled by desire, Olivia is not made selfless; her need for Cesario's love is overwhelming and indifferent to what "he" desires. She will not accept his refusal any more than Orsino will accept her rejection of his suit. In the sonnets, Shakespeare writes of a love that is completely selfless, but he does not judge his characters' affections by so absolute a standard. Even in the sonnets, moreover, the ideal of selfless, unaltering, unbending love is one that is apparently beyond man's reach; it is a guiding light that stands above the emotional tempests that shake the closest of human ties.[4] If anything there is a compassionate awareness in the comedies of the element of selfish desire that can exist in the noblest love. While Shakespeare underlines the egotism of Proteus's desires, he does not argue that Julia's unbending devotion is selfless, because, like Mariana in *Measure for Measure*, Julia *needs* to love the man who betrays her. Similarly Romeo and Juliet are not selfless in their need to join one another in death; they do not sacrifice all for love, for in dying they relinquish nothing that they value. Let us say that there is a greediness in Olivia's love, as there is also in Helena's love for Bertram in *All's Well*, that is not stressed in the affections of earlier heroines. Indeed, Olivia grows almost frantic in her schemes to win Cesario's love by gifts or bribes if necessary. But who shall say that her desire for Cesario is not love, when it is Orsino's lack of desire to possess Olivia that convinces us he does not really love her?

Unwilling to reveal her identity, Viola must continue as Orsino's proxy wooer despite Olivia's importunities. Since Sebastian, the "solution" to Olivia's hopeless love, appears very early in the play, it is only a matter of time before he or Antonio happens on someone of Olivia's household, but until then the romantic drama of *Twelfth Night* is at an impasse: Orsino will not leave his palace; Viola will not unmask herself; Olivia's pursuit of love is impossible. Even so the plot moves forward briskly, energized by the comic antagonisms and incongruences of Olivia's household, a place of tipsy revels presided over by a prudish steward, a school for husbands in which the star pupil, nay, the only matriculant, is silly and unmasculine. There is no lack of good fellowship in these scenes, but it is often tinged with mercenary calculation and sometimes edged with veiled contempt.

Money talks almost as loudly in Illyria as in Venice. Toby lives off his niece and augments his purse by gulling Andrew. Malvolio daydreams of being master of Olivia and her fortune, and Olivia wonders which jewels or presents will dazzle a page like Cesario. "How shall I feast him?" she asks Maria; "What bestow of him? / For youth is bought more often than begged or borrowed." She should know, however, that Cesario is not to be bought, because "he" refused the purse she offered in their first meeting with a disdainful "I am no fee'd post, lady." Viola will enter service as a page or singer in a noble household, but she will not be treated as a common servant who works for hire and salary. Her angry refusal of a gratuity is just one of the occasions in *Twelfth Night* in which class distinctions matter as never before in the comedies. Although Bassanio needs money to venture for Portia's hand, he does not seek to rise above his station in gaining her because they are of the same aristocratic class. Viola will not reveal her true self to Olivia, but she is ready enough to say that she is gentle born, especially after Olivia's patronizing attitude toward her. It comforts Olivia to think that she has fallen in love with one who was born a gentleman; Malvolio, on the other hand, would like to believe that differences of class do not really matter, that he can rise above his birth by wedding his mistress as other stewards have done.

Where Launce and Speed are happy to entertain for their servant's wages, and Touchstone plays the fool without angling for gratuities, Feste is always alert for a guerdon or remuneration when he offers any service—a song or a flourish of wit—and he will shamelessly try to double or triple his reward. Like Viola, he is declassé, a person of taste, discrimination, and education who by necessity has entered service and plays the role of fool even though it grates on his nature to be at the command of others. His casuistries are subtle, his wit dry and aristocratic. He can join with Toby and Andrew in a tavern round, but he is a professional entertainer and his metier is the art song. Untouched by Malvolio's arriviste ambitions, he would be content to be well paid and appreciated by his betters, but he will not cringe before anyone, especially before an officious ass like Malvolio, whose authority over him is a daily humiliation. Since it is difficult for him to have to ingratiate himself with others, his situation is precarious in Olivia's household, where he must observe an unsympathetic steward and amuse his lady or be reminded that he can be turned away, which Maria says will be "as good as a hanging" to him. There is almost always an edge in his wit, a kind of patronizing contempt for superiors that is so cleverly expressed they must smile and allow him scope as a licensed fool. What he was before he entered Olivia's pay, we do not know, but he makes it clear that he does not wear motley in his brain. A good enough companion for the while, he will join others in a drink or a song, but he is not gregarious. Alone by choice rather than circumstance, he is able to make others laugh even though he does not find the world or his situation amusing. He has an eye for affectation and pretense, not an appreciation for the comedy of human behavior.

Although crasser than Feste, Malvolio is not greedy in the way that Jonson's comic figures are; he is too sober and sensible to dream of alchemical riches. He daydreams of lording it over those who now ridicule him, and he does not feel that marriage to Olivia is impossible for one of his merits. Since he already oversees Olivia's household, why should he not rule it as her consort? If that were to occur, it would mean only that fortune has recognized its error in depriving him of the rank he richly deserves. Those who do not enjoy Malvolio would reduce him to a conventional killjoy, a scapegoat who deserves to be held up to ridicule because of his officious humorlessness. There would be a need to expose Malvolio if he pretended to be something he is not, but he never puts on a false manner; his absurdity is native and his egotism so openly displayed that even Olivia, who appreciates his talents, very early accuses him of being ungenerous and "sick of self-love." Incapable of hypocrisy or sanctimony, he is genuinely outraged by Toby's revelries, which offend his sense of propriety and defy his authority. He is a prig with an instinct for grandeur that at once muddles his statements and endows them with an ineffable grandiosity. Appalled by the consciencelessness of Andrew, Toby, and Feste's singing, he asks, "Do ye make an alehouse of my lady's house, that ye squeak out your coziers' catches without any mitigation or remorse of voice?" His orotund style changes the base metal of Armado's pomposities into linguistic gold and is more dazzling in its eccentricity than the verbal comedy of Bottom, Quince, or Dogberry because Malvolio aims at preciseness of statement and creates majestical locutions when he misuses words. Accustomed to summing accounts and drawing up inventories, he knows the need for accurate distinctions and descriptions. Questioned by Olivia about the age of Orsino's messenger, he replies:

> Not yet old enough for a man; nor young enough for a boy; as a squash is before 'tis a peascod, or a codling when 'tis almost an apple. 'Tis with him in standing water, between boy and man.

> (1.5. 156–59)

If he is not always this precise, it is because portentous constructions are second nature to him and he would be as noble in expression as he is in mind and imagination; he would have "the humor of state," "a demure travel of regard," or an "austere regard of control." This respectable, responsible, decorous prig is no Monsieur Morose who has to be tormented so that laughter may flourish. He is as amusing as any academic potentate or government bureaucrat and much less dangerous to the commonweal.

If the gulling of Malvolio merely humbled his pride and erased his social pretensions, it would pose no problems for audiences or critics. But it does not so much reveal the truth about Malvolio as dupe him into being false to his own nature and thereby an object of public mockery. To be sure, the letter that Maria places in Malvolio's path is an inspired invention that would not succeed if Malvolio were not infatuated with thoughts of making love to Olivia, wearing rich jewels, and ordering Toby and Feste about. Maria knows just how Malvolio's mnd works, what kind of murky portentous riddles will seem to him a coy, maidenly confession of passion. She knows this prig is ignorant of the human heart except as it is depicted in romantic fables, in which lovelorn maidens (like Beatrice) commit to paper the anguished desires they dare not express to the men they adore.

Maria's letter is a parody of, and tribute to, the conventions of romance that Shakespeare does not shrink from using in *Much Ado* as well as *Two Gentlemen*. Malvolio's response to the letter is one of the supreme moments of Shakespearean comedy, a variation on Morocco's wrestling with the riddle of Portia's caskets and on Benedick's comic rationalization of his decision to love. Applying the full pressure of his analytical intelligence, Malvolio first authenticates the seal and the handwriting; next he squares the style with Olivia's manner of speech and finds the two almost identical. Incurably pedantic, he is ready to identify hackneyed phrases with the spontaneous overflow of powerful feeling. He thrills to the adventure of deciphering the clues, and he rejoices in the invitation to be great and bold in word and deed. Like Benedick, Malvolio will be horribly in love, yellow stockings, cross-garters, leering, and all.

Although the asides of the eavesdroppers add to the humor of the letter scene, Malvolio is its comic star and his performance a delight from beginning to end. His next appearance as a leering amorist is a performance his gullers enjoy more than an audience can. Because he is too literal-minded to diverge from the instructions given him in the letter, his garb, manner, and speech are completely predictable. If we laugh it is not at the comedy of Malvolio's behavior but at his ignorance of the ludicrousness of the role he has been gulled into playing. He is not the only one, moreover, who can be so manipulated. Even Viola can be coerced and cajoled by Toby into attempting to play the dueler, a role that makes her look ridiculous. Watching Malvolio's ponderous attempt to court Olivia is like watching an untalented singer or comedian who has been flattered into displaying his incompetence for the amusement of others. Unaware of the reason for it, Olivia is shocked by Malvolio's grotesque behavior, and the joke threatens to turn uglier still when she commissions Toby to cure Malvolio of his madness. She would not have this scapegoat miscarry for half her dowry.

In the letter scene Fabian explained his desire to get back at Malvolio because "he brought me out o' favor with my lady about a bearbaiting here." Toby replied, "To anger him we'll have the bear again, and we will fool him black and blue." They need not bring back the bear, however, because they have Malvolio to bait in a dark room, where they fool him black and blue. Feste does the taunting in the role of a curate while Toby, the audience to this sport, is vastly amused but fearful that this "knavery" may threaten his place in Olivia's household. It is not sentimental to find the baiting unpleasant; Malvolio is helpless and reduced to abject pleading.[5] Feste and Toby have no aim in mind other than to torment the steward a bit longer before they release him and face Olivia's displeasure. This is not the kind of experience likely to make Malvolio more humane, and in fact, it has an unpleasant effect on Toby, who develops a taste for this kind of sport. Afraid to continue the baiting of Malvolio, he decides to amuse himself more safely by gulling and manipulating Cesario and Andrew, who is growing restless at his failure to win Olivia and must be distracted. If Andrew leaves, Toby, who has been taking money from him, will be out of pocket and lack a comic butt. The practical joke Toby conceives is harmless enough in its intent; he knows that no blood will be spilled when Andrew and Cesario are bullied into drawing their swords. Yet the heartlessness of the gulling and its mercenary motive make it unpleasantly similar to Iago's use of Roderigo to make a street brawler out of Cassio. In both instances the doltish mark, who is supposedly being aided in his hopeless courtship, is becoming aware of the futility of his suit and must be convinced that he can win his lady by eliminating the rival who has won her heart. Unlike Iago, Toby has at first a derisive affection for his "purse" and enjoys Andrew's company in their wassails. When Andrew threatens to remove himself and his purse, however, Toby's contempt grows more transparent. Fabian says of Andrew, "This is a dear manikin puppet to you, Sir Toby." Toby responds, "I have been dear to him, lad, some two thousand strong or so." Told that Cesario is a very devil with a rapier, Andrew would give him his horse to let the matter slip. Toby agrees to negotiate the settlement and promises in an aside, "Marry, I'll ride your horse as well as I ride you." The "hooking-on" Falstaff of 2 *Henry IV* could not have said it better.[6]

Jonson, who ridiculed Shakespeare's penchant for romantic fabling, was much taken with the gulling of Malvolio and the mock duel of *Twelfth Night,* which he imitated in *Epicene.*[7] The tormenting of Morose by clever gallants is a baroque elaboration of the baiting of Malvolio even as their manipulation of Jack Daw and La Foole is a direct plagiarism of the Andrew-Cesario-Toby scenes. What Jonson borrows he strips of humanity. Where Andrew is amusing as well as unmanly, Daw and La Foole are parody males who are merely fatuous in their boasting of family and sexual conquests. Where Olivia is frantic and yet completely feminine in her pursuit of Cesario, Jonson's emancipated Collegiate Ladies are grotesquely masculine in their aggressive sexuality. Like an amusement park mirror, *Epicene* distorts all that it reflects in *Twelfth Night,* but it does call attention to what is unconventional and daring in Shakespeare's treatment of love and gender. Perhaps Jonson was unable to see that Shakespeare does not ridicule the prudery of Malvolio and the capering of Andrew. Rather than studies of abnormal psychology, they are sympathetically drawn characters who remind us that masculinity is a spectrum that includes some whom we too easily label effeminate but who have the same erotic desires as a conventional romantic hero like Sebastian, who is ready to fight a duel or marry a lady at a moment's notice.

The richness of psychological characterization in *Twelfth Night* would seem to deny the possibility that its emotional entanglements can be resolved by a Plautine device of plot, namely, the providential appearance of Viola's twin brother. Yet the closer *Twelfth Night* comes to its denouement, the more its plotting resembles that of *Errors,* for mistaken identities, supposes, and confusions multiply until Viola stands accused of disloyalty by Antonio, Olivia, and Orsino, and of assault and battery by Toby and Andrew. At Viola's darkest moment, Sebastian enters to play a recognition scene with her that ends all (or almost all) discord and conflict. But how can this be when so few of the complications of plot are caused by the mistaking of one twin for the other? Olivia's predicament does not arise because she mistakes Viola for Sebastian; she falls in love with the beauty of Viola's nature that no disguise can alter or hide. It is not Viola's resemblance to Sebastian that dupes Olivia; rather it is Sebastian's resemblance to Viola that falsely persuades her that Cesario has suddenly become responsive to her suit. Her love is authentic if hopeless; what may be dubious is the solution to the problem that Sebastian represents.

Tillyard remarks that were it not for dramatic convention, the substitution of Sebastian for Viola as Olivia's love would be more unpleasant and difficult to accept than the bed tricks of the dark comedies.[8] Since he does not refer to any Elizabethan plays that have a dramatic situation like that of *Twelfth Night*, it is impossible to say what convention he has in mind. Most readers and audiences are not troubled by the bed tricks of *All's Well* and *Measure for Measure* because they are reported, not staged, and we do not have to think about the practical difficulties of these stealthy assignations in which one woman's body is substituted for another's. The substitution of Sebastian for Cesario as Olivia's mate, however, is far more problematical, for although brother and sister are almost identical in voice, face, and figure, that identity is limited to appearances. No dubiety would exist if Olivia were attracted to Cesario's physical beauty rather than to qualities that are not readily apparent in Sebastian, who is manly, intelligent, and able to inspire deep affection in Antonio, but who does not seem to have Viola's wit, poetry, or sympathy with others. Indeed, Sebastian is serious almost to the point of humorlessness, and he is quick to annoyance, if not to anger. Where Viola enjoys her encounter with Feste in 3.1 and appreciates the skill with which he plays the fool, Sebastian is irritated when approached by Feste, who mistakes him for Cesario. He advises Feste to vent his folly elsewhere and sends him on his way with a small remuneration and a threat of worse payment if he tarries. Sebastian's testiness is also evident when, mistaken for Cesario, he is struck by Andrew. At once he is ready to fight Andrew and to exchange blows with Toby, who tries to restrain him.

After Orsino's languishings, Malvolio's prissiness, and Andrew's doltishness, Sebastian's manliness is refreshing even in its bluntness. This bluntness makes him seem more conventional, however, than the other characters, who are colorful and idiosyncratic. His manner is courtly, his speech faintly euphuistic and self-conscious. When Antonio asks where he is bound, Sebastian answers:

> No, sooth, sir: my determinate voyage is mere extravagancy. But I perceive in you so excellent a touch of modesty, that you will not extort from me what I am willing to keep in; therefore it charges me in manners the rather to express myself.
>
> (2.1. 11–15)

After this long preamble Sebastain tells of himself and his sister:

> A lady, sir, though it was said she much resembled me, was yet of many accounted beautiful; but though I could not with such estimable wonder overfar believe that, yet thus far I will boldly publish her: she bore a mind that envy could not but call fair. She is drown'd already, sir, with salt water, though I seem to drown her remembrance again with more.
>
> (2.1. 25–32)

Sebastian, of course, is not as stiff as these speeches might suggest. His depth of feeling is evident in his greeting of Antonio in the final scene and in his reunion with Viola, both of which are crucial to the emotional resolution of the play because there is no love scene as such between Sebastian and Olivia that would persuade an audience that their marriage, though founded on a suppose, will be a loving union. Like other of Shakespeare's romantic heroes, Sebastian could have fallen in love with Olivia at first sight and exchanged hearts with her in their first meeting, as Romeo does with Juliet and Orlando with Rosalind. All he expresses, however, is bewilderment at her loving words and eagerness to marry him:

> What relish is in this? How runs the stream?
> Or I am mad, or else this is a dream.
> Let fancy still my sense in Lethe steep;
> If it be thus to dream, still let me sleep!
>
> (4.1. 60–63)

Before the marriage, Sebastian speaks of Olivia at greater length; or rather he dwells at length on the wonder of what is happening and debates whether he or Olivia is mad and decides that neither of them is. He is more than willing to enter a marriage that will change him from a penniless survivor of a shipwreck to husband of a beautiful woman and master of a great house, even though he realizes that something deceivable is at work. Shakespeare could have suggested a transference of love in this first meeting by having Olivia discern something new and even more desirable in the personality of Cesario/Sebastian. But she is too overjoyed by Sebastian's willingness to wed her to ponder this astonishing change of heart. Besides she has gained his consent after the gift of a valuable pearl and she would not care if his consent were prompted more by greed than love. She hurries him to the altar before he can have second thoughts, for only then, she says, her "most jealous and too doubtful soul / May live at peace." This hurried nuptial is hardly a meeting of true minds, but it is a necessary step in the resolution of tangled affections that allows the play to end well.

A more conventional dramatist would have prepared the way for Orsino's discovery of his love of Viola by depicting his growing realization that he does not love Olivia. Shakespeare gives us an Orsino who is still fantasizing his passion for Olivia in the concluding scene. That he is willing at last to leave his palace and confront his cruel fair is a hopeful sign, but fresh air does not make Orsino wiser or more realistic. When he realizes that Olivia loves Cesario he does not relinquish his romantic fantasy; instead he exchanges one literary posture for another. Before he was a Petrarchan lover who adored his mistress from a safe distance; now he imagines himself a love-crazed revenger ready to draw his sword against the woman who scorned

him and the minion who betrayed him. Orsino's giddiness infects Viola, who
in a moment loses her equilibrium and sense of humor; in the face of
Orsino's melodramatic threatenings, she announces her readiness to play the
self-sacrificing heroine and welcome death on the point of his sword. Only
the successive entrances of the Priest, Toby, Andrew, and Sebastian rescue
the denouement from absurdity.

Over four hundred lines in all, the concluding scene of *Twelfth Night* is
spacious enough to allow almost every character to reappear and have a last
moment center stage. Antonio can tell his story and make his accusations;
Toby has an opportunity to complain about his aching head; Andrew,
Fabian, Malvolio, and Feste are given equal time. Yet while Shakespeare
generously allows the minor characters to tell and reflect on what has
happened to them, he gives Olivia no speech in which to respond to the
stunning discovery of Cesario's true identity. After Sebastian enters, Olivia
does not speak to Viola except to welcome her at last as a sister, and she does
not register any dismay at the thought that she married, as it were, a
substitute husband. Sebastian also is not disturbed to discover that Olivia
confused him with his disguised sister, because he suspected some "error"
was involved and now he sees that Olivia's misapprehension was providential:

> So comes it, lady, you have been mistook;
> But Nature to her bias drew in that.
> You would have been contracted to a maid,
> Nor are you therein, by my life, deceiv'd,
> You are betroth'd both to a maid and a man.
>
> (5.1. 259–63)

By itself this rationalization is facile. It is easy for him to say that all is well
because he was not deceived by appearances and did not fall in love with one
Olivia and marry another. Yet all *is* well because it is very soon evident that
Olivia and Sebastian are well matched. Her kindness shows in her concern
for Malvolio; his capacity for devotion is revealed in his reunion with
Antonio:

> Antonio, O my dear Antonio!
> How have the hours rack'd and tortur'd me,
> Since I have lost thee!
>
> (5.1. 218–20)

Sebastian's response to Viola, which is more profound still, confirms his
tender heart and suggests that the stiffness of his earlier speeches masked the
anguish he felt at the loss of a beloved sister. Since Viola and Sebastian's
twinness is immediately apparent, their ritualistic exchange of information

about the shipwreck and their personal histories is almost comic in its gratuitousness. Yet this near parody of a conventional recognition scene, which includes the obligatory proof of an identifying mole, is moving in its effect and necessary to the recognition that Viola and Sebastian have the same loving hearts. "Were you a woman," Sebastian says to Viola,

> as the rest goes even,
> I should my tears let fall upon your cheek,
> And say, "Thrice welcome, drowned Viola!"
>
> (5.1. 239–41)

Olivia's capacity to love has already been amply shown. The last scene confirms her gentle heart. Perhaps before her concern for Malvolio was a fear of losing a valuable servant, but now, with Sebastian by her side, she shows a disinterested compassion for him. She is pained by the accusation in Malvolio's letter and by Fabian's explanation of how he was abused. She explains how and by whom he was duped and she promises that he will judge his own cause and what punishment his tormentors deserve. Malvolio could perhaps be placated and remain as her steward, but Feste cannot resist a last sneering reminder of how Malvolio was gulled:

> Why, "some are born great, some achieve greatness, and some have greatness thrown upon them." I was one, sir, in this enterlude—one Sir Topas, sir, but that's all one. "By the Lord, fool, I am not mad." But do you remember? "Madam, why laugh you at such a barren rascal? And you smile not, he's gagg'd." And thus the whirligig of time brings in his revenges.
>
> (5.1. 370–77)

Since Olivia clearly sides with Malvolio, Feste's scorn is dangerous as well as tactless. It leaves no doubt, therefore, of how difficult and humiliating it has been for him to live under the authority of Malvolio, who storms off stage threatening to be "revenged on the whole pack of you." Thus the spoilsport is driven away, and the comic scapegoat ritually cast out of the company of lovers and friends. Yet the ritual "expulsion" does not bring laughter and joy because Malvolio is more wretched than before, Olivia is deeply distressed by his mistreatment, and Feste's need to strike back strips the comic mask from this professional clown.

If any character has been illuminated by experience in *Twelfth Night* it is Andrew, who is poorer and a bit wiser than he was at the beginning. He knows that he was not born to court a lady, and he has learned from Sebastian that it is dangerous to pretend to be manly—a somewhat gratuitous lesson, since he knew before that he was a coward. Toby has also learned that it is dangerous to be too busy; he made the painful mistake of picking a quarrel with someone who seemed an easy mark when he was himself the worse for drink. Now he comes halting on stage in no mood for jokes. "Sot," he says to Feste, "didst see Dick Surgeon, sot?" Andrew offers to help him have their wounds dressed, but Toby pushes him away with the abusive remark, "Will you help—an ass-head and a coxcomb and a knave, a thin-faced knave, a gull?" It will be a while at least before their wounds are treated because Dick Surgeon, Feste reports, is drunk—"his eyes were set at eight i' th' morning." So much for the saturnalian vision, for the belief that a full cup, a merry song, and a carefree attitude will solve the difficulties of life. Falstaff thinks of Shallow in much the way Toby thinks of Andrew, but Toby lacks Falstaff's ability to say to his gull, "Master Shallow, I owe you a thousand pounds." The master of Illyrian revels is a bad loser and a worse friend.

Marriage to Maria portends soberer and perhaps better days to come for Toby. Orsino, who scarcely stirred to pursue Olivia, is enchanted to find that the Cesario whom he loves and with whom he shared his most intimate thoughts is a woman who adores him. He is willing to postpone any declaration of passion until he sees Viola in her woman's dress, but he is not very different from the Orsino who opened the play on a note of romantic extravagance. He promises Viola that when she assumes her maiden's garb again she will be "Orsino's mistress and his fancy's queen."[9]

A director can darken the conclusion of *Twelfth Night* by having the lovers gaily exit, leaving a dejected Antonio to trail after them, just as one can darken the ending of *The Merchant* by making it appear that Antonio is somehow forgotten by Bassanio and Portia as they exit to their wedding bed. To do so, however, is to violate Shakespeare's characterizations of Sebastian and Bassanio. Feste's fate is more dubious, for if Malvolio does not return he will have to answer to an angry Olivia, and it is doubtful that he will find Sebastian a congenial master. The ending of *Twelfth Night* is not more pessimistic or more shadowed than the endings of earlier comedies. Its joyousness is qualified, however, by the revelation of Toby's shabbiness and of Feste's smoldering resentment against Malvolio and the circumstances of his life. The circle of love and friendship is as warm here as in any other comedy but it cannot be all-inclusive because Andrew and Malvolio do not know how to love and Toby and Feste are incapable of friendship.

Where the songs of the Cuckoo and the Owl anticipate the fulfillment of love that is postponed at the close of *Love's Labor's*, Feste's song, which provides an epilogue to *Twelfth Night*, is a last reminder of the circumstances and accidents of life that cannot always be transcended.[10] One can, I suppose, say that in Feste's lyrics Shakespeare speaks of the humiliations of the professional entertainer even as in the sonnets he laments having made himself "a motley to the view." Like Feste, Shakespeare knew what it was to "strive to please" his "master," the audience, every day. But this suggestion of personal bitterness is rare even in the sonnets and is absent from his dramatic art, for of all the Elizabethan playwrights he had the least reason to complain about the audiences that applauded his work and enabled him to become a man of some wealth and property. Feste does not step out of his dramatic role to play Shakespeare's chorus. The loneliness of which he sings is very personal; he has no friend, no companion except for the moment, because he does not seek one. He is alone because he needs no one, and he is aloof from the human comedy except when his wit is disdained or his ego wounded. If his lyrics protest too much the foulness of the weather—"for the rain it raineth every day"—they accurately define the grayness of his perception of life. Despite a sometimes insolent tongue, Feste takes no risks for the sake of another as Antonio does, and he knows that the world is full of men like him, who shut their gates and purses to others. And yet he is one of the many who necessarily depend on the good will of others for food, a bit of money, and a place to lay their heads.

Unlike the clowns and fools who preceded him, Feste is never given to exuberant fancies; indeed, he is not one to whom laughter comes easily. Foolery, he tells Cesario, "does walk about the orb like the sun, it shines everywhere"; but in *Twelfth Night* high-spirited and good-natured foolery mingle at times with sharp-edged and denigrating wit. After *Twelfth Night* Shakespearean foolery will not turn its face completely to the sun until Autolycus strolls the country lanes of Bohemia in *The Winter's Tale*, enjoying his vagabond days, even though he has been turned out of doors at the palace and knows what it is to live with the wind and rain.

11

All's Well That Ends Well

It is not easy to say why Shakespeare wanted to write a play about characters as limited and uninspiring as Helena and Bertram. A relatively straightforward dramatization of Boccaccio's tale of Giletta and Beltramo,[1] *All's Well* is the only comedy that centers on a single love—or rather, a single love-hate—relationship. No Hero, Nerissa, or Celia stands by Helena's side; for most of the play she is a solitary figure who keeps her own counsel and pursues her ends without confiding them to any other person. For a time Bertram has Parolles as a companion, but he is nearly incapable of intimacy or emotional attachment. The minor characters of *All's Well* are, by and large, more attractive than its romantic protagonists, but none are as fully realized or as important to the plot as Leonato is in *Much Ado*. Nevertheless the warm-heartedness of the Countess, Lafew, the King, and Bertram's fellow officers is important to the emotional resolution of the play precisely because it is a quality somewhat lacking in Helena and completely absent in Bertram.

Compared to the comedies I have discussed already, *All's Well* seems gray if not bleak, not because its viewpoint is jaded or disillusioned but because its chief characters do not delight us by their verve or humor or expansiveness of thought. Bertram is the least philosophical and perhaps the least intelligent of the heroes of the comedies. He does not reflect on his experiences, much less on life, and he seems incapable of introspection and self-knowledge. He never wrestles with alternatives even though he finds himself repeatedly in difficult predicaments. Although his conduct appalls those who love him, he is never burdened by shame or guilt, and he can be dishonest as well as callous. Because his inner life (if he has one) is hidden from an audience, it knows and judges him by his acts, which are thoroughly unlovely. Helena is a more complex character who is revealed as much through soliloquy as through dialogue. Unlike Bertram she is thoughtful and reflective by nature, yet her speeches lack choric amplitude and range because she is as self-absorbed as he is, forever occupied with her quest to become his wife. More than any other heroine, Helena is single-minded in her romantic dedication, and yet she is the least romantic in temperament of any Shakespearean heroine. As serious as her namesake, Helena of *A Dream*, she is incapable of light-heartedness or gaiety. Love does not inspire her to flights of whimsical or ecstatic poetry, and she seems nearly incapable of spontaneity. Thus while Helena will dare all for love, the Countess's remembrance of her youthful passion is the most poignant expression of romantic yearning in the play; and the only love scene, ironically enough, is the one in which Bertram attempts to seduce Diana. The hero and heroine are alone together only once and that is when Bertram takes his leave, never expecting to see Helena again. He seems almost incapable of tenderness, and she is almost indifferent to what he desires in her determination to become his wife.

The absence of romantic idealism in *All's Well* is not an inevitable result of Shakespeare's choice of the Boccaccian tale, which ends with the loving embrace of husband and wife. Even as Petruchio is less attractive than his counterpart Ferando in *A Shrew*, Bertram is less attractive than Boccaccio's Beltramo, although he is not coarsely contemptuous of women, as Petruchio is. Immature and inexperienced, he is quite incapable of seeing through Parolles' preposterous affectations, which he takes for courtly graces. He is also incapable of seeing beyond his immediate desires, but his faults would seem pardonable enough if Helena's determined pursuit of him did not bring out the worst in his character. He wants what most young gentlemen want— to win honor on the field of battle and to sow a few wild oats before he settles down to marriage and adult obligations. His youthful male instinct for freedom and adventure is opposed by Helena's desire to turn the would-be hero into a husband and father. Having just escaped his mother's watchful eye, Bertram yearns to prove himself a man among men. The disclosure in act 5 of his earlier attraction to Lafew's daughter seems almost an after-thought by Shakespeare because one cannot imagine Bertram in love or desiring to share his life with a woman. He does not love Diana or seek to win her love; he wants only the spoil of her maidenhead, which is no less a trophy than the capture of an enemy's drum. After he has proved his gallantry, won the esteem of his fellow officers, and possessed the prize of Diana's virginity, he is ready to marry Maudlin, especially when it will redeem him in the eyes of the King, his mother, and Lafew.

Bertram does not pose any problems of interpretation; apart from his gallantry in war, he is incurably ordinary and lacking in scruple. Helena is less easily explained. As the play opens, her situation at Rossillion is comparable to Viola's situation in Orsino's household; both adore a great nobleman who is far above their station in life and who knows nothing of their love. Where Viola is resigned to her unhappy circumstances, Helena is determined to wed Bertram, and her single-minded quest of that goal inspires continuing critical debate. No critics have said of Olivia what distinguished Shakespeareans have said of Helena, that she is enthralled and degraded by sexual passion, even though Olivia's desire for Cesario is more obsessive and reckless than Helena's desire for Bertram. But then Olivia responds to what is beautiful in Viola's character while Helena's attraction to the callow Bertram must necessarily be merely physical, just as her pursuit of him must be calculated and covert. Like Olivia, Helena will accept any humiliation for the sake of love, but she is never impulsive or reckless in seeking Bertram, and she does not, like Olivia, openly declare her love and beg to be loved in return. She has adored Bertram for some time, it seems, without once speaking or even hinting of her feeling for him and without trying to draw his attention to her. When she confesses her love in soliloquy, she does not speak rapturously of Bertram the way Olivia does of Cesario or Juliet does of Romeo. She does not dream of embraces and kisses; she dwells on, even fantasizes, the hopelessness of her love in lines that seem to belie any immediate physical longing:

> I have forgot him [her dead father]. My imagination
> Carries no favor in't but Bertram's.
> I am undone, there is no living, none,
> If Bertram be away. 'Twere all one
> That I should love a bright particular star
> And think to wed it, he is so above me.
> In his bright radiance and collateral light
> Must I be comforted, not in his sphere.
> Th' ambition in my love thus plagues itself:
> The hind that would be mated by the lion
> Must die for love.
>
> (1.1. 82–92)

The verse is clumsy in movement and the statements curiously flat and lacking in emotional intensity. Whenever Helena speaks of her desire she feels compelled to abstract it from anything resembling sensual longing. As a result, her poetic figures are stilted and even grotesque in their incongruities: She is a hind that would be mated by a lion, a violent consummation indeed.[2]

It is conventional for poets to speak of a loved one as a star; so Astrophil speaks of Stella in Sidney's sonnets. But Sidney does not, like Helena, at once imagine Stella as a point of light in a distant heaven and speak of wedding this star as if he could yearn for physical union with a galactic sphere. The peculiarity of Helena's lines cannot be ascribed to a failure of Shakespeare's poetic imagination because he knows how to make the traditional conceit of "love's star" a vehicle for romantic ardor. Compare, for example, Helena's soliloquy with Juliet's soliloquy as she awaits her wedding night with Romeo:

> Come, gentle night, come, loving, black-brow'd night,
> Give me my Romeo, and, when I shall die,
> Take him and cut him out in little stars,
> And he will make the face of heaven so fine
> That all the world will be in love with night,
> And pay no attention to the garish sun.
>
> (3.2. 20–25)

Helena's statement that she cannot live without Bertram does not express a comparable immediacy of longing but rather a determination to be his wife. Even when she is alone her responses are guarded; instead of a spontaneous rush of feeling there is cautious appraisal of possibilities and practicalities. If her passion for Bertram were not all-consuming, it would seem jejune because she dwells on his features as an adolescent might linger over the publicity photo of a movie star. What she describes she reduces to conventional epithets, thereby robbing Bertram of any distinctiveness of face or form:

> 'Twas pretty, though a plague,
> To see him every hour, to sit and draw
> His arched brows, his hawking eye, his curls,
> In our heart's table—heart too capable
> Of every line and trick of his sweet favor.
>
> (1.1. 92–96)

Since she will not allow herself to imagine kissing, embracing, and joining bodies with Bertram, Helena's deepest longing for him is expressed not in soliloquy but in her teasing, riddling conversation with Parolles about losing her virginity to her liking. The more directly she thinks of sexual union with Bertram, the more blurred her lines become, until she recovers her self-control and remarks of the pity that "wishing well had not a body in't,"

> Which might be felt, that we, the poorer born,
> Whose baser stars do shut us up in wishes,
> Might with effects of them follow our friends,
> And show what we alone must think, which never
> Returns us thanks.
>
> (1.1. 181–86)

She knows what Parolles is but can appreciate the flair with which he pretends to valor and courtesy. She gives him scope for his scurrilous argument against virginity and pretends to fear the loss of her maidenhead when in fact she is thinking of making love to Bertram; that is, wishing him well with a body that might be felt. She also manages with smiling, gentle mockery to suggest that Parolles is an absolute coward without seeming to insult him. When she is alone again, she represses all sensual longing and coolly assesses in soliloquy the difficulty of the task that lies before her:

> Our remedies oft in ourselves do lie,
> Which we ascribe to heaven. The fated sky
> Gives us free scope, only doth backward pull
> Our slow designs when we ourselves are dull.
> What power is it which mounts my love so high,
> That makes me see, and cannot feed mine eye?
> The mightiest space in fortune nature brings
> To join like likes, and kiss like native things.
>
> (1.1. 216–23)

This kind of rhyming sententiousness is more customary in a choric speech than in a personal meditation, but the very stiltedness of Helena's images is an intimation of the emotional turmoil that lies beneath her seemingly measured and generalized statements. Since she can look up to her high love and feed her eye with Bertram's sight, the unsatisfied appetite that she is determined to "feed" is not for his sight but for his body, an appetite that is half-acknowledged in the murky lines about joining "like likes to kiss like native things."

Helena's incapacity to express her sensual longing for Bertram is analogous to Angelo's recoil from his sexual desire for Isabella in *Measure for Measure*. Convinced of his superiority to the common sensual herd of men, Angelo is shattered by his longing for a virginal novitiate, and yet an audience realizes that his desire, unlike Helena's, is not immediately physical in origin. He responds to the beauty of Isabella's spirit, her religious ardor and anger at his complacency, even as Olivia responds to Viola's liveliness of mind and depth of feeling. For though Isabella is fair, her physical beauty is in large part hidden by her novice's habit. Only a woman like Isabella, Angelo says, could have aroused his desire, and we believe him, for any calculated or sophisticated sensual appeal would have aroused his contempt and disgust. He hungers to possess Isabella's purity, and since that desire horrifies him, he must hate her for inspiring it. If he could freely accept his passion, he could ennoble it by his genuine admiration for her and turn desire to love. Unable to accept his passion, he is like Helena incapable of appealing for the love he desires. Just as Helena never hints to Bertram of her love, Angelo does not woo Isabella with tender vows or seductive praise. Revolted by his longings, he cannot voice them and would have Isabella catch the drift of his veiled suggestions and submit to his lust without his having to make it explicit. Her ignorance of his desire infuriates him because it forces him to speak frankly; and when he finally does it is with a desire to drag her innocence down into the mire of his lust, to prove that she is like him despite her show of purity. Like Bertram with Diana, he would have Isabella stop playing the modest virgin and put on the destined livery of all women—the soiled garment of a whore.

Like Helena's soliloquies, Angelo's soliloquies have a detached quality, even when he immediately confronts his passion, because he must seek to maintain control or lose his sense of self. His lawyerly assessment of his case is, like Helena's stilted conceits, an attempt to distance himself from sexual desire.[3] When that attempt fails, he necessarily has to satisfy that desire in a way that degrades Isabella and himself. Because Helena can turn sexual longing into a quest to prove her worthiness, she can channel it into a goal that engages the best of her intelligence and daring. And because she can separate that goal from Bertram's nature, she can endure insult and humiliation from him without feeling degraded. We cannot speak then of Helena's love as demeaning her when it expresses what is essential in her nature. Apart from that love, she does not exist for us in the way that Portia, Beatrice, Rosalind, and Viola do. She lacks their warmth and imagination, their pleasure in others and responsiveness to their worlds. Except for the comedy of the denouement, which she invents and stage manages, and apart from her brief sparring match with Parolles, Helena is without humor. Of couse, she is more burdened by circumstances than other heroines but one doubts that she would be playful even if her situation allowed it because she is too earnest and practical by nature.

In fairy tales Cinderellas live happily ever after with their princes because love and fairy godmothers annihilate barriers of money and class. In *All's Well*, as in Boccaccio's tale, these barriers are not easily waved away with a magic wand. Although Giletta is a wealthy heiress in Painter's version of Boccaccio's tale, she is not of noble blood. The King, therefore, "was very loath" to grant Beltramo to her and would not have allowed it had he not pledged to do so earlier. Beltramo is shocked by the command to marry Giletta and protests that she is not of "a stock convenable to his nobility."[4] Shakespeare increases the disparity of rank between Helena and Bertram by turning Boccaccio's rich heiress into a ward in the Rossillion household whose only dowry is the medical cures left to her by her father. Yet the difference of rank matters only to Bertram in *All's Well*. The King does not hesitate at Helena's choice of Bertram as a husband, and he immediately condemns Bertram's snobbery in refusing Helena. Praising Helena's virtues, he promises to make her honor and estate at least as great as Bertram's. Lafew, who watches while Helena chooses a husband, thinks her worthy of the best in France, and the Countess, learning that Helena loves her son, welcomes her as a daughter. Only Bertram finds Helena too mean to be his wife, and his objection is prompted less by aristocratic hauteur than by distaste for a woman who was no better than a dependent in his household—"a poor physician's daughter," from whom he parted in scene 1 with the command one gives to a servant, "Be comfortable to my mother, your mistress."

Bertram's contemptuous attitude toward Helena is not supported by the choric commentary in the play on aristocratic values. The King's complaints of the decline of courtesy and chivalry invoke a standard of gentility that is the opposite of Bertram's disdain, one of gracious respect for inferiors. Indeed, the King's praise of Bertram's father in 1.2 measures Bertram's failing as a courtier, not Helena's lack of nobility. To be sure, Bertram is not by nature rude or arrogant; he does not demand a cringing obedience from servants and retainers. If he were infatuated with the idea of great rank, he would not reject Helena but rather rejoice in having a wife who is a royal favorite and will bring him great wealth and esteem. One suspects that Bertram would have turned as angrily on any marriage that was going to be forced upon him.

If Shakespeare wanted an audience to recognize Helena as a social climber he had only to give her some of Malvolio's hunger for money and status or allow her to lord it over others when she becomes the Countess of Rossillion. Nothing in her words or manner intimates that wealth and title mean much to her. She wants Bertram, not his estates; the goal she aggressively pursues is to submit to Bertram, to surrender her virginity—her body—to him and be accepted as his wife. Parolles, not Helena, is the upstart of the play, the dependent who affects aristocratic airs. Indeed, it is doubly ironic that Bertram, unable to appreciate Helena's virtues, despises her baseness but accepts Parolles, who is all sham and bluster, as his mentor in chivalry. It is doubtful, moreover, that Shakespeare's audiences were scandalized by Helena's desire to wed Bertram, for the vitality of their society depended on its relative openness, on the opportunity it offered men of talent and energy to rise above their birth and enter the ranks of a nobility that had not grown moribund. The New Men whom Elizabethans and Jacobeans despised and feared were the unworthy royal minions who gained power and wealth through a monarch's thoughtless largesse or granting of monopolies.[5]

I have suggested elsewhere that if Hamlet did not keep accusing himself of failing to revenge his father, no reader would think that he hesitates or delays taking revenge against Claudius.[6] Similarly, no reader would be inclined to label Helena a social climber if she did not persist in accusing herself of ambitious and overreaching love. It is she who keeps harping on her humble origin and on Bertram's great height above her and who feels a continuing need to apologize for her presumptuous desire when no one impugns her motives. Proclaiming that she is unworthy of Bertram, she stalks him relentlessly, without seeming to be hypocritical, and she resorts to a bed trick without seeming to degrade herself. If she were conniving by nature, she would rely on the King to make Bertram accept her as wife after their marriage. But she turns neither to him nor to the Countess and Lafew, who would willingly aid her if she asked. She never desires something for nothing; she offers good value to the King for the reward she seeks, and she is scrupulous in fulfilling the letter of the terms Bertram sets for accepting her as his wife. She would not have him, she says, without deserving him. Since he is a radiant star she will shine forth with her own glowing achievement. She will be a fairy tale heroine who wins her love by daring and skill as so many fairy tale heroes win a king's daughter. To succeed she must use guile and deception because his terms leave her no other alternative; or rather the only other choice she has is to be revolted by his mistreatment of her.

It never seems to occur to Helena that success in winning Bertram might depend on his feeling for her; assuming that she is nothing to him, she never attempts to gain his affection. Because she says nothing to him of her love before she publicly chooses him as her royal reward, he is utterly unprepared for and dumbfounded by her choice. Because she conceals her love from everyone it is only by accident that it is discovered and brought to the attention of the Countess; even then she will not readily admit it. Boccaccio's heroine is not, like Helena, a loner by nature as well as circumstance. She is surrounded by relatives before she marries and wins the love and loyalty of all her people after the Count rejects her and departs. From the beginning Shakespeare makes Helena a solitary figure, one who grew up alone on the periphery of a great household in which she had no assured place or station. Accustomed to this aloneness, she does not reach out to anyone except when an alliance with the King or with Diana and her mother will further her goal of obtaining Bertram. Her joyful greeting of the Countess in the final scene is the single occasion when she openly returns the affection of those who love her. At other times she hoards her emotion as if she must channel it all toward Bertram and the task of achieving him.

As soon as she learns of Helena's love for her son, the Countess makes clear her approval by inviting Helena's confidences. When she asks Helena to think of her as a mother, the response is that the Countess is her "honorable mistress." The Countess persists in speaking of her as her daughter, and Helena persists in denying the possibility of such a relationship. Although she has already concluded that she can deserve to become Bertram's wife, she speaks here as if she would never dare link her name with the Rossillions:

> The Count Rossillion cannot be my brother:
> I am from humble, he from honored name;
> No note upon my parents, his all noble.
> My master, my dear lord he is, and I
> His servant live, and will his vassal die.
> He must not be my brother.
>
> (1.3.155–160)

Helena's equivocations are transparent to the audience; she cannot allow Bertram to be her brother because she would be his wife, and she hints more directly at her yearning for him when she says that she wishes the Countess were her mother, "so that my lord, your son, were not my brother . . . So I were not his sister." The Countess, having offered her sympathy and love is annoyed by this evasiveness. She declares that Helena's looks, sighs, and tears express her love of Bertram, and "only sin / And hellish obstinacy tie thy tongue, / That truth should be suspected." Although the Countess charges her to speak truly, Helena continues her zigzag course, begging for pardon, refusing to say she loves Bertram until finally she slips to her knees and "confesses":

> Here on my knee, before high heaven and you,
> That before you, and next until high heaven,
> I love your son.
> My friends were poor, but honest, so's my love.
> Be not offended, for it hurts not him
> That he is lov'd of me; I follow him not
> By any token of presumptuous suit,
> Nor would I have him till I do deserve him;
> Yet never know how that desert should be.
>
> (1.3.192–200)

Since she cannot believe by this point that the Countess will be offended by her love of Bertram, Helena's evasiveness must be prompted by her own emotional needs rather than a fear of rebuke. Her humility is genuine and yet equivocal because she kneels only to declare her intention to pursue Bertram—but not in "any token of presumptuous suit." That is, she will not "have him" till she deserves him. This is the humbleness of one who will not claim great merit as yet, but who is absolutely certain that one day she will deserve a place among the best. This kind of self-effacement is slyly glossed by Lavatch just before Helena enters:

> Though honesty be no puritan, yet it will do no hurt; it will wear the
> surplice of humility over the black gown of a big heart.
>
> (1.3.93–94)

Ordinarily humility and simplicity go hand in hand, but there are times when plainness becomes ostentatious and a sign of self-righteous superiority. Repelled by the rich panoply of Anglican worship, the puritan minister wears a simple black gown beneath the showier surplice church law required, thus making his disdain for episcopal finery a gesture of spiritual pride. To say there is a like pride in Helena's humbleness is not to accuse her of hypocritical earnestness, for she must be certain of what she can achieve to dare what she does, and she must also believe in her inferiority to Bertram to bow before his abuse and rejection. If she did not keep telling herself that she is unworthy of him, she could not accept the contemptuous conditions he sets for accepting her as his wife. At the same time, once she has proved her worthiness to be his wife, she is determined to enjoy the prize she has won. Sometimes Helena plays the poor little waif for herself and others, but she invariably slips from this self-image to that of a female knight-errant who will accomplish impossible tasks to win her curled darling.

Helena's proud humility and kneeling pride are vividly expressed in her audience with the King, who must be convinced that he can be cured when his learned doctors have given him up as lost. First she is all humbleness, ready to accept his denials; then she refuses to be denied because she is heaven's emissary, an agent of providence, an instrument of miracles as great as the parting of the Red Sea. Finally she is a high priestess of mysterious powers and incantatory prophesies who promises a cure in less than forty-eight hours. She will wager all on belief in her father's cure, aware, no doubt, that the melodramatic punishments she names as her forfeit would not be imposed should she fail. When she asks what reward she will obtain if she succeeds, she specifies nothing until the King has pledged his scepter and hopes of heaven on his good faith. Then she avoids any hint of guilty presumption by declaring that she would not think of joining her "low and humble name" to the royal blood of France but seeks as husband only a vassal whom the King is free to bestow.

The public ceremony in which Helena pretends to pick and choose among the young noblemen at court before settling on Bertram is not in Boccaccio. It is invented by Shakespeare—or, rather, it is invented by Helena as an ostentatious show of humility in her choice of a husband, and as such it wins the hearts of all save Bertram, who is ignorant of his role in the charade. It also allows him no time to digest the stunning news and no way to protest his fate without open defiance of the King. Since she cannot be sure of Bertram's response, her timidity may be real. She acts as if she were so fearful of rejection that she prefers not to choose, yet she knows that she cannot be refused by any of the lords because the King informs them that Helena has power to choose any and they "none to forsake." When Helena hesitates, the King insists that she make a choice and turns a threatening eye on the assembly: "Make choice and see, / Who shuns thy love shuns all his love in me." So reluctantly, blushingly, shamefacedly, Helena is "forced" to do what she has set her mind on doing. She could choose Bertram outright, but that would be too obvious; she will settle on him only after considering various other young noblemen. One lord, she says, deserves a wife twenty times above herself. Another she would not wrong, for he deserves a fairer fortune in bed. A third she says is "too young, too happy, and too good" to be the father of her son. Only after these lords have protested their willingness to be her husband does she humbly turn to Bertram:

> I dare not say I take you, but I give
> Me and my service, ever whilst I live,
> Into your guiding power.—This is the man.
>
> (2.3.102–4)

What she says is heartfelt but it does not alter the fact that that though she dares not "take" Bertram, she does take him.

Bertram's outcry is understandable. Just before he was deprived of an opportunity to fight in the war by the King, who said he was too young. Now he is being deprived of his right to choose his own wife; although not old enough to be a soldier, he is old enough to be given away in marriage as a royal reward. This is especially bitter to one who complained to Parolles that he must remain at court in the service of women as "the forehorse to a smock." Bertram is probably the only lord foolish and heedless enough to refuse Helena, but his refusal is frank and prompted by the fact that he does not love her. Shall he be denied the right to choose his own wife because Helena is a worthy choice? Or can he not rebel against an enforced marriage with the same justification that Silvia, Hermia, and Juliet rebel? The abuse of wardships through enforced marriages was a scandal in Shakespeare's time, and the misery of enforced marriage was poignantly depicted by contemporary playwrights. The moral issue does not change because a man rather than a woman is thrust into a loveless marriage by a guardian's prerogative.[7]

When Bertram asks leave "in such a business . . . to use / The help of mine own eyes," he is a sympathetic figure. When he speaks scornfully of Helena as one who would bring him down, his snobbery is nasty because he speaks of her as if she were a horse or a dog who "had her breeding at my father's charge." This arrogance merits the King's angry reply about the superiority of Helena's active virtue to a dropsied inherited honor. Nevertheless, *honor* and *dishonor* become slippery terms when they depend merely on the King's favor or disdain. Helena says she is glad of the King's cure and would let the rest go. That is not possible, however, because his honor is engaged on her behalf and he cannot allow himself to be publicly humiliated. "Obey our will," he commands Bertram,

> Or I will throw thee from my care for ever
> Into the staggers and the careless lapse
> Of youth and ignorance; both my revenge and hate
> Loosing upon thee, in the name of justice,
> Without all terms of pity.
>
> (2.3. 162–66)

Threatened in this fashion, Bertram asks pardon, and with just a bit of insouciance declares that Helena, who just before seemed most base to him, is now with the King's praise as noble as if born so. It would be sensible for Bertram to marry Helena and learn to cherish her qualities, but it would also be sensible for Hermia to marry Demetrius rather than risk death by eloping with Lysander. It is not shameful of Bertram to state his feelings openly; what is shameful is the cowardly revenge he takes on Helena afterward.

Furious at Bertram's response to being chosen by Helena, Lafew takes out his rage on Parolles as if Parolles were responsible for Bertram's callowness. An audience knows, however, that Parolles' influence on Bertram is limited. When he sneers at Lafew as an idle lord, Bertram bluntly disagrees: "I think not so." His decision never to sleep with Helena or live with her is made without Parolles' assistance, and he shows his contempt for his wife by having Parolles inform her that there will be no wedding night before she returns to Rossillion. Enjoying his role as messenger, Parolles mockingly addresses Helena as "fortunate lady," and assures her that he prayed for her success. He probably also embroiders Bertram's message with a few rhetorical flourishes of his own, promising that the postponed pleasures of the wedding night will be sweeter still when enjoyed later. Helena shows immense composure in the face of Bertram's rejection of her. Wanting Parolles' good will she does not tease him, nor does she protest the fact that she learns her fate from him, not her husband. The quiet with which she accepts Bertram's will suggests a resilience and perhaps a heart already prepared for the blow. Her responses are simple and matter-of-fact: "What's his will else? . . . What more commands he? . . . In everything I wait upon his will." It is as if she continues to regard herself as Bertram's vassal even after she has become his wife. Her parting from Bertram is equally restrained; she shows no self-pity and makes no appeal. Bertram seems, if anything, more uncomfortable than she, and makes his lame excuses in lines that are sinuous, stilted, and patently insincere:

> You must not marvel, Helen, at my course,
> Which holds not color with the time, nor does
> The ministration and required office
> On my particular. Prepar'd I was not
> For such a business; therefore am I found
> So much unsettled.
>
> (2.5. 58–63)

Here, as later in the play, Bertram proves to be a bad liar—one of the more hopeful signs of his nature. He is unable to be brutal to Helena face to face, and he is unable to withstand her long-suffering patient humility. When she replies to his threadbare excuses, "Sir, I can nothing say / But that I am your

most obedient servant," he says, "Come, come; no more of that." But she
has much more to offer; she swears that she shall ever,

> With true observance seek to eke out that
> Wherein toward me my homely stars have fail'd
> To equal my great fortune,

(2.5 74–76)

a statement that inspires in Bertram an overwhelming desire to cut short the
interview.

Once again Helena's humility seems sanctimonious and manipulative, a
denial of self calculated to make Bertram squirm. Yet the acceptance of her
situation is real; she timidly begs for a parting kiss as if she recognizes that
affection cannot be earned or "achieved," it can only be given or begged for.
The Countess's response to the letter in which Bertram swears never to have
Helena as his wife is unequivocal. She is angry and also fearful for this "rash
and unbridled boy" who risks the King's wrath by "misprising of a maid too
virtuous / For the contempt of empire." When Helena reads aloud her
"passport" from Bertram, the Countess is ready to disown him: "He was my
son." Helena will not permit herself any outcry; the most she will say is that
Bertram's decision is a dreadful sentence and "bitter." Even when she rereads
the letter alone on stage she cannot acknowledge its brutality. She must pity
Bertram rather than pity herself; indeed, she must accuse herself of being the
reason he fled his home and country for the Italian wars or else face the
reality of his contempt. Her pity is like the pity Julia feels for Proteus when
she discovers his faithlessness to her. Julia, however, can admit the ugliness
of Proteus's behavior, whereas Helena must heap abuse upon herself so that
she can blot out the callousness of Bertram's actions. Melodramatizing her
guiltiness, she declares that it will be her fault if he dies in battle. For his sake
she will renounce all claim to him and steal away like a "dark, poor thief" so
that he can return to Rossillion; yet like the Countess she speaks of him as if
he were a defiant child who has run away from home because she was too
harsh, one whose "tender limbs" are being exposed "to the event / Of the
none-sparing war." It would be more appropriate, she thinks, if she met a
ravenous lion than he be a mark for smoky muskets. Helena's self-accusations become more unctuous still in the letter she leaves for the Countess
when she departs Rossillion. Once again she speaks of the offense of her
ambitious love that only a barefooted pilgrimage can expiate. Ignoring
Bertram's mistreatment of her, she promises to sanctify his name "with
zealous fervor," begs forgiveness for driving him to the war, and declares that
she will go away because "he is too good and fair for death and me." Can
Helena believe that such a letter will soften the Countess's anger at Bertram
and bring him home from the war? The Countess notes the "sharp

stings . . . in Helena's mildest words" and sends a letter to Bertram that is full of praise of his saintly wife.

No letter from the Countess will reform Bertram, who is now openly defiant of his wife and the King. If he is to be redeemed, it will have to be by Helena, who is willing to meet his mocking demands and win him twice. Her pretense of a holy pilgrimage is no more devious than Portia's pretense that she intends a religious retreat when she sets off with Nerissa for Venice. Her attitude of self-sacrifice is very different, however, from Portia's refusal to praise herself or be praised for her effort to rescue Antonio. But then one could not be like Portia and accept the humiliations that Bertram heaps on Helena. To undertake and accomplish Helena's venture, one must have immense self-confidence but not much pride, for one must believe that this "god" has the right to set whatever terms he pleases for his wife.

More alone in Florence than at the start of the play, Helena confides in no one. She will not admit to the Widow that she knows Bertram, much less that she is his wife. When she hears that Parolles has spoken coarsely of her, she agrees that Bertram's wife "is too mean / To have her name repeated." Boccaccio's heroine is more open and direct in managing the bed trick, but Shakespeare does not emphasize Helena's craftiness so much as he does the viciousness of Bertram's attempted seduction. Mariana warns Diana of the deceitfulness of men like Bertram, whose oaths and promises are merely "engines of lust" and who leave the maids they have despoiled to the misery of a ruined reputation. Her appraisal of Bertram's motives is painfully accurate because he is callous as well as unskilled at seduction. First he attempts some conventional Petrarchan flatteries and a bit of Parollesian casuistry about the value of losing one's virginity. When these fail, he swears that he will be her servant, and when she ridicules these vows, he discards the pose of courtly lover and bluntly demands her surrender:

> Stand no more off,
> But give thyself unto my sick desires,
> Who then recovers. Say thou art mine, and ever
> My love, as it begins, shall so persever.

(4.2. 34–37)

Later Bertram will boast of this night's work to his comrades, but it is he—not Diana—who surrenders. Instructed by Helena, she insists on having his ancestral ring—his honor—in exchange for her maidenhead—her honor. He holds out for only a moment and then barters for one night's lust the ring that was "bequeathed down from many ancestors"; such is the regard for name and lineage of one who disdained a poor physician's daughter. The mention of vows and holy oaths and the exchange of rings turn the supposed seduction into a mock nuptial in which Diana acts as Helena's proxy even as Helena will serve as Diana's substitute in bed with Bertram.

The ironies and moral ambiguities that surround the bed trick in *Measure for Measure* are absent in *All's Well*. There is no surrender to unlawful coercion, no bribery of justice, no soliciting of a woman for a stealthy assignation by a mock friar. The Widow and Diana will be rewarded by Helena for their part in the duping of Bertram, but they do not agree merely for the sake of reward. The Widow would not put her reputation "in any staining act" and must first be convinced that Helena's purpose is legitimate and will not harm her daughter. Then she and Diana join with Helena as women, as natural allies, against predatory men like Bertram. After listening to Bertram's lying protestations, Diana decides that it is "no sin / To cozen him that would unjustly win." More candid with herself and others than Duke Vincentio is about the bed trick, Helena does not attempt to invest it with high moral purpose. It is lawful, she says, and yet it involves on Bertram's part a "wicked meaning" (that is, vicious intention); she and Bertram will not sin in making love because they are married, and yet the act she knows is "a sinful fact." Diana risks very little and because of Helena's generosity will no longer be dowerless and prey to the enticements of men like Bertram; Helena will lose her virginity to her liking and gain Bertram in the bargain. She has no illusions anymore about her bright star; she knows him well enough now to wager that he will give his ancestral ring "to buy his will," but she does not recoil from that knowledge. Perhaps it is comforting to know the full extent of his shabbiness, because the shabbiness justifies the means she uses to gain him.

While Bertram ensnares himself in lust, his fellow officers plot to free him from the influence of Parolles, who they know to be a cowardly braggart. By placing the scenes in which Bertram and Parolles are duped side by side, Shakespeare artfully balances the emotional effects. On the one hand, Parolles' readiness to betray his comrades to the enemy is worse than Bertram's attempted betrayal of Diana. On the other hand, Bertram is at his worst in lying to Diana while Parolles achieves a kind of comic grandeur in the scene in which he is exposed. Even before he is captured, he is shrewd enough to realize that he has trapped himself by blustering over the captured drum, which he knows he cannot recover. One of his captors is astonished to discover that Parolles knows exactly what he is but has no intention of changing his ways. He also knows that except for Bertram everyone sees through him and "disgraces have of late knock'd too often at [his] door." His imagination takes wing as he considers how he might fool others into thinking he fought to recover the drum—by cutting his garments, breaking his Spanish sword, shaving his beard, stripping his clothes, and so forth. The mention of torture by his captors is enough to make him turn his coat and volunteer to betray all the secrets of the camp. Yet the mock interrogation scene is not an unpleasant game of cat and mouse like the taunting of the "mad" Malvolio by Feste and Toby, for the gullers are not vindictive and

Parolles does not whimper. Instead he grows expansive, almost Falstaffian, in slandering his comrades. Captain Dumaine, he says, was

> . . . a botcher's prentice in Paris, from whence he was whipt for getting the shrieve's fool with child, a dumb innocent, that could not say him nay.
>
> (4.3. 185–88)

When he warms to his task, he is a slanderer non pareil who adds to his previous description of Dumaine the information that he will

> steal, sir, an egg out of a cloister. For rapes and ravishments he parallels Nessus. . . . He will lie, sir, with such volubility, that you would think truth were a fool. Drunkenness is his best virtue, for he will be swine-drunk, and in his sleep he does little harm, save to his bed-clothes about him; but they know his conditions, and lay him in straw. I have but little more to say, sir, of his honesty. He has every thing that an honest man should not have; what an honest man should have, he has nothing.
>
> (4.3. 250–61)

Dumaine, who has a sense of humor, can appreciate Parolles' genius at calumny. He remarks to Bertram that he begins to love Parolles for this, for he "hath outvillained villainy so far that the rarity redeems him." The humorless Bertram finds nothing funny in Parolles' description of him, which comes all too close to the truth:

> . . . the young Count [is] a dangerous and lascivious boy, who is a whale to virginity, and devours up all the fry it finds.
>
> (4.3. 219–21)

It is good of Parolles to send a letter warning Diana against Bertram, but the advice he gives is as cynical as Bertram's professions of love: get your money before you submit because Bertram "never pays the score." Bertram, who would like to have his boon companion "whipped through the army," writhes at Parolles' words and like a sulky child keeps repeating that he cannot stand cats, nor can he stand a Parolles who is a cat to him, "more and more a cat." When his blindfold is removed, Parolles' first instinct is to bluster: "Who cannot be crushed with a plot?" When his captors leave, however, he expresses something like relief in being found out, which he regards as the fate of every braggard. Now, at least, he does not have to live in fear of being "smoked" or of dying on the battlefield. He can still brag to himself of his cunning, confident he will "eat and drink and sleep as soft" as a captain though no longer pretending to be one; but he protests too much and next appears at Rossillion in stinking rags.

Bertram is not shaken by the realization of how much he misprised

Parolles and he is not moved to self-examination by the humiliation of the exposure scene. A fellow officer says that the Countess's letter to him about Helena stung his "nature, for on the reading it he changed almost into another man." If any moral illumination occurred, there is no trace of it in Bertram's speech or behavior. One of his comrades describes his pursuit of Diana as a perverting "of a young gentlewoman in Florence, of a most chaste renown." Bertram's view is different; he boasts of his recent activities without a sign of remorse for the supposed death of Helena or shame at having despoiled a virgin:

> I have congied with the Duke, done my adieu with his nearest; buried a wife, mourn'd for her, writ to my lady mother I am returning, entertain'd my convoy, and between these main parcels of dispatch [effected] many nicer needs. The last was the greatest, but that I have not ended yet.
>
> (4.3. 87–92)

The only retribution he pretends to fear is the possibility that Diana may become pregnant, but that "fear" is a boast of his virility.

If redemption is possible for Bertram and Parolles it will come at Rossillion, where they may be forgiven and guided by those who have more wisdom and decency. The first to recognize Parolles for what he is, Lafew is also the first to pity him; when Parolles comes begging, he extends his hand and promises that though Parolles is a fool and a knave, he shall eat. Lafew is also willing to trust that Bertram, disgraced by his mistreatment of Helena, will make a worthy husband for his daughter Maudlin. This time Bertram consents to the betrothal, but this second marriage is, like the first one, arranged by others and ratified by the King. If Helena were dead, as all think, Bertram's wedding to Maudlin would put the seal on his supposed reformation and provide a reasonably satisfactory denouement for the play. But Helena lives and Bertram is not wiser or humbler than before, merely suaver. Although the King is willing to forget his misconduct, Bertram makes a silken apology for his past deeds; nay, he uses his avowed love of the fair Maudlin to explain his mistreatment of Helena. At first, he says, he loved Maudlin,

> ere my heart
> Durst make too bold a herald of my tongue;
> Where the impression of mine eye infixing,
> Contempt his scornful perspective did lend me,
> Which warp'd the line of every other favor,
> Scorn'd a fair color, or express'd it stol'n,
> Extended or contracted all proportions
> To a most hideous object. Thence it came
> That she whom all men prais'd, and whom myself,

Since I have lost, have lov'd, was in mine eye
The dust that did offend it.

(5.3. 45–54)

This is not as strained and patently false as his explanation to Helena of why he had to leave her on his wedding day. It has, nevertheless, a facile ring and a rehearsed artificiality. The King appreciates the refinement of the excuse but still reminds Bertram that belated love is "like a remorseful pardon slowly carried," a sour offense to the sender.

In Boccaccio the ending of the story of Giletta and Beltramo is simple and straightforward. She arrives at his household during a great feast, falls weeping at his feet, and shows him his ring and her twin sons as proof that she has met all the terms he set down for accepting her. On hearing her words, Beltramo realizes Giletta's nobility and loving devotion, and in response to the pleas of all his people, he raises her up, embraces her, and acknowledges her as his lawful wife. Knowing what she does of Bertram, Helena does not risk all on a sudden appeal to his better nature. As before she will by indirection find direction out; all of her ingenuity and resourcefulness are employed in contriving a baroque dramatic interlude of supposes and false accusations that so unnerves Bertram that he is overjoyed when she finally appears to rescue him from calamity.

Most of the comedy of the final scene derives from Helena's artful choreographing of Diana's accusations against Bertram and her provocative riddling about Helena's ring. Shakespeare aids Helena's cause by allowing Diana to enter just as a bewildered Bertram, suspected of wicked deeds, is being led away under guard. But Helena does not need much help from Shakespeare because she is able to contrive her own masterly version of the discovery scenes that close *Errors* and *Twelfth Night*, one in which the clamor of false accusations mounts until the entrance of a single character— Antipholus S. or Sebastian or Helena—resolves all difficulties. Except for Bertram's mistaken assumption that he made love to Diana, none of the supposes in this discovery scene is the result of mistaken identities. Moreover, the crucial issue is not the discovery that Helena is alive but the unmasking of Bertram's moral nature, which resembles the exposure of Parolles down to the extravagant lies each one tells when caught in the trap. Where Parolles rises to heights of comic calumny, Bertram descends to depths of falsehood and vicious slander, but the comic confusion that surrounds his possession of Helena's ring and Diana's saucy manner keep the revelation from becoming so nasty that a happy ending is impossible.[8] The tone is as artfully balanced as in the analogous ring episode in *The Merchant*, although the dramatic circumstance and moral issue are far more serious.

Things go wrong from Bertram as soon as his love token for Maudlin is recognized by the King as a ring he gave Helena. Although the Countess and

Lafew confirm the identity of the ring, Bertram is convinced that they are mistaken, because he knows that he got it from his Florentine dish. Too tactful to brag of his sexual conquests, he invents the facile lie that the ring was thrown to him from a window by a woman who desired him. Since Helena told the King she would not part with the ring except to her husband in bed, he is incensed by Bertram's falsehood and begins to have dark suspicions about how Bertram obtained the ring. After Diana enters to accuse Bertram of seducing her with false promises of marriage, the King wonders why Bertram wishes to marry Maudlin when he has apparently fled from two other "wives," and Lafew decides to "buy me a son-in-law in a fair." Bertram admits that he knows Diana but will not admit he attempted her seduction. Even granting his shock and panic, his lines suggest that his view of women has not changed:

> My lord, this is a fond and desp'rate creature,
> Whom sometime I have laugh'd with. Let your Highness
> Lay a more noble thought upon mine honor
> Than for to think that I would sink it here.
>
> (5.3. 178–81)

Sinking lower, Bertram describes Diana as "a common gamester to the camp," but she shows his ancestral ring, and that is enough to convince the Countess that Diana is his wife. Bertram reaches his nadir with the lie that Diana obtained his ring by angling for him, madding his desire with "infinite cunning" until he gave it for that "which any inferior might / At market-price have bought." Since Parolles, who is called to testify, can expose this falsehood, Bertram must also vilify his former companion as

> a most perfidious slave,
> With all the spots a' th' world tax'd and debosh'd,
> Whose nature sickens but to speak a truth.
>
> (5.8. 205–7)

Bertram seems all the more shabby when Parolles proves reluctant to condemn him and charitable in his assessment of Bertram's character: "My master hath been an honorable gentleman. Tricks he hath had in him, which gentlemen have." According to Parolles Bertram loved Diana "as a gentleman loves a woman . . . He lov'd her sir, and lov'd her not." This explanation is less equivocal than the King supposes, for Parolles implies that gentlemen marry ladies but make love to women of no birth without loving them and have no intention of marrying those who surrender to them. If Bertram had been more sophisticated he would not have pursued a virgin; he would have made love to a woman who had already lost her maidenhead and honor and who could not be further degraded by a gentleman.

Parolles' statement, like those which Diana, Helena, and Mariana make about men, make the battle of the sexes in *All's Well* more explicit than it is in earlier comedies, for here the aggressiveness and callousness of male appetite is opposed to the woman's need to lose her virginity to her liking or husband it as a priceless commodity. Like the cynical Lavatch, the ruttish Bertram travesties romantic ideals by reducing the "service" of love to that which a bull offers a cow. Portraits like Bertram and Lucio of *Measure for Measure* do not imply, however, that Shakespeare has lost faith in the romantic ideal that informs his earlier comedies; they simply confirm that the ideal of love depends on an ability to cherish others and a capacity for generosity that Bertram does not possess.

Since too much emphasis on Bertram's failings will make a shambles of the denouement, Shakespeare focuses attention on the mystery of Helena's ring after Parolles has spoken. Coached by Helena, Diana, who has already given false testimony about Bertram, responds to the King's questions with such riddling equivocations that Lafew and the King believe she is, as Bertram claimed, "some common customer," "an easy glove" that goes off and on at pleasure. Threatened with death, Diana grows more impudent; she is cheekily familiar with the King, and hinting that she is still a virgin, she suggests also that Bertram is "guilty and he is not guilty." Her impudence is a welcome note given Helena's willingness to abase herself before Bertram in earlier scenes, for at last the women in the play do not bow before the will of men. At the last moment Diana plays her trump card: she produces a Helena whose pregnant state is the simple truth hinted at by her equivocations: "one that's dead is quick."

No one is more overjoyed at Helena's appearance than Bertram, for she alone can rescue him from ignominious disgrace. Like Hero in the last scene of *Much Ado*, Helena does not dwell on the wrongs that were done her. When the King asks, "Is't real that I see?" she answers:

> No, my good lord,
> 'Tis but the shadow of a wife you see,
> The name, and not the thing.
>
> (5.3. 306–8)

To which Bertram cries out, "Both, both. O, pardon!" Reminding Bertram that she found him "wondrous kind" when he thought he was making love to Diana, she also reads aloud the conditions he set down for accepting her as his wife and asks, "Will you be mine now you are doubly won?" This is not the Helena of earlier scenes who bowed before Bertram's scorn; instead of timidly begging for affection, she asks Bertram to acknowledge publicly that she deserves him. In a last attempt at masculine pride Bertram makes his answer not to her but to the King:

> If she, my liege, can make me know this clearly,
> I'll love her dearly, ever, ever dearly.

Keeping her emotional distance from Bertram, Helena embraces the Countess, whom she can at last acknowledge as her "dear mother." Diana's future seems assured, for the King promises to provide a dowry when she marries. Wiser than before, he does not propose to enforce her choice of husband with his prerogative, and still wary of her glibness he makes his promise as conditional as Bertram's to Helena: if Diana is still a virgin, he will see that she marries well. Too ready before to jump to erroneous conclusions, now he is cautious about assessing the outcome of events:

> All yet seems well, and if it end so meet,
> The bitter past, more welcome is the sweet.

If all is well it is not because Bertram is more mature or more sensitive in the last scene than in the first, but because, after his narrow escapes, he is no doubt ready for a quiet life at Rossillion.[9] He promises that he will love Helena dearly, and no doubt he will, insofar as "loving dearly" can be a matter of deliberate choice. Helena's progress is more certain and significant. She knows more about Bertram than any wife should know about a husband and yet she loves him still. She is not revolted by his desire for Diana because she knows how circumstance affects sexual longing and pleasure. He rejected her out of anger and spite but enjoyed her body in Florence, thinking she was a prize that had been won with difficulty. She can acknowledge the lure of stealthy illicit sex without feeling the need to justify Bertram's lust. Once too ready to proclaim her unworthiness, she now is fully assured of her self-worth. At the beginning, she imagined the attaining of Bertram as an achieving of the impossible, a striving for a star. After the bed trick, she no longer speaks of what she can achieve by a determined will. In a speech to Diana and the Widow, she puts her faith in the passing of time that brings life again to barren twigs and that will confirm the new life that exists in her womb:

> . . . the time will bring on summer,
> When briers shall have leaves as well as thorns,
> And be as sweet as sharp. We must away:
> Our waggon is prepar'd, and time revives us.
> All's well that ends well! still the fine's the crown;
> Whate'er the course, the end is the renown.

> (4.4. 31–36)

Helena's alliance with Diana and the Widow is important to the denouement of *All's Well* because she is no longer apart from others, absorbed in her

determination to have Bertram. When she embraces the Countess, the familial drama of the play reaches its happy conclusion: an orphaned child raised
as a ward in a great household has found a mother as well as a husband at
Rossillion. Despite the earlier melancholy sense of lost values, there is hope
of better days to come. Bertram is in good hands and Helena carries the child
that will assure the future of the noble lineage he very nearly compromised.
Although they play a small part in the dramatic action, the presence of the
Countess, Lafew, and the King matters in the final scene of *All's Well* because
their kindness assures that experience can lead to maturity and some measure
of wisdom. Although one can exaggerate the somberness of the play by
quoting the King's early speeches out of the context of his despairing illness,
it is not a very dark comedy. But it is clearly a "later comedy," one that is
linked in various ways to *Twelfth Night* and *Measure for Measure* and that
anticipates the poignant interdependence of youth and age in the last of the
comedies.[10] In the late romances Shakespeare will recapture the radiance of
youthful love that is absent in *All's Well*, but he will never again make the
trials and rituals of wooing the central theme of comedy. Like *All's Well*,
Cymbeline and *The Winter's Tale* will deal with the violent shattering of a
marriage bond and the slow painful process by which a husband redeems
himself after the betrayal of his wife.

12

Cymbeline

Cymbeline is for most readers a puzzling and unsatisfying play. Its tone is often uncertain, its plot changes shape and direction abruptly and arbitrarily. It has some remarkable characterizations and a few marvelous scenes, but many of its dramatic figures are vapid or unconvincing, and some of its scenes almost ludicrous. Although it deals with the clash of mighty nations and with a struggle for power that touches the throne of Britain, it is not, as the First Folio would have it, a tragedy. The deaths of the Queen and her son Cloten are cause for general rejoicing, and the play ends happily for all the major characters after many trials and hairbreadth escapes from catastrophe. It is also not a comedy in any ordinary sense, although it ends happily, because it contains only one unmistakably comic scene, that between Posthumus and a Jailer who seems to have learned his trade from Pompey and his philosophy of life and death from the Clown who brings Cleopatra a basket of figs. Other apparently serious moments are likely to provoke laughter either because they are too preposterous to be taken at face value or because, as in the final scene, Shakespeare seems to wink at the audience and invite it to enjoy a deadpan parody of Fletcherian plotting at its sensational worst. But though *Cymbeline* draws to a farcical conclusion, it began, I think, as a serious experiment in the mode of Fletcherian tragicomedy, one that taught Shakespeare how to adapt Fletcherian theatricality to nobler artistic purposes. Indeed, for all its flaws, *Cymbeline* merits critical attention because it directly foreshadows the daring treatment of sexual jealousy in *The Winter's Tale*.

One can only speculate, of course, about Shakespeare's artistic intention in *Cymbeline*, because its historical-tragical-pastoral-lyrical plot is neither unified nor coherent in effect. Its first two acts unfold a drama of false accusation and sexual jealousy that rivals the finest scenes in *Othello*. As the third act begins, however, this taut drama begins to unwind, and its moral realism gives way to melodramatic fantasy.[1] The improbable becomes ordinary, coincidences multiply, and sober characters turn giddy and unreliable. Peripeteia piles on peripeteia as the major figures escape the frying pan of mortal danger only to fall into the fire of imminent execution, from which they are rescued at the last moment by a final extraordinary twist of fate or turn of event. Like Fletcher's tragicomic heroes and heroines, they are accomplished equilibrists who, swaying on the high wire of thrilling adventure, seem always about to fall but reach the safe platform of a happy ending clasped in each other's arms.

Although critics will continue to argue about Fletcher's influence on Shakespeare, there is to me irrefutable evidence that Shakespeare was trying his hand at Fletcherian tragicomedy because the borrowings from and imitations of *Philaster* in *Cymbeline* are specific and explicit.[2] The vapid Cymbeline resembles none of the monarchs who appear in earlier Shakespearean plays, but he is remarkably like the cardboard king of *Philaster* and has the blustering emptiness of the king in *Henry VIII*, a play that is more Fletcherian than Shakespearean in temper.[3] The loutish Cloten, who makes Caliban seem like a thing of beauty and grace, has no analogue in Shakespearean drama but is almost a twin to the coarse lustful Pharamond of *Philaster*, who also is a suitor for the king's daughter. Closer still is the resemblance of Posthumus to Philaster: both are orphans exiled by the king; both are victims of febrile imaginations and strained sensibilities that provoke them to attempt the murder of the innocent women who love them. The first two acts of *Cymbeline* have the moral and psychological seriousness of other Shakespearean plays; the remainder of the play takes place in a Fletcherian never-never land, where rude mountaineers have a princely grace and a Roman general picks posies to adorn the grave of a man he has never seen.

It is not surprising that Shakespeare would be fascinated by Fletcher's sophisticated stagecraft and attempt to adapt Fletcherian romance to his own more elevated artistic purposes.[4] What is baffling is Shakespeare's willingness to mimic the unreality of Fletcherian romance in the latter half of *Cymbeline* and his decision to parody its theatricality in a dramatic conclusion that abandons all pretense of artistic seriousness. None of Fletcher's tragicomedies are as badly flawed because he never allows his attention to wander from his goal of fashioning a fluent and exciting plot. His plays are as skillful as they are empty of meaning, meretricious but artfully constructed to keep the attention of a not-too-demanding audience. At first the Fletcherian echoes in *Cymbeline* are relatively unobtrusive. One notes an uncharacteristic self-consciousness and artificiality in the opening dialogue between unnamed Gentlemen at Cymbeline's court, who embroider their speech with parentheses and circumlocutions. It is the style that Osric tries to imitate and that seems to the modern ear arch and overrefined. One gentleman describes Posthumus as a paragon of men. Another objects, "You speak him far." The first continues:

> I do extend him, sir, within himself,
> Crush him together rather than unfold
> His measure duly.
>
> (1.1. 25–27)

The figure of speech barely escapes preciosity; it takes the measure of a man the way a tailor unfolds a bolt of cloth for a customer's inspection. Where the choric speeches of *All's Well* set forth an ideal of aristocratic virtue and courtesy, the choric dialogue of these Gentlemen introduces us to a world of aristocratic snobbery in which rank and name are all important but which lacks a genuine standard of noble behavior. Although the Gentlemen see how Imogen is wronged by Cymbeline and is threatened by the Queen and Cloten, they will not speak out on her behalf or hazard any opposition to the abuses they describe. They speak of Imogen and Posthumus only in whispers, and they are amused rather than disgusted by Cloten's animality, which they make the subject of their witty asides. These Englishmen are not blunt and outspoken in the way of a Faulconbridge or a Kent; their sotto voce mockeries are almost Italianate, closer in temper to Jachimo's sophisticated manner of speech than to the simplicity and directness of the decent Pisanio.

The blurring of moral attitude and atmosphere at Cymbeline's court is made necessary, in a sense, by the blurred characterization of the King. If none of Cymbeline's followers attempts to enlighten him about the wickedness of his queen, it is perhaps because her wickedness is so blatant that only someone as obtuse as Cymbeline could fail to see it. He rails at Posthumus's baseness but he is blind to the grossness of Cloten, and he seems incapable of recognizing the nobility of Imogen, at whom he hurls his small arsenal of nearly inarticulate vituperation: "O disloyal thing. . . . O thou vile one! . . . Thou foolish thing! . . . away with her / And pen her up . . . let her languish / A drop of blood a day, and being aged, / Die of this folly." Such is the King's affection for his only child, and such is the usual form of his speeches, which are made up of expletives and seriocomic fulminations that out-Capulet Capulet. Although he is the titular hero of the play, he is too blank to play a major role in the dramatic action. At best he is capable of expounding conventional patriotic sentiments, but his political convictions are shaped by his wicked consort and do an about-face at the conclusion.

The supreme figure of *Cymbeline* is Imogen, who, disguised as a boy, wins the instinctive worship of the princely Guiderius and Arviragus and the admiration of Jachimo as well as Lucius. She has dared her father's wrath to marry Posthumus and she accepts her loneliness and abuse without regret or self-pity. Lacking the precocious wisdom and ironic insights of earlier heroines, she is more vulnerable in her innocence than most of them. Her gravity is almost childlike but it is allied to a strength and clarity of vision that makes her the noblest figure at Cymbeline's court, for she is unwilling to cringe before his furies and unterrified by Cloten's animalistic wooing. Posthumus's character is less clearly etched before he falls victim to Jachimo's provocations and falsehoods. Cymbeline's gentlemen speak of his notable chivalry, and his love of Imogen is expressed in the brief scene of their parting. The full revelation of his character, however, comes only in his encounter with Jachimo, and there his salient traits seem to be egotism and rashness. There would be a similar problem in assessing Othello's character if it were mainly revealed in the scene in which Iago poisons his mind against Desdemona and Cassio rather than in the scenes in Venice in which he demonstrates his nobility of mind, self-control, and confidence in his beloved wife. Cymbeline's gentlemen, the good Philario, and Imogen's devotion testify to Posthumus's worth, but what we see in him is immaturity and an appalling willingness to help Jachimo attempt Imogen's chastity.

Where Imogen stands apart from the sophisticates at court in her clear-spirited innocence, Posthumus is very much of their temper and a distant relation of such Fletcherian heroes as Philaster and Amintor.[5] He lacks Jachimo's cynical worldliness, but he is a gentleman among gentlemen, ready to boast of his lady's incomparable virtues as Hector does in *Troilus and Cressida* when he makes Andromache the theme of his chivalric challenge to the Greeks. His vulnerability is different, then, from that of Claudio, who is uncertain of his judgment of women, and from that of Othello, who is an alien in Venetian society and ignorant of its ways. He is sensitive to any slight and too ready to accept a challenge because he has an uncertain status in a world where rank is paramount. Exiled from Britain for having presumed to marry a royal princess, he cannot bear any suggestion that he is an upstart. He will prove himself noble and worthy of a king's daughter even if he must wager on her fidelity as a wife. Jachimo is not an Iago smarting at his lack of recognition or his inferior rank. He is every inch the well-born courtier, who sneers at Imogen for taking a beggar for husband and at Posthumus as one who is admired because of his marriage. Where Posthumus seems not very different from Laertes or other headstrong gallants in Shakespeare's plays, Jachimo is a very original portrait of a courtliness that is at once refined and debased. He is not an antique Roman like his countryman Lucius; he seems, rather, a compatriot of Machiavelli but his arrogance will not allow him to pretend a false friendship when he sets about to destroy Posthumus's faith in Imogen. His manner is immediately provocative and he makes clear his desire to bait this parvenu. In the Boccaccian tale that served as a source for *Cymbeline*, the challenger is contemptuous of women and their pretenses to virtue; he knows that all of them are weak and pliant and will fall if solicited. Jachimo is more vain about his seductive powers than cynical about women. His target, moreover, is Posthumus, not Imogen. A jaded sophisiticate who has seen all and believes in almost nothing, he is irritated that a fool like Posthumus should be so certain of his wife.

The good-hearted Philario sees that Jachimo is goading Posthumus and tries to end the discussion of women. Posthumus also sees that Jachimo means to bait him and agrees:

Sir, with all my heart. This worthy signior, I thank him, makes no stranger of me: we are familiar at first.

(1.4. 100–102)

But Jachimo presses home the attack, sneering at Posthumus's confidence and boasting that he would attempt any lady in the world. In Boccaccio, the husband, enraged by the cynicism of the braggard, proposes the test of his wife's chastity. Posthumus is, superficially at least, in control of himself when he agrees to Jachimo's wager. His pride and honor as a gentleman are at stake; he has been challenged and must accept even though the trial risks his wife's integrity and his marriage. At first he would wager anything except the ring that Imogen gave him as a token of her love, but he submits when Jachimo calls this scruple "fear." After all, what is aristocratic confidence without a show of negligent disdain for the possibility of losing? Deaf to Philario's good counsel, Posthumus is obsessed with his reputation and blind to the shamefulness of exposing his wife to the importunities of Jachimo, whom he will recommend to Imogen with a personal letter. The gentleman's code demands that he give Jachimo a sporting chance, and besides, he knows that Jachimo cannot succeed. Or, rather, he does not see how he could lose whatever the result. If by chance Jachimo should seduce Imogen, he will take nothing of value from Posthumus because such a wife was not worth the whistle to begin with. Thus Posthumus promises that if Jachimo succeeds he will no longer be an enemy because Imogen will not be "worth our debate." If Jachimo fails, however, he will have to answer to Posthumus with his sword for his slander of Imogen and his assault on her chastity. There's honor for you!

It is necessary for Iago to keep telling himself and others that Desdemona can be seduced even though he knows that she is chaste. Jachimo does not lie to himself about Imogen. He sees immediately her rareness and for a moment is tempted to give up his venture but decides that audacity may work. Utterly without vanity, she cannot be moved by his rapturous praise of her beauty, and she is too pure-minded to catch the filthy insinuations that Posthumus is wallowing in lust, especially when those insinuations are expressed in such affected hyperboles:

The cloyed will—
That satiate yet unsatisfied desire, that tub

> Both fill'd and running—ravening first the lamb,
> Longs after for the garbage.
>
> (1.6. 47–50)

Still she listens anxiously to the slander of Posthumus, for it comes from one who knows her husband well and whom her husband calls of "noblest note." She is, moreover, so unaware of her beauty that she had wanted Posthumus to swear at their parting not to betray her with the "she's" of Italy. Fearing that he might "forget Britain" in Rome, she does not pay attention to the coarseness of Jachimo's description of Posthumus's supposed debauchery, his slavering

> with lips as common as the stairs
> That mount the Capitol; join gripes with hands
> Made hard with hourly falsehood (falsehood, as
> With labor); then by-peeping in an eye
> Base and illustrious as the smoky light
> That's fed with stinking tallow: . . .
>
> (1.6. 105–10)

When he finally comes to the point and proposes that she take her revenge by sleeping with him, she knows at once that he is a scoundrel and is ready to expose him to Cymbeline. She cannot resist, however, his swelling praise of Posthumus, for whom, he says, he made this test of her loyalty. Like a cat, Jachimo is agile enough to land on his feet, and he is also shrewd enough to know that he will never corrupt her. To win his gentleman's wager he will have to obtain seeming evidence of Imogen's "looseness" by treacherous means.

The scene in which Jachimo emerges from a trunk to gaze at the sleeping Imogen is so close to fairy tale that one wonders at first why Shakespeare chose to stage it rather than have Jachimo report it as Borachio describes the window scene in *Much Ado*. The answer, I imagine, is that this scene has the emotional and thematic significance of the willow song scene in *Othello*, which makes unforgettable Desdemona's innocence just before she is murdered by Othello. Jachimo does not crow over his clever strategem; his soliloquy is an awed response to the sleeping Imogen's beauty:

> Cytherea,
> How bravely thou becom'st thy bed! fresh lily,
> And whiter than the sheets! That I might touch!
> But kiss, one kiss! Rubies unparagon'd,
> How dearly they do't! 'Tis her breathing that
> Perfumes the chamber thus. The flame o' th' taper
> Bows toward her and would under-peep her lids

To see th' enclosed lights, now canopied
Under these windows, white and azure lac'd
With blue of heaven's own tinct.

(2.2. 14–23)

Only a villain of refined sensibility could respond to Imogen with such lyric grace. Here is the first instance in the play of an almost metaphysical yoking of contrarieties—of naturalness and artificiality—that will recur in later scenes and in the comedies to follow. The note of wonder struck here will sound again in the mourning of Guiderius and Arviragus over the body of Imogen, and it will return, transmuted, in Florizel's admiration of Perdita and in the wondering responses of Perdita and Leontes to the statue of Hermione in *The Winter's Tale*. The eroticism of Jachimo's desire to touch, kiss, and possess Imogen's beauty is subdued to a connoisseur's admiration for a perfection that is beyond artificial adornment: her lips beggar the price and redness of rubies; her breath perfumes the chamber, her eyes are very heavens. The familiar hyperboles of praise give Jachimo's soliloquy a consciously literary flavor and thereby call attention to the transmutation of Petrarchan clichés. This peeping tom is not excited sexually by the nearness of Imogen's beautiful body; like the taper's flame that bends to underpeep her lids, he is a silent worshipper, and she is the glorious sun toward which even a candle bows and yearns. She is another Juliet but he is not Romeo: he savors the freshness of the lily he intends to sully. Indeed, his sensitivity to Imogen's beauty will serve his villainous purpose because he will remember all he sees and use it to hoodwink Posthumus.

Jachimo thinks of Tarquin as he approaches the sleeping Imogen because his gaze is a rape of beauty that will make her like Philomel, of whom she has been reading, a victim of male brutality. A more immediate threat appears in the next scene, in which Cloten comes to woo Imogen with an aubade. His grossness is both the antithesis of Jachimo's sophistication and its complement. His instructions to the musicians make palpable and reduce to obscenity the sensuality implicit in Jachimo's soliloquy: "Come on, tune. If you can penetrate her with your fingering, so; we'll try with tongue too." Following directly upon this coarseness, the beauty of "Hark, hark the lark" is another "metaphysical" surprise because the song is very sophisticated in sensibility, completely innocent in attitude. Its lyricism is stylized if not artificial; it describes what is fresh and bright in nature as if it were being recreated by a master craftsman in fabric and metal. The chaliced flower is a blossom delicately woven in a tapestry. Phoebus and his steeds have the beauty of figures chased on a gilt bowl; they are as diminutive as butterflies that sip from dew-drenched flowers, as gleaming as a polished surface of silver and gold. The wonder of ancient myth is recaptured and Englished in the thrilling ascent of the lark, which sings its song at heaven's gate, high above an imaginary landscape where drovers awake at dawn to water their teams before the day's work begins. The unadorned beauty of wildflowers is exalted in the description of "winking Mary-buds" whose "golden eyes" are as precious as any treasure fashioned out of bullion by the goldsmith's art.

As soon as the song ends, Cloten reminds us of the ugliness of a world in which he is a king's favorite:

> If this penetrate, I will consider your music the better; if it do not, it is a [vice] in her ears, which horsehairs and calves'-guts, nor the voice of the unpav'd eunuch to boot, can never amend.
>
> (2.3. 27–31)

Although he is coarser than dirt, Cloten has the attributes of the courtier that Touchstone and Autolycus catalog: he games, swears, drinks, quarrels, wears his clothes badly, offers bribes, and shows his aristocratic arrogance in despising Posthumus as "a base slave, / A hilding for a livery, a squire's cloth, a pantler." The vehemence with which Imogen defends Posthumus against Cloten's insults makes all the more terrible his readiness to believe she is a whore in the scene that immediately follows.

The fact that Posthumus is separated from Imogen makes Jachimo's task of defaming her a bit easier than the task Iago faced; but Jachimo, one feels, could handle Othello as well as Posthumus because he knows, like Iago, how to tantalize his victim, how to make him eager to hear the worst about his cherished wife. He does not enter gloating of his victory; he praises Imogen's beauty in an offhand way and gives Posthumus some letters but refuses to broach the subject of his venture. When Posthumus asks, he boasts of the sweet night he spent in Britain for which he deserves Posthumus's ring. Iago would have embroidered his story with a few obscene details— how Imogen put her leg over his, or embraced him and kissed his inner lip. The more refined Jachimo does not, like Iago, enjoy inflicting pain; it is enough for him to win the wager by duping Posthumus with his tissue of lies and scraps of evidence. He begins with the flimsiest proof of his success, a description of Imogen's bedchamber, knowing that Posthumus will be a bit rattled by it but not convinced. Information of this kind can be obtained in various ways. As he describes very minute details of the room, however, Posthumus must grant that Jachimo was in the bedchamber, and afterward Posthumus is on the defensive and almost prepared to surrender when Jachimo produces the "ocular proof" of Imogen's unchastity—the bracelet that he took from her while she slept. Philario suggests that the bracelet might have been stolen by a suborned waiting woman, but Jachimo can earnestly protest that he had it from Imogen's arem.

When Othello's faith in Desdemona is shaken, chaos comes again in his uncontrollable rages and fits of irrationality. The degradation of Posthumus is more gentlemanly and decorous. He and Jachimo debate the chastity of Imogen with ironic politesse, with many "sirs" interposed in their speeches. Since Imogen fears that Posthumus can be seduced by the she's of Italy, it is understandable that he may fear she will not remain faithful to a husband exiled for life. Is is appalling, however, that he can imagine her submitting to someone like Jachimo. He knows Imogen well enough to be certain she will not lose the bracelet he gave her; therefore, his twisted logic proceeds, she must have given it away when she made love to Jachimo. Because he can still recall her loving nature, he must now conclude she is a whore, especially when Jachimo can describe the curious mole under her breast. Thus the discovery scene of antique romance and Renaissance comedy is turned seamyside out, and handy-dandy the matchless wife is revealed as a common slut. After the intense anxiety of this encounter, Posthumus almost rejoices in the sickening lie that ends all doubting. Like Claudio and Othello before him and Leontes after him, he relishes his discovery of the true nature of this seeming innocent, so much so that he would kill Jachimo if Jachimo tried now to change his story.

Because he is more knowing, more sophisticated than Claudio and Othello, Posthumus's vulnerability is a fascinating revelation of the ambivalence of men toward the sexuality of women. He can license Jachimo's attempt on Imogen because in the great world women must, for courtesy's sake, accept the gallantries, even the importunities, of men but not surrender their bodies to anyone but their husbands. They should be soft, delicate, alluring, and also chaste as ice; once they fall they sully forever the innocence that makes them goddesses and are no different from the rankest punk who sells her wares in public. Thus Posthumus can treat courteously the man he believes seduced his wife because the "honest" Jachimo has merely freed him of illusions. Very like Troilus, who cries out self-pityingly against Cressida, Posthumus rages at the memory of how Imogen restrained his sexual advances with seeming modesty when she must have submitted to Jachimo's boarish lust like a sow in heat. The Imogen Posthumus imagines is the eternal whore of male pornographic fantasies, as innocent in appearance as a child, as abandoned in her lust as the most practiced sensualist.

Jachimo's descent to outright villainy is not surprising. Posthumus's fall is astonishing because he not only believes Jachimo's lies but also plans a cowardly villainous revenge on his faithless wife. It would be logical enough for him to hurry back to England to play a "closet scene" or a "brothel scene" with Imogen. But no, he will not confront her or punish her with his own arm. He decides upon a revenge that makes Othello's strangling of Desdemona seem almost honorable by comparison. Imogen will be murdered without being accused and given any opportunity to refute the charges. Posthumus will lure her to her death by the lie that he has returned to England. Knowing that this whore will risk all to see him again, he is certain she will follow Pisanio to some remote place where he can murder her and escape suspicion. Nothing in Posthumus's soliloquy at the end of his second encounter with Jachimo anticipates this Italianate treachery, which violates the integrity of Posthumus's character by suddenly transforming him into a giddy Fletcherian hero who, lacking any moral or psychological stability, is ready here to plot Machiavellian murder and ready there to kill himself out of remorse.[6] As Pisanio reads Posthumus's instructions at the opening of act 3, the dramatic action of *Cymbeline* suffers a sea change. Although Pisanio's decency saves Imogen from Desdemona's fate, it does not save the plot of *Cymbeline* from melodramatic extravagance, for Imogen turns theatrical and self-dramatizing at the knowledge of Posthumus's murderous purpose. Before, she seemed simplicity and honesty incarnate, a character incapable of exaggeration or affectation. Now she waxes operatic in a longing to end her wretched existence. That she is suddenly weary of living is plausible, but her insistence that Pisanio prove himself an honest servant by murdering her rings false. It is the kind of posturing that abandons all pretense of emotional reality but is common in Fletcherian tragicomedy.[7] One moment Imogen is sickened by the false accusations laid against her; the next moment they infect her reason because she demands that the noble Pisanio turn villain—an impossibility—and she calls him coward when he refuses:

> Why, I must die;
> And if I do not by thy hand, thou art
> No servant of thy master's. Against self-slaughter
> There is a prohibition so divine
> That cravens my weak hand. Come, here's my heart:
> Something's [afore't]. Soft, soft, we'll no defense.
> Obedient as the scabbard. What is here?
> The scriptures of the loyal Leonatus,
> All turn'd to heresy? Away, away,
> Corrupters of my faith! You shall no more
> Be stomachers to my heart.
>
> (3.4.74–84)

Imogen's scruple against self-slaughter is ludicrous given her desire to die by Pisanio's hand. Her discovery of Posthumus's letters next to her heart is almost comic but not as sentimental as her self-pitying Fletcherian death wish:

> Prithee dispatch,
> The lamb entreats the butcher. Where's thy knife?
> Thou art too slow to do thy master's bidding
> When I desire it too.
>
> (3.4.95–98)

Rescued from such attitudinizing by Pisanio, Imogen disguises herself as a boy to escape the court and hopes to find refuge in the service of the Roman general Lucius. The way to the Roman army leads through a mountainous neverland in which Guiderius, Arviragus, and Belarius live like noble savages. In this enchanted country almost anything can happen. Although disguised as a boy, "Fidele," Imogen turns into Snow White, happens on the mountaineers' cave, eats their food, and falls asleep. What Shakespeare intends in this fairy tale pastoral is not quite clear, but he does not make a joke of the pastoral as Fletcher does in describing Philaster's desire to find refuge in a simple rural existence:

> Oh, that I had been nourish'd in these woods
> With milk of goats and acorns, and not known
> The right of crowns nor the dissembling trains
> Of women's looks; but digged myself a cave
>
> . . . .
> And then had taken me some mountain-girl,
> Beaten with winds, chaste as the harden'd rocks
> Whereon she dwelt, that might have strew'd my bed
> With leaves and reeds, and with the skins of beasts,
> Our neighbors, and have borne at her big breasts
> My large coarse issue! This had been a life
> Free from vexation.
>
> (4.2.38–50)[8]

Guiderius and Arviragus are set apart from all others by their instinctive, unsophisticated nobility. Ignorant of their royalty, they are more kingly than Cymbeline—and more intelligent. Belarius would have them rejoice in a low content; he tells them of the tawdriness of court life, in which treachery and ingratitude thrive, but, like Orlando, they are not convinced that pastoral ignorance is bliss. They want to know more of life than a mountain cave and to learn more than the skill of the hunter. Belarius's descriptions of the cringing, corrupting, uncertain ways by which courtiers rise and fall provide the moral perspective that was absent in the scenes at Cymbeline's palace, but Belarius is a flawed moral chorus because he has taken a savage revenge on Cymbeline for the wrong he suffered by stealing the King's sons and depriving Britain of its royal heirs.

The coincidence of Imogen's meeting with her brothers is as gratuitous as it is improbable. The meeting does not affect the outcome of the play to any degree and it does not add an emotional resonance to the denouement, in which they meet again. Indifferent to the larger design of his play, Shakespeare seems to have no purpose other than to experiment with lyric effects, and the experiments are themselves puzzling in their incongruities. To Arviragus and Guiderius, Fidele is wondrous, a "fairy: this angel, earthly

paragon, divineness / No elder than a boy." Despite the rudeness of his
unlettered existence, Arviragus is capable of a poetic response to Fidele that
is as exquisite as Florizel's response to Perdita:

> Nobly he yokes
> A smiling with a sigh, as if the sigh
> Was that it was for not being such a smile;
> The smile mocking the sigh, that it would fly
> From so divine a temple to commix
> With winds that sailors rail at.
>
> (4.2.51–56)

For the sake of such lyricism Shakespeare piles improbability on improbability. Imogen sickens, takes a restorative given her by Pisanio, who
had it from the Queen, who intended to poison him, but the poison was
tempered by the suspicious Physician so that it produces only a deathlike
trance. All this romantic filagree of plot exists so that Fidele can fall into a
trance so deep that her companions think she has died and mourn her in a
scene of exquisite lamentation. In their ritualized expressions of grief,
Belarius, Arviragus, and Guiderius cease to be individual characters and are
so many antiphonal voices of choric sorrow:

> *Arv.*   The bird is dead
> That we have made so much on. I had rather
> Have skipp'd from sixteen years of age to sixty,
> To have turn'd my leaping time into a crutch,
> To have seen this.
> *Gui.*   O sweetest, fairest lily!
> My brother wears thee not the one half so well
> As when thou grew'st thyself.
> *Bel.*   O melancholy,
> Who ever yet could sound thy bottom? find
> The ooze, to show what coast thy sluggish [crare]
> Mightst easil'est harbor in? Thou blessed thing,
> Jove knows what man thou mightst have made; but I,
> Thou diedst, a most rare boy, of melancholy.
>
> (4.2.197–208)

Since Belarius, Arviragus, and Guiderius are not realistically drawn—they
are storybook figures, noble attitudes rather than dramatic personalities—
they fall easily into the role of choric voices.[9] Their mourning is formal and
stylized and thereby distanced from immediate anguish. The brothers are as
solemn as children conducting a funeral service for a bird that is to be buried
in the back of a garden. "With fairest flowers," Arviragus says,

Whilst summer lasts and I live here, Fidele,
I'll sweeten thy sad grave. Thou shalt not lack
The flower that's like thy face, pale primrose, nor
The azur'd harebell, like thy veins; no, nor
The leaf of eglantine, whom not to slander,
Outsweet'ned not thy breath.

(4.2.219–24)

This lyric simplicity is the antithesis of Jachimo's sophisticated rhetoric, but like Jachimo, Arviragus plays tribute to Imogen's beauty with conceits made conventional by Elizabethan love poets: no flower that blows is as exquisite as the garden in Fidele's face. Like "Hark, hark, the lark," the great dirge that is recited over Imogen's body owes its mysterious exaltation to metaphysical wit: its simplicity is very artful and its unclouded vision of life is at once very direct and uncomplicated and compounded of worldly ironies:

Fear no more the heat o' th' sun,
Nor the furious winter's rages,
Thou thy worldly task hast done,
Home art gone, and ta'en thy wages.
Golden lads and girls all must,
As chimney-sweepers, come to dust.

(4.2.258–63)

The humor of the dirge is tender and affectionate. It rejects all high-sounding talk of the meaning of life and death. The moralist warns that the wages of sin is death, but here the quiet of the grave is a reward for a life well lived, a release from restless striving and vain ambition, a refuge from arrogance, envy, and malice. The great lady who masked her delicate cheek against the sun need not fear for her complexion in the shadow of death. The chimney sweep, used to dark cramped spaces, need not shudder at his meeting with dust. The beggar and the king take equal wages when they return to the clay from which they were made.

The sublimity of the funeral scene ends when Imogen awakes beside Cloten's headless corpse. If a momentous symbolism inheres in the tableau of bodies on stage, it is confused by and lost in the contrived grotesquerie of Imogen's awakening, which is almost a parody of Juliet's discovery of Romeo's body in Capulet's tomb. For one agonized moment, she might mistake the headless corpse dressed in Posthumus's clothes for her husband. The next moment, however, she must recognize that the brutish body is Cloten's, not Posthumus's, especially since she makes a limb-by-limb examination of the corpse (while an audience inevitably titters) and finds here the shape of Posthumus's leg, there his hand, "his foot Mercurial, his Martial thigh, / The brawns of Hercules." Either this is a Shakespearean attempt at ironic comedy or a Quincean attempt at tragic pathos. "Damn'd Pisanio hath," she thinks,

> From this most bravest vessel of the world
> Strook the main-top! O Posthumus, alas,
> Where is thy head? Where's that? Ay me! Where's that?
> Pisanio might have kill'd thee at the heart
> And left this head on.

(4.2.317–23)

She falls on the body lost in grief, but recovers her composure as soon as Lucius enters. Without hesitation she invents a smooth tale about herself and her dead master that wins his immediate sympathy. Indeed, he is so moved by her pathos that, forgetting his Roman dignity, he volunteers to look for "the prettiest daisied plot" in which to bury the corpse. Roman generals should be made of sterner stuff, and Shakespearean heroines should be more familiar with their husbands' limbs.

Lest an audience have time to reflect on such events, Shakespeare quickens the tempo of his plot. In one scene alone Cloten is killed, Imogen seems to die, and the Romans land in Britain. In the next scene Cymbeline is dismayed by the invasion and unable to act without the counsel of Cloten and the Queen, who is maddened by her son's disappearance. Then Guiderius and Arviragus persuade Belarius that they should fight for the king who wronged him, and as act 5 begins, Posthumus enters, anguishing over a bloody handkerchief Pisanio sent him as proof of Imogen's death. Since a bracelet could convince him of Imogen's lustfulness, a bloody handkerchief is more than enough to persuade him of her death. His lamentations over the handkerchief, his apostrophes to Pisanio, Imogen, the Gods, and Britain, and his direct address to "you married ones in the audience" give his Fletcherian death wish a slightly comic aspect. Yet he has a clearer sense of his guilt than Othello, who thinks, like Claudio and Don Pedro, that he erred only in mistaking, and finds life unbearable only after he discovers that Desdemona was wrongly slain. Posthumus has the greater moral recognition that he had no right to murder Imogen, even if she had been unfaithful. Like Imogen he is unable to kill himself and therefore decides to seek death in battle against the Romans by suiting himself as a Briton peasant.

Posthumus's moral realization is as sudden and unexpected as his earlier descent to Machiavellian treachery. He sets forth on a pilgrimage of expiation that is a bit gratuitous because he is already penitent and that will lead to melodrama and muddledom as well as heroic exploits. His desire to die, moreover, runs counter to the tide of events that promises a happy ending. The Queen will join her son in death; Belarius, Guiderius, and Arviragus will join with Posthumus against the Romans, and all must meet on the field of battle. Having eliminated his most dangerous villains and redeemed his sinning romantic hero, Shakespeare decides to amuse his audience and himself by inventing complications that give the plot of *Cymbeline* the busyness of a French bedroom farce, in which one lover enters the closet while another knocks on the door and the jealous husband peers through the window. When Imogen joins the Romans, Posthumus leaves their side to fight among the Britons. Seeking only death, he is inspired by the bravery of Belarius, Guiderius, and Arviragus, and he joins them in defeating the Romans, who had routed Cymbeline's forces. After the battle it seems for a moment that Posthumus has transcended his death wish because he can speak only of the valor of the "old man and two boys" and the shamefulness of the Briton noblemen who fled from Roman swords. When his anger subsides, however, he feels no chivalric pride in his deed, only regret that he could not find death in battle. Still yearning to die, he decides to resume his Roman garb in hope that he will be executed by the Britons.

If the many disguises and exchanges of clothing in *Cymbeline* have a symbolic import, that import is too murky to decipher. When Jachimo is defeated in battle by Posthumus disguised as a peasant, he moralizes the event as only an inveterate snob would:

> The heaviness and guilt within my bosom
> Takes off my manhood. I have belied a lady,
> The Princess of this country; and the air on't
> Revengingly enfeebles me, or could this carl,
> A very drudge of nature's, have subdu'd me
> In my profession?
>
> (5.2. 1–6)

Since Posthumus is not "a very drudge of nature's," Jachimo's moral self-discovery is as misguided as it is fatuous, but that does not matter very much since few moments in the last act of *Cymbeline* can bear any close scrutiny. One of the most perplexing is the dream vision that appears to Posthumus on the eve of his execution by the Britons. The assemblage of ghosts, the ceremonial stage movements, and antiphonal speeches plagiarize and parody the dream visions that appear to Richard and Richmond in the penultimate scene of *Richard III*. Unlike the ghosts of Richard's victims, the ghosts of the Leonati have no clear dramatic function either as moral chorus or prophets. They are querulous complainers who would blame Jupiter for every mishap suffered by their family, including Posthumus's gulling by Jachimo. The Leonati, it would seem, do not believe in free will and moral responsibility for one's acts; they are also irreverent enough to mention various of Jupiter's pecadilloes when they ask him to stop tormenting "mortal flies." They suggest that he "With Mars fall out, with Juno chide, /

That thy adulteries / Rates and revenges." If that were not sacrilegious enough, they warn Jupiter that if he does not mend his ways, they will complain against him to the other gods "and from [his] justice fly." Understandably annoyed, Jupiter descends on an eagle's back and hurls a thunderbolt. He rebukes the hubris of the ghosts and tells them that "mortal accidents" are none of their concern. He also assures them that in this best of possible worlds calamity is a sure sign of divine favor:

> Whom best I love, I cross; to make my gift,
> The more delay'd, delighted.
>
> (5.4. 101–2)

Jupiter's explanation of the sweetness of adversity is not half as reassuring as the Jailer's following explanation of the benefits of hanging. His homily on the consolations of the gibbet echoes the ironic humor of "Fear no more the heat of sun":

> A heavy reckoning for you, sir. But the comfort is, you shall be call'd to no more payments, fear no more tavern-bills, which are often the sadness of parting, as the procuring of mirth. You come in faint for want of meat, depart reeling with too much drink; sorry that you have paid too much, and sorry that you are paid too much; purse and brain both empty; the brain heavier for being too light, the purse too light, being drawn of heaviness. O, of this contradiction you shall now be quit. O, the charity of a penny cord! it sums up thousands in a trice.
>
> (5.4. 157–67)

A good hanging, the Jailer suggests, prevents many a bad hangover. Who can dread the noose with such a comedian by one's side?

Summoned to Cymbeline's presence with the other Roman prisoners, Posthumus appears on stage with Imogen, Pisanio, and Jachimo, all of whom should recognize him despite his Roman uniform and by doing so bring the play to a happy conclusion. But too simple a recognition scene would make an obvious joke of the portentous dream vision. To prove that Jupiter works in mysterious ways, Shakespeare undertakes to out-Fletcher Fletcher in a tragical-comical denouement that has the flair of a gymnastic performance on the uneven parallel bars. Singly and in groups the characters are brought to the edge of doom only to be rescued at the last moment and then threatened again by extinction. First the Roman prisoners face execution; Imogen is spared on the plea of the noble Lucius, who assumes that his page will in turn beg for his life. No doubt she would if she did not suddenly gain the eyesight of an eagle and spot the ring she gave Posthumus on Jachimo's finger. "Your life, good master," she says, "must shuffle for itself." Questioned about the ring, Jachimo is incapable of a simple answer. He wishes to confess his villainy, but his "false spirits / Quail to remember"; he faints, he fails, he has just enough breath to launch into some fifty bravura lines embellished with digressions, parentheses, hyperboles, and compliments to Posthumus and Imogen that try the patience of his listeners. Ordered by Cymbeline to "come to the matter," he waxes more operatic. Ordered to speak "to the purpose," he says that Posthumus spoke of Imogen "as Dian had hot dreams" and staked his ring on her chastity "And would do so, had it been a carbuncle / Of Phoebus' wheel." Who could doubt such simplicity?

Like remorse, hyperbole is catching. Jachimo's extravagance inspires Posthumus to a grandiloquent confession of guilt and to call for immediate death in a manner that out-Philasters Philaster:

> O, give me cord, or knife, or poison,
> Some upright justicer! Thou, King, send out
> For torturers ingenious; it is I
> That all th' abhorred things o' th' earth amend
> By being worse than they.
>
> (5.5. 213–17)

He is so absorbed in expressing his grief for Imogen that when she tries to reveal herself to him, he strikes her down.[10] A true aristocrat, he will not have his histrionic guilt upstaged by a "scornful page" who wants a part in his melodrama. Pisanio revives Imogen, who accuses him to trying to poison her, a turn of events that makes Cymbeline cry out, "New matter still." The Physician rushes forth to explain about the potion; Imogen embraces Posthumus and kneels before her father. Soon the happiness of all will be trebled by the revelation that the two young heroes of the battle are the long-lost princes. Before that joyous moment, Shakespeare manages to fabricate one last crisis. When he admits that he slew Cloten, Guiderius is sentenced to death, but Belarius proves that he is Cymbeline's son by pointing to a mole on Guiderius's neck. That mole puts a new complexion on Guiderius's deed. Whereas a commoner would die for defending his life against a stupid son of a wicked queen, a king's son can kill as queen's son with impunity. Rank must have its privileges, Belarius implies, and undoubtedly Guiderius "is better than the man he slew." With these dangers passed, Imogen can save Lucius's life; Posthumus can reveal that he was the valiant peasant who helped defeat the Romans; and Jachimo can claim the death wish Posthumus relinquishes. If any doubt remains that this is comedy, the Soothsayer steps forward to misconstrue Jupiter's murky oracle with the aid of outrageous etymologies. Justifiably dubious, Cymbeline pronounces that "this hath some seeming." Inspired by this prophecy of peace and plenty, he decides to submit to the defeated Romans and pay them the usual tribute. He blames his defiance of Rome on his wicked queen, whom the heavens have punished. Earlier Cymbeline had seemed to gain some nobility as England's champion against the power of Rome, but the value of patriotism shrank in the battle scenes when the Romans showed themselves more civilized than most of the Britons. Now it seems right for Cymbeline to submit again to Rome because his royal abilities are questionable at best. Unable to see his queen's blatant evil, he was astonished by the Physician's report that she died horribly and confessed her hatred of her husband and her plots to poison him and Imogen. Another monarch might have begun to question his judgment at this point, but Cymbeline is unenlightened:

> Mine eyes
> Were not in fault, for she was beautiful;
> Mine ears, that [heard] her flattery, nor my heart,
> That thought her like her seeming. It had been vicious
> To have mistrusted her.
>
> (5.5. 62–66)

Fortunately, Cymbline's subjects are wiser and nobler than he; he is saved from ruin by Belarius and Posthumus, whom he had wronged and driven from his sight.

The silliness of the denouement of *Cymbeline* is far more ingenious and entertaining than the silliness of the denouement of *Two Gentlemen*, but it is not more artistically defensible, for in parodying Fletcherian tragicomedy, Shakespeare makes a joke of his own play. Yet he did not turn away from tragicomedy after *Cymbeline* as he turned away from prose romance after *Two Gentlemen*. He fashions a greater drama of false suspicion and murderous jealousy in *The Winter's Tale;* he transforms Posthumus's febrile self-dramatizations into Leontes' tormented delusions, and he reincarnates Imogen's grave beauty in Hermione and Perdita. He does not eliminate the muddle of *Cymbeline* in *The Winter's Tale;* rather he turns what is meretricious in the former into what is mysterious and sublime in Leontes' guilt and spiritual pilgrimage. He aims again at the theatrical in the conclusion of *The Winter's Tale* and achieves it greatly in the statue scene that brings Hermione "back" to life. Even Fletcher must have been awed by this bit of Shakespearean alchemy.

13

The Winter's Tale

It was not too long ago that critics explained *The Winter's Tale* as the work of a Shakespeare who had all but retired from the stage and indulged his poetic fancies and love of fairy tale at the expense of dramatic coherence and psychological verisimilitude. Just how this Shakespeare, dreaming away his afternoons in the garden of New Place, managed to create the highly disciplined dramatic structure of *The Tempest* these critics do not say. It is always possible, of course, that he pulled himself together after the self-indulgence of *The Winter's Tale* and paid strict attention to the unities in *The Tempest* to atone for a ramshackle plotting that allows sixteen years to elapse between the close of the third act and the start of the fourth. It is now generally agreed that *The Winter's Tale* is a masterpiece of Shakespeare's artistic maturity, one that enlarges our awareness of the possibilities of dramatic form by seeming to ignore its necessities—indeed, by committing the sins against common sense that Sidney held up to ridicule in his *Apology.* No doubt the rambling incoherence of most pre-Shakespearean plays made some Elizabethans long for the decorums stipulated by neoclassical theorists. Yet the instinct of the popular dramatists to ignore those decorums was largely correct, as any comparison of Elizabethan academic tragedies to those of Shakespeare, Marlowe, and Kyd will testify.

Although *The Winter's Tale* is daring in its conception, it is not a tour de force that artfully disguises its improbabilities and failures of coherence. An audience does not have to make allowances for its supposedly splintered dramatic action, because the play coheres in performance. Only in a study does the passing of sixteen years between the third and fourth acts seem a violation of artistic unity that is clumsily excused by a doddering Father Time, who informs the audience that he can do what he pleases with chronology. It is worth remembering that the dramatic fable of *The Tempest,* that paradigm of artistic unity, encompasses some twelve years in the lives of Prospero and Miranda, almost as many as pass in the dramatic fable of *The Winter's Tale.* The artistic unity of *The Tempest* does not depend on the fact that its playing time is identical to the time that elapses in its dramatic action; it depends on a conviction that the history of Prospero's exile is complete and coherent, that we know "all" that has happened to him on the island as well as the events that occurred in Milan for which he now seeks some form of retribution. Just as *The Tempest* convinces us that nothing has been arbitrarily omitted or passed over in the lives of its characters, so too *The Winter's Tale* convinces us that it encompasses the entire drama of Leontes and Hermione's lives even though its plot skips over sixteen years and temporarily changes its focus from Sicily to Bohemia. Unlike Greene's *Pandosto*, which tells of the reunion of the King with the daughter he tried to kill many years before, *The Winter's Tale* tells of the reunion of Leontes and Hermione, who are the preeminent figures of the last scene, as they are of the first three acts.

Shakespeare could have handled the plot of *The Winter's Tale* as he handled the plot of *The Tempest* by presenting on stage only the scenes of act 5 and by allowing his characters to sketch in the history of past events through dialogue and soliloquy. To do so, of course, he would have had to sacrifice the drama of Leontes' tyranny and the poetry and humor of the sheepshearing feast. He would also have had to burden the audience with expository speeches much longer than those that make Miranda's eyelids heavy. Even then it is doubtful that any expository narration could capture the moral and psychological nuances of Leontes' self-delusion. It is ironic that some critics complain of Shakespeare's indifference to psychological verisimilitude in the depiction of Leontes' jealousy, when he devotes three acts of *The Winter's Tale* to tracing that obsession from its first faint stirrings to its full-blown horror. More than in any earlier play, the emphasis falls here on the irrationality of sexual jealousy. Leontes is not victimized, as Claudio, Othello, and Posthumus are, by deception, insidious suggestion, and seeming "ocular proof" of his wife's adultery. No subtle villain poisons his mind, torments him with doubts about his manhood, or dares him to face the truth about the wanton he loves. Without provocation of any kind, Leontes convinces himself that the chaste Hermione is a hobby horse ridden by his childhood friend Polixenes. Once the delusion becomes fixed in his mind, no denial or appeal to reason can move him. He does not, like Othello, murder his innocent wife, nor is he guilty of Posthumus's treacherous plotting, but his intent is more heinous than theirs. Were it not for the opposition of his courtiers he would have sent his infant daughter and wife to the stake. Because of his murderous rage against Hermione, his son sickens and dies; his infant daughter is abandoned to the elements on a distant shore, and his wife apparently dies of the shock of her son's death. And yet Leontes seems to us a far nobler figure than Claudio or Posthumus, one whose anguished pilgrimage of remorse ends, not in Posthumus's histrionic self-accusations, but in an almost saintly humility and loving care of others.

In the first scene, Leontes seems one of those specially favored by the gods. His kingdom is peaceful, his courtiers honest and devoted to him. His young son is the joy of his life and his gracious wife is big with their second child. His boyhood companion Polixenes has remained in Sicily for nine months, although his duties as king of Bohemia and his love of his young son beckon him home. Unlike Claudio, who is inexperienced in love, and unlike Posthumus and Othello, who must be uncertain of their place in their societies, Leontes has no uncertainty of self or of place that would make him vulnerable to false suspicion. He is not, like some of Fletcher's heroes, an emotional weathervane that swings wildly as he imagines some disloyalty or nurtures some fantastic misconception about those he knows best. Although Emilia shrewdly observes that jealousy needs no cause and feeds on its own suspicions, it is not an inexplicable delusion, a virus that suddenly infects the mind. Iago's brilliant manipulations might not succeed if Othello had not already been angered and perhaps a bit shaken by Cassio's dereliction. Like Othello, Posthumus is somewhat vulnerable because he is newly married and no sooner married than separated from Imogen, whom he may never see again. Leontes, on the other hand, has been married for years and knows his wife as Othello and Posthumus do not. Nothing in Hermione's and Polixenes' behavior attracts attention, much less suspicion. She is never coquettish with Polixenes, he never gallant in Cassio's fashion with her. They are fond of each other but clearly they are drawn together by their mutual love of Leontes. Hermione never speaks to Polixenes except to ask about her husband, and she does not slight Leontes by allowing Polixenes to engross her conversation. Thus Leontes' jealousy does not spring from some imagined slight or petty misunderstanding; it comes into being very suddenly as a tumultuous conviction of Hermione and Polixenes' adultery.

Leontes is not an enigma for scholars who believe that Elizabethan dramatists were uninterested in psychological motivation and aimed at the creation of striking theatrical situations, not at the revelation of the human heart. They can erase any problem of critical interpretation by demeaning Shakespeare's artistic intention and achievement—by turning him into a more artful Fletcher—but their reductive assumptions cannot explain why a Shakespeare uninterested in the psychology of sexual jealousy should treat it at length in so many plays. If Shakespeare lacked psychological insight or interest, he would have provided some obvious if mistaken reason for Leontes' jealousy: Greene does so in *Pandosto* by emphasizing the intimacy of the king's wife and friend. Or he would have made Leontes' jealousy plausible by depicting him as insecure and suspicious by nature, too ready to find an insult or innuendo in an innocent remark. Where other Elizabethan dramatists customarily simplify and externalize the motivations of their characters, Shakespeare again and again makes the motivations of his characters more oblique and mysterious than they are in his source materials. It is not the absence or vagueness of psychological revelation in Shakespeare's characterizations that challenges us, but rather the profundity and seemingly contradictory nature of his depiction of motive and emotional response. No explanation is possible or needed for Cymbeline's failure to see the blatant evil of his queen because he is a cardboard figure; his obtuseness is simply a donné of plot. Leontes is a fully realized character, however, and his jealousy is projected in hundreds of lines; indeed, it is as fully represented as is Hamlet's spiritual malaise in the scenes that lead up to the killing of Polonius. Freudian critics argue that these extended revelations of a character's thought and emotion are merely the tip of the iceberg of personality, the data which can be used to infer necessarily hidden or unconscious motivations. Hamlet, they explain, suffers from an oedipal fixation that makes him unable to kill Claudius while his mother lives; Leontes, they surmise, suffers from a homosexual panic and tries to repress his sexual attraction to Polixenes by imagining that Hermione desires him.[1] Since it is impossible for an audience to grasp Hamlet's oedipal fixation or Leontes' homosexual panic from the lines which Shakespeare wrote, the Freudian solutions are not relevant to the plays as works of dramatic art, although they may point toward the psychological intuitions that underly Shakespeare's conception of these characters.

If the oedipal theory of Hamlet is correct, there can be no resolution of his tragic angst, no possibility of personal illumination or transcendence, because he does not know what torments and paralyzes him. Similarly, if Leontes' jealousy of Hermione is a displacement of his repressed homosexual attraction to Polixenes, it is a subject for clinical diagnosis and expert therapy, and as such it lies outside the realm of moral judgment. Yet the play allows no extenuation of Leontes' guilt as a behavior which he cannot control. Leontes never attempts to explain or justify his acts as the result of delusion or madness, and at every moment the emphasis falls on the moral repugnance of his deeds, which are so terrible that only a lifetime of remorse can suffice for their expiation.[2]

Leontes' tyrannical behavior would be easier to explain if he were an autocrat like Lear or a blusterer like Cymbeline. Hermione is not afraid of her husband's moods or accustomed to obeying peremptory commands. She is frank, playful, often teasing with him in their first scene together. His courtiers, though sophisticated in speech, are unlike the witty sotto voce mockers of Cymbeline's retinue. Accustomed to speaking their minds freely to the king, they openly oppose his vicious purposes and are not cowed by his threats. That he has such a wife and such courtiers is evidence enough of his fundamental decency. Nevertheless he is the kind of person who is determined to have his own way. Although Polixenes has put aside his royal responsibilities and personal attachments to stay in Sicily, Leontes is not grateful or sympathetic to Polixenes' longing to return to his kingdom and son. When he importunes Polixenes to stay longer, it is not because he cannot bear to part with his company; it is because he wants to prevail in this contest of wills. Since Polixenes has been in Sicily nine months, it is childish to insist he stay another week or day, but Leontes will have him stay and is annoyed that Polixenes reasonably and affectionately refuses. Although not a bully by nature, Leontes is one of those who measure the affection of friends by their willingness to be imposed upon.

Leontes' first words to Hermione are somewhat petulant. "Tongue-tied, my queen?" he asks, as if she were remiss in not badgering Polixenes. Wise and gracious, Hermione gives Polixenes a perfect excuse to return home—the love of his son—but offers that if he stays another week, she will let Leontes stay a month longer in his royal visit to Bohemia than custom dictates. When he agrees to stay, she does not crow over her success but immediately changes the subject by asking what Leontes was like as a boy, what pranks he and Polixenes were guilty of. Polixenes remembers their boyhood as a time of innocence when they could not even imagine how to be bad: they knew not the doctrine of doing ill and suspected evil in no one. One doubts the accuracy of the report, but given the nature of the world in which we live, a nostalgia for the paradise of childhood, like the dream of Edenic innocence, is necessary and precious. Polixenes laughingly suggests that Hermione and his wife played Eve to their Adam, tempted them to love and desire and thereby made them fall. Hermione will accept the blame if Polixenes will swear that he and Leontes slipped with no one else.

Throughout this conversation Leontes is silent, perhaps distracted by an attendant or some court affairs, but he half-attends, half-hears the joking about sexual innocence and guilt. When he rejoins the conversation it is to ask the brusque question "Is he won yet?" His choice of words makes clear his view that this is a contest of wills, and therefore his pleasure in getting his way is spoiled by the fact that Hermione gained the victory. "At my request," he says, "he would not." Here is the first small, understandable pinch of jealousy; although Polixenes is his boyhood friend, he surrendered to Hermione's entreaty. The "winning" of Polixenes reminds Leontes of his courtship of Hermione, when he sued to her for "three crabbed months" before he "could make her open her white hand," an unpleasant metaphor that makes her hesitation seem like niggardly denial, and her acceptance of him a physical surrender. Where he had to beg for her love, she was willing to entreat Polixenes to stay, and she succeeded where he failed.

Up to this point, Leontes seems a bit restless, somewhat insensitive and childish in his annoyance at Hermione's success. His sulky resentment would probably pass except for the coincidence of Hermione and Polixenes' joking about sex. Theirs is an open good-humored bantering, the kind that is possible when men and women speak as friendly equals without conventional priggery or fear of innuendo. Such moments are rare because the wise world does not believe in friendship between men and women; or rather it is inclined to believe that a married woman will have such "friends" as Lavatch describes to the Countess in *All's Well*. To be sophisticated, after all, is to have few illusions about men and women but not to be liberated from anxiety about sexual fidelity, for the sophisticate is alert to the possibility that a touch of a hand, a smile, a murmured conversation may be the outward shows of a cleverly concealed adultery. For a moment, Leontes (and perhaps many other men) could suspect that his wife and best friend are playing a subtle game to deceive him; the next moment, common sense and trust in those one loves should prevail over this ugly conjecture. It does not prevail, however, because the thought of such a betrayal is immensely disturbing, almost physically distressing, to Leontes. He *feels* it sickeningly in the pounding of his heart; therefore, it must be real. Although he is too rational simply to give in to fantasy, the effort he has to make it push it aside and smile and converse with others makes him wonder what others are pretending at that moment, what faces his wife and friend are putting on to mask their deeper emotions:

> Too hot, too hot!
> To mingle friendship far is mingling bloods.
> I have *tremor cordis* on me; my heart dances,
> But not for joy; not joy. This entertainment
> May a free face put on, derive a liberty
> From heartiness, from bounty, fertile bosom,
> And well become the agent; 't may—I grant.
> But to be paddling palms and pinching fingers,
> As now they are, and making practic'd smiles,
> As in a looking-glass; and then to sign, as 'twere
> The mort o' th' deer—O, that is entertainment
> My bosom likes not, nor my brows!
>
> (1.2. 108–19)

He tries to be reasonable, to tell himself that Hermione and Polixenes' friendliness may be innocent, but their innocence is only one possibility now, and a tenuous one that does not ease his acute distress. In one sense Leontes' self-dramatizing soliloquies and asides are like the overwrought speeches of Posthumus and Jachimo in the last act of *Cymbeline*. But Leontes is never merely theatrical or ludicrous; where Posthumus and Jachimo's operatic emotionality is a parody of Fletcherian attitudinizing, Leontes' surrender to delusion is an absorbing portrayal of the acute self-consciousness that fastens on imagined overtones and insinuations. Once the thought of cuckoldry enters his mind, he can find a hint of horns in every casual thought, so that the mere act of wiping his son's nose leads to a play on the word "neatness."[3] He sees his features in his son's face; he knows that

Mamillius is a collop of his own flesh, and yet his delight in his son is poisoned by the possibility of Hermione's infidelity. Now he finds a bitter pleasure in seeing through the cunning shams of women, who say that he and Mamillius are "almost as like as eggs; women say so, / That will say anything." He gives in to obsession at least half-aware that it is obsession, but he must tell himself that he is dealing with reality or acknowledge that he is losing himself in disordered fantasy, and that is too frightening to allow. What he "affects" must be true—it must be, even though he knows that affection (i.e., passion) makes possible "things not so held,

> Communicat'st with dreams (how can this be?),
> With what's unreal thou co-active art,
> And fellow'st nothing.
>
> (1.2. 139–42)

At first Leontes' fantasy is disarmingly comic. Rejoicing in his Machiavellian mastery of the situation, he will stealthily observe the adulterers, who think he suspects nothing. He enjoys a private game of word play and punning that hints at and conceals his masterful game of cat and mouse. He sends Hermione and Polixenes to walk in his garden, admonishing her to "let what is dear in Sicily, be cheap." He adds:

> To your own bents dispose you; you'll be found,
> Be you beneath the sky. *[Aside.]* I am angling now,
> Though you perceive me not how I give line.
> Go to, go to!
> How she holds up the neb! the bill to him!
> And arms her with the boldness of a wife
> To her allowing husband!
>
> (1.2. 179–85)

This is not Othello's heroic passion; he does not strike his hand against his heart and feel the pain, nor does he anguish at the pity of it. His fantasy is closer at this moment to Posthumus's absurd dream of Imogen and Jachimo making love over the sty. Yet such a fantasy of barnyard copulation would be too gross for Leontes, who appeals directly to the audience for understanding and sympathy, convinced that many who are watching him are familiar with his predicament and can appreciate the delicacy with which he describes it: For everyone "plays" and plays various roles to hide the fact of their "playing."

> There have been
> (Or I am much deceiv'd) cuckolds ere now,
> And many a man there is (even at this present,

> Now, while I speak this) holds his wife by th' arm,
> That little thinks she has been sluic'd in s'absence,
> And his pond fish'd by his next neighbor—by
> Sir Smile, his neighbor. Nay, there's comfort in't,
> Whiles other men have gates, and those gates open'd,
> As mine, against their will.
>
> (1.2. 190–98)

There is even a comic shrug of the shoulders in this soliloquy, a resigned awareness that there is "no barricado for a belly," which will "let in and out the enemy, / With bag and baggage."

In most Jacobean plays adultery has a decadent hothouse flavor; it is part of the rankness of courtly life that is fed by luxury and sensual indulgence. Leontes' fantasies of country matters are uniquely pastoral; in his mind adultery has a fresh rosy complexion, as befits an outdoor sport and rural pastime. His rage at Polixenes is that of a petty freeholder who bites his lip when his aristocratic neighbor assumes the right to fish in his private pond. The sheer number of allusions to rural life in the dialogues at Leontes' court is remarkable, given the subjects being discussed. References to horses and riding, to barns and stables, drainage ditches and sluices, eggs, hens, lambs, and heifers abound. Thus the sophistication of language at Leontes' court is never as brittle as the courtly dialogue of *Cymbeline*. The recurrent allusions to farms and farm animals create the impression that just outside Leontes' palace is a countryside as rural as the coast of Bohemia, and that is only appropriate since Sicily was the original setting of the Greek pastoral.

Posthumus would cure the sickness in his heart by having Imogen murdered. Leontes would proceed more honorably against Hermione; although certain she is an adulterer, he wants confirmation of her guilt from others; he wants his courtiers to agree that he has been wronged and can justly take revenge. He has no doubt that they see what he sees, and he fears they are already smirking about his horns. How could they not see? How could they not smell the fault? He speaks to Camillo as if the sluttishness of Hermione were as blatant as the rancid odor of a whore. Once he grasps the import of Leontes' sneering insinuation, Camillo maintains Hermione's honesty in the face of hectoring abuse. His obstinacy infuriates Leontes, who will not be made a fool of by his courtiers as well as his wife. Either Camillo is obtuse or too crafty-ignorant to see the reason for Polixenes' willingness to stay. Surely, he thinks, Camillo must be smirking when he explains that Polixenes remains in Sicily "to satisfy your Highness, and the entreaties / Of our most gracious mistress." "Satisfy / The entreaties of your mistress?" Leontes asks, "Satisfy? /Let that suffice." Leontes' questioning of Camillo is very like Othello's questioning of Emilia about Desdemona, except that the Moor tells himself that he is seeking for truth even though he is already convinced of Desdemona's guilt. Leontes does not pretend to objectivity; he demands agreement with his version of the truth:

> Ha' not you seen, Camillo
> (But that's past doubt; you have, or your eye-glass
> Is thicker than a cuckold's horn) or heard
> (For to a vision so apparent rumor
> Cannot be mute), or thought (for cogitation
> Resides not in that man that does not think)
> My wife is slippery?
>
> (1.2. 267–73)

The rhetorical starts and stops, parentheses, and broken syntax of this speech are similar to the mannerisms of Jachimo's arias of remorse except that now these rhetorical mannerisms express the feverish self-consciousness of delusion. Since belief in Hermione's looseness has become the bedrock of Leontes' reality, he must cling to it at all costs. When Camillo protests that he would not tolerate this slander of his mistress from another person, Leontes presents his "evidence":

> Is whispering nothing?
> Is leaning cheek to cheek? is meeting noses?
> Kissing with inside lip? stopping the career
> Of laughter with a sigh (a note infallible
> Of breaking honesty)? horsing foot on foot?
> Skulking in corners?
> . . . .
> Is this nothing?
> Why then the world and all that's in't is nothing,
> The covering sky is nothing, Bohemia nothing,
> My wife is nothing, nor nothing have these nothings,
> If this be nothing.
>
> (1.2. 284–96)

The manic rush of these lines is frightening because Leontes is now inventing his reality with feverish words, not simply distorting the reality he sees and hears. At the same time, his obsession seems as childish as a temper tantrum. When Camillo will not accept his view of Hermione, Leontes replies:

> . . . you lie, you lie!
> I say thou liest, Camillo, and I hate thee,
> Pronounce thee a gross lout, a mindless slave.
>
> (1.2. 299–301)

He would have Polixenes murdered, but he cannot broach the matter without making the assassination sound more like a practical joke than a heinous crime. Since Camillo can see "plainly as heaven sees earth and earth sees heaven" how his master is galled, he

> mightst bespice a cup,
> To give mine enemy a lasting wink;
> Which draught to me were cordial.

> (1.2. 315–18)

Whereas Pisanio's refusal to murder Imogen is an isolated instance of integrity in a world where men do not openly oppose the evils they see, Camillo's defense of Hermione is the first ripple of a swelling tide of moral opposition to Leontes' tyranny. His nobleman beg him to reconsider even though he warns that anyone who defends Hermione "is afar off guilty." One would stake his life that the Queen is spotless. Antigonus is so confident of Hermione's chasteness that he promises to geld his daughters before the age of fourteen if she be false; he will also pawn his life to save the infant Perdita from the fire. Unable to bully his courtiers Leontes is reduced to complaining that no one listens to him or respects his majesty. He has less success still in silencing Paulina, who brings him the infant daughter, the "bastard" he does not want to see or acknowledge as his own. Rebuked for letting Paulina come to the king, Antigonus replies that she is not one to be led by a bridle:

> When she will take the rein I let her run,
> [Aside.] But she'll not stumble.

> (2.3. 51–52)

The implication is that Paulina may be headstrong but she is not confused or blind. When Leontes sneers at Paulina's mention of the "good queen," she responds:

> Good queen, my lord, good queen, I say good queen,
> And would by combat make her good, so were I
> A man, the worst about you.

Leontes would have her thrust out with the bastard, but no man dares touch her unless he is willing, she says, to make "trifles of his eyes." So the would-be tyrant is reduced to blustering and name-calling:

> Traitors!
> Will you not push her out? Give her the bastard,
> Thou dotard, thou art woman-tir'd, unroosted
> By thy Dame Partlet here.

> (2.3.73–76)

If, as allegorizing critics suggest, Paulina's name has momentous significance, it is curious that she is not identified by name before the fifth act.[4] It is also odd that a supposed symbol of Christian otherworldliness should be so gruff and obstinately earthy. Like Hermione and the women around her, Paulina knows what it is to have given birth and nurtured children; it is inconceivable to her that Leontes will disown or seek to destroy his infant daughter. Her faith is not in things unseen but in Hermione's innocence. Certain of that obvious truth, she has no patience with the fanaticism and casuistries of men; indeed, her anger at Leontes has hardly a drop of Christian forbearance. The central issues of *The Winter's Tale* are not religious; what is at stake here, as in *Othello*, is human trust and confidence in the nature of another, the knowing that love affirms even though there is no possibility of absolute proof. Since men and women are fallible, love is an act of faith that can at times rightly be expressed in the language of religious conviction. When Brabantio hurls a parting insult at Desdemona, Othello stakes his "life upon her faith." When he turns unbeliever, Emilia stakes her hope of heaven on Desdemona's innocence and truth. No religious text is needed to gloss Emilia's or Paulina's love of their mistresses: they will not have an innocent woman maligned and brutalized by a man.

I suggested earlier that the horror which the Inquisition inspired among Elizabethans is relevant to the enforced baptism of Shylock. There are explicit allusions to that horror in *The Winter's Tale*. Threatened by Leontes that she will be burned, Paulina replies:

> I care not:
> It is an heretic that makes the fire,
> Not she which burns in't.
>
> (2.3.114–16)

Paulina summons up again the memory of the Inquisition when she enters with the news that Hermione has died:

> What studied torments, tyrant, hast for me?
> What wheels, racks, fires? What flaying, boiling
> In leads or oils?
>
> (3.2.175–77)

If this is hyperbole, so too is Leontes' fanaticism, which is born of a failure of belief, not an excess of conviction. The opposition of his nobles might reassure Leontes and provide a foundation on which he could stand again, but he will not retreat once his authority is challenged, whatever doubts he may begin to have about his "truth." So it is also with Creon in *Antigone*, whose determination hardens as others oppose him, because he must prevail in this struggle or be nothing.[5] In defense of his delusion Leontes marshalls

all his skill as casuist and all his sophistication with word and image.
Although he need not try to ensnare Hermione in legalisms, he plays the
brilliant attorney, intimidating, jeering, and twisting her every response. He
lives now in a world reduced to elemental truths: what he says exists;
nothing else is. Hermione says:

> You speak a language that I understand not.
> My life stands in the level of your dreams,
> Which I'll lay down.

He craftily retorts:

> Your actions are my dreams.
> You had a bastard by Polixenes,
> And I but dream'd it.
>
> (3.2.80–84)

He has sent to the oracle at Delphos, not because he is uncertain of his
judgment, but because he is certain that his truth and the oracle's will be
identical. When the oracle contradicts him, he must reject its lie even as
Creon rejects the advice of Teiresias. Yet the news that Mamillius has died
shatters Leontes' arrogance and he immediately confesses his sin. The
swiftness with which he surrenders suggests that his defiance required a
tremendous effort of will and there is immense relief, not tortured resignation, in his submission:

> Apollo's angry, and the heavens themselves
> Do strike at my injustice.
>
> (3.2.146–47)

  Leontes' sudden complete recovery is less surprising than the hysteria
with which Paulina announces Hermione's death, for up to this moment her
gruff simplicity had stood against Leontes' histrionic casuistries. Now
Leontes speaks frankly of his guilt and his desire to right the wrongs he has
done while Paulina is strident in her grief and accusations. As he grows
reasonable, she turns fanatical and shouts of wheels, racks, and fires, although she cannot really believe that the penitent Leontes will have her
boiled in oil or lead. Perhaps at the moment she does believe Hermione is
dead; in any event, she is determined, like Leontes, to impose her "truth" by
sheer insistence:

> I say she's dead; I'll swear't. If word nor oath
> Prevail not, go and see. If you can bring
> Tincture or lustre in her lip, her eye,

Heat outwardly or breath within, I'll serve you
As I would do the gods.

(3.2.203–7)

Her rage against Leontes is pitiless because she proclaims that his crime is
beyond the forgiveness of men or the mercy of the gods:

> . . . betake thee
> To nothing but despair. A thousand knees,
> Ten thousand years together, naked, fasting,
> Upon a barren mountain, and still winter
> In storm perpetual, could not move the gods
> To look that way thou wert.

(3.2.209–14)

Shocked by Paulina's bitterness, a courtier bids her say no more, and
immediately her hysteria subsides. She asks pardon for her folly and seeing
that Leontes is touched to the heart, bids him put this grief behind him:

> What's gone and what's past help
> Should be past grief. Do not receive affliction
> At my petition; I beseech you, rather
> Let me be punish'd, that have minded you
> Of what you should forget.

(3.2.222–26)

Her tone is gentle and forgiving but her advice is not practical; Leontes
cannot forget and should not forget. He must live with the realization of
what he has done, study to know himself, and gain what wisdom this bitter
knowledge can bring. The danger is not that he will soon forget but that he
will grow accustomed to self-lacerating remorse and substitute a fanatical
penance for his fanatical delusion; indeed, he promises to perform a daily
ritual of sorrow at Hermione's grave as his "recreation."

When Posthumus acknowledges his crime against Imogen, he begins his
pilgrimage of expiation. When Leontes admits his tyranny, he comes to as
full a recognition of his guilt as he will ever attain, one that is untainted by
theatrical posturing. Acknowledging the goodness of Hermione, Polixenes,
and Camillo, he accepts responsibility for the deaths of Mamillius and
Hermione. Unlike Posthumus, who melodramatizes his guilt to the last,
Leontes achieves genuine contrition at the moment he hears that his son is
dead, but that contrition is not enough to prevent continuing calamity.
Apollo is angry, and the heavens strike at his injustice, but the blows fall on
the innocent, not the guilty, and more guiltless lives will be lost on the
seacoast of Bohemia. The oracle is true, but it does not promise anything
except barrenness for Sicily unless the lost child is found.

The multiple calamities of the third act are stunning because an audience does not believe that Leontes will commit the terrible acts he threatens. His rage is often seriocomic, his evil purposes are opposed by his courtiers, and surely the oracle will establish Hermione's innocence. Yet the blows fall, perhaps have to fall to rid Leontes of his obsession. At the moment of catastrophe, moreover, there is assurance that simple decency matters in the grand scheme of things and can shape the course of the future. Antigonus's kindness costs his life, but his sacrifice is not in vain because Perdita is rescued by the Shepherd and his son. A balance is struck between lives lost and saved that is at once grotesque and sublime. The Shepherd's son describes the gruesome death of Antigonus and the drowning of the seamen; the Shepherd tells of the foundling babe, whose dowry is the fairy gold left with her by the shore. "Now bless thyself," he says, "thou metst with things dying, I with things new born." No one survives to tell Sicily that Perdita lives or to explain to Bohemians why the infant was abandoned in this way. Nevertheless the future of Perdita in Bohemia is also the future of Sicily, and in the fullness of time her destiny will converge with Leontes' and Hermione's.

When the Shepherds exit, Time walks out on stage to introduce act 4 and explain away the indecorum of letting sixteen years slip by between one scene and the next. He is not the best of casuists: his verse is a trifle halting, his statements a bit muddy, and his arguments unconvincing. In the course of centuries, Time may indeed overthrow civilizations and alter law and custom—who would deny the fact of mutability? But Time cannot alter its own nature: it cannot brush aside a decade or two because its minutes must follow one another as ceaselessly as the waves beat toward the pebbled shore. By presenting Time as a slightly doddering figure, Shakespeare suggests to his audience that no turgid sophistries are needed to justify the unorthodox plotting of *The Winter's Tale*. Indeed, he can use an inept apologist precisely because the design of his play needs no apology. His plot does not suddenly change course and begin again, as it were, in the fourth act in a new setting and with a new cast of characters. The movement from Sicily to Bohemia is accomplished before Time makes his entrance, in the scene in which the fate of Antigonus and the seamen is described by a Bohemian shepherd. The transition is effortless and seamless; while the dramatic perspective turns 180 degrees it does not seem to change at all. The countryside of Bohemia is not a strange new world like the forest of Arden in which shepherds are literary swains. The Shepherd enters muttering about the lecherous behavior of Bohemian youth, and his first thought is that Perdita is an abandoned bastard—some stairwork, some trunk work or behind-door work.[6]

When Polixenes and Camillo enter in the following scene, their wigs probably streaked with gray, they reenact a moment that occurred "sixteen years ago"—or rather that occurred perhaps an hour ago on stage at Leontes'

court. Then Polixenes wanted to return to Bohemia after a nine-month stay
in Sicily. Now, after years of exile, Camillo longs to return to Sicily to
comfort the penitent Leontes, who has sent for him. Polixenes is as stubborn
and selfish now in his desire to keep Camillo by his side as Leontes was in
trying to detain Polixenes. Camillo has become too useful, too necessary,
Polixenes claims, to be let go. Polixenes' insensitivity to Camillo's desire to
see Leontes again and die in his homeland reminds us that he can be as
peremptory as Leontes. Years ago in Sicily he grew furious when Camillo
hesitated to explain Leontes' frowns:

> How, dare not? Do not? Do you know, and dare not?
> Be intelligent to me, 'tis thereabouts:
> For to yourself, what you do know, you must,
> And cannot say you dare not.
>
> (1.2.377–80)

After so many years, he has not forgiven Leontes and has, it seems, no
compassion for Leontes' "feeling sorrows." He speaks sneeringly of "that
penitent (as thou call'st him)," as if he could not believe Leontes capable of
remorse. Where calamity has made Leontes humble and gracious, prosperity
has been less kind to Polixenes. He is as possessive of his son Florizel, on
whom he has set spies, as he is of Camillo. Like Leontes, he will angle: he
and Camillo will assume disguises to discover why Florizel spends so much
of his time at a shepherd's cottage.

Although Polixenes' wishes to gain "intelligence" of his son's behavior by
devious means, the expedition to a cottage has romantic overtones: the king
and his chief counselor will take a holiday from affairs of state to mingle with
ordinary Bohemians. They will be joined at the cottage by a more carefree
pretender, Autolycus, erstwhile servant of Florizel, who wins a haphazard
living peddling ballads and notions, cutting an occasional purse, and gulling
the country bumpkins. A born entertainer like Touchstone, he is too cowardly to rob and not especially greedy; he is not, therefore, very dangerous
to the commonweal. His wants are simple—a bit of ale, some dicing and
drabbing, some sheets to filch from the hedges, and some "aunts" to tumble
in the hay. It is now summer, a happy time for rogues and vagabonds, and
like all true pastoralists Autolycus refuses to worry about harsher weather or
reckonings: "Beatings and hanging are terrors to me; for the life to come, I
sleep out the thought of it." He will not find any banquet of venison in the
sheepcotes of Bohemia; its festive luxuries are homelier: saffron-colored
warden pies, mace, nutmeg, ginger, raisins, and prunes. At the sheep-
shearing feast no Amiens will sing art songs to the lute; instead there will be
country hays and peddler's songs, and new ballads guaranteed to astonish
and amaze rustic listeners.

Autolycus's taste for doxies is the kind of loose behavior that makes the Shepherd mutter about the younger generation. What we see of sexual desire and jealousy at the sheep-shearing feast is not very disturbing, however. At the worst some dresses are torn and some faces scratched, because country folk lack the sophistication that breeds prurient imaginings and egotistical rages in their betters. Although the Shepherd complains that young women "wear their plackets where they should bear their faces," a frank loving sexual impulse can be as chaste as Perdita's desire to cover Florizel with garlands of flowers

> like a bank, for love to lie and play on;
> Not like a corse; or if—not to be buried,
> But quick and in mine arms.
>
> (4.4.130–32)

At the beginning of the play Polixenes spoke of boyhood innocence as a paradise lost at the advent of sexual desire. Perdita's desire for oneness with Florizel is no less pure, however, than the childhood Polixenes sentimentalizes. Unlike the heroines of the romantic comedies, she does not joke about cuckoldry; she probably cannot imagine the possibility of adultery, and it would not occur to her to be coy about her love of Florizel. Totally unself-consciousness, she puts no store in cleverness, and like Imogen she is almost childlike in her gravity and in her clear direct response to others. It disturbs her to wear a festive gown as queen of the festival because she cannot bear an artificial showiness in herself or in the flowers she grows in her garden. Reared at court, Florizel is more sophisticated in speech but his loving delight in Perdita is expressed in a poetry unadorned by conceits or Petrarchan comparisons, indeed by adjectives of any kind. His is a lyricism of monosyllables even as her thought is simplicity incarnate:

> What you do
> Still betters what is done. When you speak, sweet,
> I'ld have you do it ever; when you sing,
> I'ld have you buy and sell so; so give alms;
> Pray so; and for the ord'ring your affairs,
> To sing them too. When you do dance, I wish you
> A wave o' th' sea, that you might ever do
> Nothing but that; move still, still so,
> And own no other function.
>
> (4.4. 135–43)

Florizel's joy gives phrases as flat and bureaucratic as "the ord'ring your affairs" the freshness of meadow flowers. Similarly the exuberance of the sheep-shearing feast assimilates the artifice of the court masque in an antimasque of satyrs performed by "three carters, three shepherds, three neat-herds, three swineherds that have made themselves all men of hair" (4.4. 324–26).[7] The dialogue is rich with Ovidian allusions but never learned; the only conscious verbal cleverness is the casuistic arguments that Polixenes musters against Perdita's distaste for flowers beautified by a gardener's skill.

Enchanted by Perdita, some critics would make her the supreme figure of the play, an incarnation of the power of rebirth and renewal that revives a desolate Sicily.[8] They forget that for three acts Hermione, big with child, is the embodiment of fertility and fruition[9] and that Paulina presides over the denouement as the surrogate of great creating nature, one who restores Hermione to Leontes and to life. Perdita is not a mythic figure but her unsophisticated response to the natural world does recapture the pristine wonder of seasonal change, the miracle of metamorphic renewal that ancient mythologies celebrated. Scientists explain that rising temperatures and lengthening days make daffodils sprout and birds migrate northward. Per-dita sees cause and effect differently; she knows that spring would not come into being if daffodils did not show their lovely faces and "take the winds of March with beauty." The taking of the wind is active as well as passive. The slender stems bow in the breeze, and by their grace and beauty make a loving conquest of wintry winds, warming and gentling them. What red and white can compare to the daffodils' amorous green? What blue-veined eyelid as sweet as violets dim?

Perdita's loveliness of mind and spirit is apparent to Polixenes, but he cannot accept a low-born country girl as Florizel's wife. When he casts off his disguise he blusters and threatens in the manner of the old Leontes but with more cause, for his son, Bohemia's heir, has denied the responsibilities of his birth. Asked why his father is not present at his plighting of troth, Florizel is pained and unable to give an honest answer. He knows, of course, that a nuptial is a public ceremony in which family, church, and state have a legitimate interest. For marriage demands the assumption of legal obliga-tions; it entails matters of dowry and estate, the hope of future heirs, and the continuance of society. No doubt Polixenes would have refused consent if asked by Florizel, but the fact remains that Florizel did not reveal his love to his father; and Polixenes, like Brabantio, is wounded and enraged by this lack of trust, this "betrayal." Once again Perdita might be the innocent victim of a king's tyranny, but Polixenes' threat to have her beauty "scratched with briars and made / More homely than thy state" is not very convincing; it associates royal tyranny with the other calamities that spoil picnics and festive outings: poison ivy, ants, thistles, and bad weather. Perdita is not terrified by the prospect of a cruel punishment; she knows that the King's sneers at churls and herdsmen are unworthy and she is tempted to remind him that "The selfsame sun that shines upon his court / Hides not his visage from our cottage." Her dislike for pretense prepared her for this moment because she never quite believed that she and Florizel could marry. Now that the dream is shattered, she'll "queen it no inch farther."

Once again it is Camillo's role to stand against royal tyranny and protect the innocent. He will guide the young lovers as sixteen years before he guided Polixenes away from Leontes' rage. Then he saved his own life in saving Polixenes; now he would satisfy his yearning to return to Sicily by counseling Florizel, who is determined to flee Bohemia, to seek refuge at Leontes' court. Florizel has a ship nearby but no plan or destination in mind. So long as he can be with Perdita, he is willing to be a slave of chance, a fly "of every wind that blows." With gentle irony, Camillo suggests that Florizel follow his direction—that is, if his "more ponderous and settled project / May suffer alteration." The symmetry of Camillo's roles in Sicily and Bohemia makes the memory of the past the guiding force in the lives of Florizel and Perdita even as later they will be the means by which the long winter of Leontes' sorrow will end. Their flight will be Camillo's homecoming and Florizel's denial of his father will be the means by which Leontes and his daughter are reunited. The young do not breathe new life into the old in *The Winter's Tale;* it is Camillo's desire for a small measure of personal happiness that shapes the destiny of Florizel and Perdita and finally enables Hermione and Leontes to live again in the world.

The gravitational pull of the past is strong enough to ensnare Autolycus, who, having exchanged clothes with Florizel, prevents the Shepherd and his son from informing the King about Perdita's childhood. He likes his former master and does not believe in aiding the authorities; besides, he finds profit on all sides. He has sold his ballads and trinkets, picked the rustics' purses, obtained rich garments, and now he has a prospect of bribes. Like Touchstone's explanation of the code of duello, Autolycus's satiric impersonation of a courtier is a prelude to the exiles' return to court. Like Touchstone he knows that courtliness is skin-deep: its proof lies in the cock of a hat, the cut of a doublet, the curl of a lip, the picking of a tooth. There are no truer evidences of courtliness than an overbearing manner and an outstretched palm. The Shepherd notes that Autolycus wears rich garments "but he wears them not handsomely." The Clown, more knowing about lordliness, remarks, "He seems to be the more noble in being fantastical. A great man, I'll warrant; I know by the picking on 's teeth." This comedy is not all fooling, because were it not for Perdita's infant garments, she would never be acknowledged as a princess despite her innate nobility.

Autolycus's clowning will be a welcome addition to Leontes' court, where time apparently stopped at the moment of Hermione's death. Sixteen years have passed and yet nothing seems to have changed in Sicily; the first scene of the fifth act seems a continuation of the discussion of Leontes' guilt and repentance that began in act 3, scene 2, when his lords rebuked Paulina for harping on the King's crimes. She is as fanatical as before in her devotion to the memory of Hermione and he is as obsessed with the horror of his guilt as he once was obsessed with the fantasy of Hermione's adultery. Now, as sixteen years before, Leontes' courtiers plead for an end to morbid dwelling on the past because the King's withdrawal from life threatens the well-being of Sicily. No choric exposition of past events is needed to bridge the gap between 3.2 and 5.1, because except for some graying of the characters, they are the same; the history of Leontes resumes without any sense of hiatus because now as before he is paralyzed by remorse. Only when Hermione steps down from the pedestal will he be able to escape the bondage of the past; only when she is restored to life will he live again in the present. His courtiers give practical reasons why the King must look to the future, but Paulina will not have it. The erstwhile apostle of common sense seems to have become the high priestess of a cult devoted to the worship of the martyred Hermione—a cult that has a shrine, a sacred statue, and a royal flagellant.

The metamorphosis of Paulina is more astonishing than the transformation of the ironic Beatrice into the unreasoning champion of Hero's wounded reputation, because Beatrice's rage against Claudio does not last, whereas Paulina's fanaticism only momentarily gives way to the courtiers' appeals in act 3 and apparently dominates her life afterward. Leontes' courtiers rightly argue that the King must marry again for his and the kingdom's sake but Paulina will not allow it. No woman, she claims, is worthy of taking Hermione's place; besides, a second marriage will not provide an heir to the throne, which will be barren, according to the oracle, unless the lost child is found. Yet even while Paulina cites the authority of the oracle, she admits that the prospect of the child surviving is dim, indeed, "monstrous to our human reason." Unlike Leontes' courtiers, an audience can appreciate the beauty of Paulina's devotion to Hermione and the poignant bond that now exists between her and Leontes. An audience may also perceive that Paulina speaks of Hermione not as a dead martyr but as a living beautiful woman. Had he listened to the good Paulina, Leontes says, he might even now "have look'd upon my queen's full eyes, / Have taken treasure from her lips—" and Paulina completes the thought, "And left them / More rich for what they yielded." Now the hinting of Hermione's survival begins, for Paulina does not insist that Leontes not remarry; she asks only that he not marry until she gives him leave, and then only if his new wife is "as like Hermione as is her picture." Cleomines objects, but Paulina continues and her hinting becomes more insistent:

> . . . I have done,
> Yet if my lord will marry—if you will, sir,
> No remedy but you will—give me the office
> To choose you a queen. She shall not be so young

As was your former, but she shall be such
As (walk'd your first queen's ghost) it should take joy
To see her in your arms.

(5.1. 75–81)

On the one hand, Paulina seems to avoid reality by insisting on things that are impossible or nearly so. On the other hand, she is very aware of practicalities; she accepts that Leontes must marry again—there is "no remedy" for him or Sicily but remarriage. Knowing that Perdita lives, we are ready to believe in possibilities that seem monstrous to human reason. If the oracle is true, then Paulina's prophecy may be no less true; there may be another woman as like Hermione as her ghost. The more Paulina speaks, the more evident it is that she is the voice of hope, not of despair; of love, not hatred. She would have Leontes hold Hermione again in his arms, and that can be only if he does not forget her and remains true to the anguishing memory of the past.

The memory of the past becomes more vivid and immediate when Perdita and Florizel enter. The joy of greeting Polixenes' son is bittersweet because Leontes must remember how he wronged Polixenes, and he speaks with feeling sorrow of the wife, son, and daughter he caused to die. If Shakespeare conceived of *The Winter's Tale* as a play in which the innocence of youth redeems the sins and ends the suffering of age, the arrival of Florizel and Perdita at Leontes' court would provide a satisfying conclusion, cast no doubt in the form of an extended recognition scene like those that end *All's Well* and *Cymbeline*. Imagine the lovers being welcomed and then their hopes dashed by the arrival of a furious Polixenes. The good Camillo will be accused of treachery by both Polixenes and the lovers, and the wrangling and recriminations will multiply until Autolycus enters with the shepherds and the proof that Perdita is Leontes' lost daughter. In an instant all animosities end, the characters embrace and rejoice in the prospect of a royal wedding that will unite Sicily and Bohemia. A recognition scene like this does take place, but not on stage; it is described to Autolycus and the audience by a courtier who was present. He reports that admiration and wonder grew as Leontes and Camillo gazed at each other, as Leontes greeted his daughter and begged forgiveness from Polixenes. He tells how Paulina locked Perdita in her embrace "as if she would pin her to her heart, that she might no more be in danger of losing."

Only an incompetent dramatist would withhold from an audience the joyous emotional resolution of his play. By reporting this discovery scene, not staging it, Shakespeare signals that the ultimate resolution of his play is yet to come.[10] Indeed, the reunion that is described is not one that ends emotional tensions, for the memory of Hermione is ever-present. Leontes, we hear, could not look at Perdita without remembering Hermione. Thus "being ready to leap out of himself for joy of his found daughter, as if that joy were now become a loss, [he] cries, 'O, thy mother, thy mother!' " We hear also that when Leontes "bravely confessed" how Hermione died, Perdita "did (with an 'Alas!'), I would fain say, bleed tears." By the time the account draws to a close, it is clear that this reported scene is only the prelude to another discovery scene, which will occur in Paulina's gallery. There all will see a statue of Hermione so lifelike that one might "speak to her and stand in hope of an answer." If an account of Hermione's death can make those most marble there change color, what will be their response to this miracle of art?

With hindsight one can point to the clues in Paulina's speeches that Hermione is alive, but acceptance of the ending of *The Winter's Tale* does not depend on a deciphering of her riddling statements. On the contrary, Shakespeare does not give away the surprise of the final scene because he wishes it to be as magical a moment for the audience as for those on stage. When Hero unveils herself in the last scene of *Much Ado*, only Claudio and Don Pedro are astonished at her resurrection. When Hermione's statue is unveiled, only Paulina knows that it is Hermione posed as a statue ready to descend from the pedestal. Yet the audience is not manipulated or deceived because the memory of Hermione pervades every scene of act 5. The wonder of her statue is redolent of pagan fable and Christian legend. Its immediate literary analogue is Ovid's tale of Pygmalion's statue; it also echoes medieval tales of religious statues that miraculously wept or bled or came momentarily to life. The religious aura of the statue scene for a time borders on superstitious veneration. The gallery is a shrine in which Perdita kneels and begs to kiss the statue's hand. Before she draws the veil, Paulina tells her visitors to prepare

> To see the life as lively mock'd as ever
> Still sleep mock'd death. Behold, and say 'tis well.
>
> (5.3. 19–20)

There is a tantalizing illogic and imprecision in Paulina's description. She should claim that the statue mimics life as death mocks sleep, for if the statue is to Hermione as sleep is to death, it must inevitably "awaken" to life. Paulina's lines make sense only if it is death, not life, that is being "lively mock'd"—by a woman pretending to be a statue. But then this monument to a dead woman refuses to acknowledge that she is dead, for it portrays Hermione as if she were alive now, sixteen years older than when she swooned at the news of Mamillius's death. Leontes is so moved by the sight that Camillo pleads with him to cast away his unnatural sorrow, and Polixenes begs to share some of the blame for his jealous acts. Paulina would draw the curtain again, but Leontes would stand and gaze forever because this affliction is as sweet as any cordial comfort.

Just as Paulina's description of the statue hints at its aliveness, Leontes and Perdita's responses create the expectation that the statue will move; indeed, it seems incredible that Hermione should stand as motionless as marble when her lips, eyes, flesh and veins are instinct with life—when she seems almost to breathe, for an air seems to come from her lips that no chisel is fine enough to cut. In the first scene of the play, Leontes recalled the three crabbed months he wooed Hermione before she agreed to be his wife; in the last scene, Hermione is the suitor. When she descends from the pedestal, she holds out her hands to Leontes, embraces him, and hangs about his neck. She is not miraculously restored to life; she has been preserved from death by an art "as lawful as eating."[11] She need not explain her sixteen years of seclusion: how could she look at the husband who wished her dead and whose tyranny destroyed her children? Only the hope that the oracle offered, she explains, made her preserve herself, and only when Perdita stands before her can she live again in the world as Leontes' wife. The miracle is not that Hermione lives but that she did not succumb to despair and that she is able to love Leontes as Perdita loves Florizel—as a wife loves a husband, not as a saint loves sinning mankind. If the story of Hermione's preservation were merely told, it "should be hooted at / Like an old tale." It is not told or reported, however; an audience sees her return to life and need not take anything on faith. To those ignorant of the rescue of the infant Perdita, her life is a miracle beyond reason. To those ignorant of Hermione's survival under Paulina's care, her life is also a miracle. By the time the play ends, however, the audience and those on stage know the human means by which these miracles were wrought and the cost of such miracles—years of loneliness and misery, and the sacrifice of the good Antigonus and those on his ship. Heavenly joy and sorrow mingle in the reunion of Hermione and Leontes as they mingle when Edgar reveals himself to the dying Gloucester in *King Lear*. Edgar's deception of his blind father, who thinks he has survived a terrible fall, is as "lawful" as Paulina's deception of her audience in the statue scene because both seeming resurrections testify to the miraculous powers of the human heart, to its strength to endure and not surrender to hopelessness or bitterness. In *The Winter's Tale* as in *King Lear* ripeness is all.

Confident of the artistic coherence and unity of his play, Shakespeare offers a last sly comment on its unorthodox time scheme in the conversation between Autolycus and the Clowns in act 5, scene 2. Who can doubt the plasticity of Time when a royal decree instantaneously transforms the Shepherd and his son into gentlemen born. For the low are not merely raised; rather their life histories are magically altered, their lineage retrospectively gentled by the breath of kings as so many lineages were (for a fee) in Shakespeare's days. If kings can tinker with what has been, surely play-wrights can pass over sixteen years in the lives of their characters without leaving a gap in the matter.[12]

14

The Tempest

It is impossible to ignore the special place of *The Tempest* in the Shakespearean canon. As the last play of Shakespeare's sole authorship, it has a particular significance, even a poignancy, for all who treasure his art, and some of its greatest speeches suggest that it may have had a like meaning and poignancy for Shakespeare when he wrote it. Nevertheless, the belief that *The Tempest* is Shakespeare's farewell to the stage rests on the slender evidence of two memorable passages very near its close. If these forty or so lines were intended to provide a clue to the play's essential meaning, they are too belated to serve their purpose in a theatrical production, and one must wonder why Shakespeare was willing to use his last play to make the kind of personal statement that cannot be found in any other. Apart from the brief reflection on his achievement in the history plays in the epilogue to *Henry V*, Shakespeare never calls attention to his role as dramatist in any play; he never chooses one character or another to be his spokesman or raisonneur. He may, of course, have made an exception to his artistic rule in a last valedictory work, but one must wonder, then, why a playwright whose gentleness was lovingly remembered by his colleagues should choose as his dramatic alter ego a cranky peremptory old man.[1] If Prospero is a self-portrait, it is a sly as well as unflattering one, a springe to catch sentimentalists and to baffle literary detectives bent on discovering the autobiographical significances of his art.

Attempts to convince us that *The Tempest* is Shakespeare's maturest statement on life and art only make it seem blurred and pretentious. It succeeds as fairy tale where *Cymbeline* fails because it creates a wholly consistent imaginative world; it does not intermingle realism and fantasy, moral drama and Fletcherian theatricality.[2] Caliban is more convincing than Cloten because he is not supposed to represent anything human. His lust for Miranda is neither coarse nor brutish, but rather the instinctive reproductive urge of a creature incapable of conscience and untouched by Cloten's licentiousness. There are some critics, of course, who would turn Caliban into Cloten by making him an allegorical representation of human animality, even though the play unequivocally declares him unhuman in birth and nature. Those who allegorize *The Tempest* seem to forget that allegory justifies its radical simplification of experience by a clarification and crystallization of essential truths, for their interpretations of the play make it seem as ambiguous as ink blots. What is to some an allegory of spiritual regeneration is to others an allegory of art; what some think is a drama of compassion, others consider an allegory of colonial discovery and exploitation.[3]

Although the allegorizers cannot agree, and their interpretations often seem cloudy, arbitrary, and overingenious, allegorical readings of *The Tempest* continue to appear because other critical approaches are not particularly rewarding. Character analysis is hardly appropriate to figures as slight as Ferdinand and Miranda, Alonso and Gonzalo. A discussion of theme is handicapped by the absence of moral and intellectual issues. To be sure, some critics speak of the conflict between vengeance and compassion in Prospero's soul, but it is clear from the outset that he does not intend to punish anyone, especially not Alonso, the father of the man he intends to be Miranda's husband. Although Prospero huffs and puffs and threatens dire retribution on almost everyone in the cast, we know there will be no perdition in a hair, not even the fading of a single doublet despite the drenching those on shipboard endure in the opening scene. For Prospero is not Hamlet or Posthumus or Leontes, though he may briefly enjoy the power he has over those who wronged him. The passing of years has blunted much of his rage, and he was never a man of action or one quick to strike out at others. Retiring in temperament as well as bookish, he has the powers of a Faustus and the reclusive instincts of a library researcher. He has Theseus' sobriety without his sense of humor and is comic only in his zeal to protect Miranda's virginity from the undangerous Ferdinand. A failed educator of Caliban, he has a desire for order that makes him a splendid timekeeper for the play, one who continues to remind the audience that the time which elapses in the plot is identical with the time that a performance of the play requires.

If it seems strange that the mighty magician of *The Tempest* should be reclusive and unworldly, it is stranger still that this most romantic of Shakespearean comedies, that includes in its dramatic fable a tempest, two shipwrecks, two murderous conspiracies, a monster, spirit, and host of magical spectacles, should also have a deliberately classical form and strictly observe the unities of time and place. Having endured (in silence, one imagines) Jonson's gibes about his implausible plots and want of art, Shakespeare demonstrates in his last work a mastery of the kind of dramatic structure that Renaissance literary theorists called ideal at the same time that he invents a plot calculated to set their classical teeth on edge. Or perhaps he simply pays an artist's tribute to Roman comedy in his last play as he did at the start of his career as comic dramatist by adapting *Menaechmi* in *Errors.* There is nothing Plautine, however, in the plotting of *The Tempest,* which lacks the busy complications, supposes, and confusions of Roman farce. Where the characters of *Errors* repeatedly bump into one another in the streets of Ephesus, each collision generating another bit of comic bewilderment or future wrangling, the characters in *The Tempest,* though marooned on the same island, remain in separate groups that come together only in the final scene. Ferdinand is the only one from the marooned ship to encounter Prospero and Miranda before the denouement. Trinculo and Stephano share a drunken adventure with Caliban that keeps them from meeting Alonso, Gonzalo, Sebastian, and Antonio, who are ignorant of Prospero's presence on the island and his control of events until he greets them in the last scene, dressed again as Duke of Milan. Thus Shakespeare accepts the formal discipline of Roman comedy without exploiting the kinetic energies of plot that customarily flow from that discipline,[4] and the unity of action in *The Tempest* derives less from its "classical" structure than from Prospero's domination of all the other characters.

Prospero's powers are formidable enough to ensure that nothing goes seriously or comically astray. Ariel watches over and frustrates Antonio and Sebastian's wicked conspiracy; Trinculo and Stephano are too liquorous to pose a threat to Prospero's well-being. The only danger he faces is the possibility that he may grow bored or careless in his mastery of others and forget what he has to do. Where Duke Vincentio of *Measure for Measure* must constantly alter his plans to cope with Angelo's unpredictable responses and connivances, Prospero knows his adversaries so well that he is never surprised by anything they do and he is never pressed to use the full scope of his power to achieve his ends. On the other hand, he does not attempt or accomplish as much as Vincentio, who masterminds an intricate denouement that stuns Angelo into repentance. Perhaps because he is still unreconciled to his failure to educate Caliban to moral responsiblity, he makes no serious attempt to reform Antonio and Sebastian while he thwarts their vicious schemes. They will not be moved to remorse by a disappearing banquet, and they do not hear the call to repentance in the billow's roar that Alonso does. In the final scene he is content to intimidate the conspirators by threatening to expose them if they should again plot any evil.

I do not mean to suggest that Prospero's powers of moral suasion should be as impressive as his feats of magic. A control of the elemental forces of nature does not imply a similar control of the working of the human heart or an ability to alter moral character. The climactic moment of the play comes not when Prospero provides a dazzling display of his magical powers but when he decides to abjure them. The more one ponders his magic, the more paradoxical seems its reach and limitations. Although he can raise a mighty storm at sea, he is apparently unable to free himself from his island exile. It is not altogether clear, moreover, whether in this instance he commands the forces of nature or merely commands the minds and imaginations of his adversaries. Either he raises a furious tempest at sea that wrecks Alonso's vessel, but he miraculously preserves it and all who sail on it from even the stain of salt water, or the storm and shipwreck are as illusory as the banquet that Ariel causes to appear and disappear.[5] Where Paulina's "magic" is nothing more than trompe l'oeil, Prospero can create the semblances of goddesses and spirits out of airy nothing; yet nothing in Prospero's repertory of magical effects is as stunning as the living statue of Hermione. Indeed, Paulina's faithfulness to Hermione and her unbending conviction that the lost will be found have more grandeur than Prospero's domination of the castaways. For hers is a devotion that transcends all claims of ego and rationality while his magic is a private intellectual pursuit that has no relation to other humans and no need of collaboration with anyone but Ariel.

Learned attempts to distinguish Prospero's "white" magic from Faustus's "black" magic seem gratuitous given the difference between Prospero's moral character and Faustus's.[6] There is no hint in Prospero of the sensuality and blasphemous pride that prompt Faustus to sell his soul. He was so little interested in worldly sway that he gave over the care of his dukedom to his treacherous brother. Years of exile and a mastery of magical arts have not changed his nature. Now as before he is accustomed to solitude and his quirks of personality—an irritability and readiness to hector those about him—are understandable in one who is growing old without the company of men and women of his age. He is not used to sharing his thoughts with any one, not even with Ariel, who carries out his instructions without knowing what the larger purpose is. Where Faustus is cut off from others by egotistic self-absorption, Prospero is inured to a brooding isolation, and he does not look forward to resuming the life of the court even as he prepares to return to Milan. Yet his essential kindliness is never in doubt, and his rejection of revenge is inevitable almost from the beginning.

For much of the play the role of Prospero does not make exceptional demands on an actor. If he has the presence and voice to play a great magus, he can master the part, which does not involve much in the way of psychological complexity or nuance. As the play draws to a close, the role of Prospero grows more challenging because the prospect of return to Milan makes him suddenly aware of his age and what he must relinquish to resume his place in society. Even then, the revelation of inner turmoil is very limited, and one is moved by the splendor and spaciousness of Prospero's visionary insight, not by the poignancy of his personal fate. The role of Miranda offers fewer challenges and rewards to an actor. The most childlike of Shakespeare's heroines, she is totally ignorant of the world, having known no human other than the father who has reared and protected her, and upon whom she is utterly dependent. Even so she is more vivid in her intensity of feeling than

Ferdinand, who is bland enough to play the romantic lead in any operetta or musical comedy. A few brush strokes suffice for Alonso and for the good-hearted garrulous Gonzalo, and not many more for Antonio and Sebastian, who are too languid in their depravity to chill an onlooker.

Not blatantly malevolent like Cymbeline's queen, they are something like the sophisticated gentlemen of Cymbeline's court, only they are complete cynics who have seen everything (and found it tiresome) and believe in nothing. Incapable of ordinary sympathy or any more exalted emotion, they are heartless to the grieving Alonso and vie with one another in baiting and belittling Gonzalo. Since Antonio has already betrayed his brother Prospero, it is not surprising that he would invite Sebastian to murder his brother Alonso while he undertakes to kill Gonzalo. Yet the casualness of their decision to murder sleeping men robs it of moral impact because they agree to the most vicious of acts as if they were deciding on a fashion for doublet and hose. Jachimo is coldly calculating in his assault on Posthumus, but he is not off-hand or casual in his villainy because he is determined to humiliate this upstart. Antonio and Sebastian, in contrast, seem congenitally incapable of intense emotion. They would be content, like the gentlemen at Cymbeline's court, to amuse themselves with clever asides about the fools around them; when the opportunity for treachery arises, however, they seize it without hesitation because they are conscienceless and as such capable of any atrocity. Their amorality would express the decadence of the court that created them if they were characters in a play like *The Revenger's Tragedy*. In *The Tempest* they are inexplicable figures—defectives rather than decadents or degenerates.

It is not easy to say what comment such languid villainy makes on the thirst for power, which is a continuing theme in Shakespearean drama. The murderous conspiracy has an almost dreamlike quality and no more chance of success than Trinculo and Stephano's inebriated plot to murder Prospero and possess his island. Such evil ambition is a joke only to a Lear not quite in his senses who thinks of it as a child's game of "who's in and who's out." It is no joke to Cordelia, who weeps because she knows that losing that game will cost their lives. *The Tempest* does not suggest a final indifference to politics or to the evil that ambition engenders. Prospero might prove a tyrant in the little world of his island if he enjoyed the exercise of power over those who wronged him, but the politics of revenge do not interest him any more than did the politics of Milan. Because Faustus is infatuated with the things of this world, he wishes to display his power at the courts of emperors and popes. Prospero's quest for supernatural power can be fully realized on his island because it has nothing to do with the prizes for which men compete and conspire. His realm is the elemental world of nature that drawfs ordinary human strivings. Faustus's achievements seem paltry at least in part because Marlowe's conception of the fabulous does not transcend the reports of exotic kingdoms and riches that travelers brought back to Europe from Asia and Asia Minor. Prospero's magic escapes these confines because Shakespeare's imagination reaches westward toward the undiscovered countries of the Americas, toward new found lands still unravaged by European greed and corruption. Thus Prospero's island, though supposedly located in the Mediterranean somewhere between Italy and Africa, seems to European eyes as strange and mysterious as the tropical islands of the Caribbean.[7]

For Europeans awed by the virgin beauty and fertility of the New World, the journey westward was like a journey backward in time to an age when England and Europe were still wilderness. They could see in the New World an image of what the Old World was like before populations expanded and forests were cut for timber and firewood, before fields and meadows were cleared and fenced in, and towns and cities began to dominate the landscape. Glowing accounts of noble savages, great forests and rivers, and exotic birds and animals inspired utopian dreams of a second chance—a new start—for a Europe ravaged by civil and religous warfare. Gonzalo can imagine a new commonwealth on Prospero's island in which men and women live as the myth of the golden age envisioned, without artificial laws or customs, on the abundance that nature provides. With rare exceptions, however, the voyages of exploration and settlement were not prompted by idealistic motives; they were commercial enterprises if not expeditions of plunder and exploitation.

For Prospero the island has not been a refuge or a "second chance." It has not made him one with nature or given him tranquility of mind. He and Miranda are strangers on this speck of land, dependent for their survival on the grumbling labor of Caliban, who showed them how to find water and gather food. He does not rejoice in an exile that keeps him from the malice and treachery of the court anymore than the crazed Lear rejoices in a return to nature that teaches him the brutishness of the natural order: Let copulation thrive, for the gilded fly lechers in his sight. Caliban's desire to populate the island by mating with Miranda is perfectly natural, although his attempt to force her sexually is horrifying by civilized standards. Just as the innocence of Arden is a virtue that the exiles from the court bring with their other baggage, Miranda's innocence is a result, not of a life lived according to nature, but of her inherent purity of spirit and Prospero's watchful care. He has kept her ignorant of the vices of civlization, so much so that he must assure her of a virtuous husband before they leave the island.

Having protected his daughter against Caliban's lust for so long, Prospero instinctively hectors Ferdinand on the need to respect Miranda's virginity as if the young prince were as ruttish as Bertram. But then he is unable to think of Miranda except as a vulnerable defenseless child even though he knows that she has grown into womanhood. He is not a possessive father who clings to the daughter who has been his only human companion for many years, and he is not an overbearing one who would dictate her choice of a mate. He arranges her meeting with Ferdinand but is content to allow them to fall in love while he pretends to scowl at Ferdinand and treat him as an enemy. The matchmaking is his last act as a parent and one that he performs, characteristically, without taking his daughter into his confidence. During all the years on the island, he has never shared his thoughts with Miranda, never thought of her as one in whom he might confide. Until the opportunity came to have his enemies at his mercy, he told her nothing of the events that brought them to the island, and when he does at last recount them, he puts her to sleep so that she will not know what he nows plans to do with the aid of Ariel.

Like Egeon's relation of his sorrowful past to the Duke of Ephesus, Prospero's account of the past to Miranda is a long, undramatic, and not very artful means of communicating information to the audience. Egeon's account of his lamentable history, as we have seen, necessarily precedes the farcical action of *Errors* and serves to deepen its emotional tone. Why the dramatic exposition of *The Tempest* must be delivered in one long harangue by Prospero is less easy to say because Shakespeare and Prospero know that this exposition is somewhat tedious. The latter keeps reminding Miranda to pay attention even though she claims that his tale could cure deafness. Of course, Shakespeare wisely opens his play with the excitement of the storm in which Alonso's ship seems to be foundering. Then the following scene in Prospero's cave is inherently interesting because it reveals that the fury of nature is at the command of a magician who is quite human in his frailties. He dwells on the wrongs that were done to him, but he does not see that in pursuing his "close" studies he shrugged off his obligations as a ruler. He is also ready to browbeat Ariel and Caliban when they object to their servitude or question him about their freedom. Unable to accept Caliban's unhuman nature, Prospero answers his grumbling with a stream of invective and threatens to torment him with stitches, cramps, and assorted afflictions.

If Ariel did not exist, Prospero's pettiness of temper would seem impossible in one who commands the elements. He transcends human limitations only through the services of Ariel and even then he remains earthbound while Ariel races with the wind. Ariel is not a Puck who has to be instructed carefully lest he make an error in carrying out his assignment, nor is he simply an instrument of Prospero's will. He is glorious in his own right, a creature who can sip nectar from a flower or join himself to wind, lightning, and rain, the forces that teach proud man what he truly is. He is also the nonpareil musician of the play and composer of the heavenly lyrics he sings. With sophisticated lighting, sound, and stage effects, modern productions of *The Tempest* can create an effective illusion of a storm at sea in the opening scene, but nothing in modern stagecraft can mimic Ariel's performance on shipboard:

> I boarded the King's ship; now on the beak,
> Now in the waist, the deck, in every cabin,

> I flam'd amazement. Sometimes I'ld divide,
> And burn in many places; on the topmast,
> The yards and boresprit, would I flame distinctly,
> Then meet and join. Jove's lightning, the precursors
> O' th' dreadful thunder-claps, more momentary
> And sight-outrunning were not.
>
> (1.2. 196–203)

The wonder here is the airy flight of language and image that makes Ariel seem a poet in thought and movement. He is less inspired when at Prospero's command he harangues his master's enemies in the shape of a harpy:

> You are three men of sin, whom Destiny,
> That hath to instrument this lower world
> And what is in't, the never-surfeited sea
> Hath caus'd to belch up you; and on this island
> Where man doth not inhabit—you 'mongst men
> Being most unfit to live. I have made you mad;
> And even with such-like valor men hang and drown
> Their proper selves. You fools! I and my fellows
> Are ministers of Fate. The elements,
> Of whom your swords are temper'd, may as well
> Wound the loud winds, or with bemock'd-at stabs
> Kill the still-closing waters, as diminish
> One dowle that's in my plume.
>
> (3.3. 53–65)

This has a grandiloquent, almost Chapmanesque ring. The style is conventionally elevated and conventionally rhetorical. There are no flights of metaphysical fancy, only commonplace epithets. The sea is "never-surfeited," the winds "loud," the waters "still-closing." The wonder of the natural world is reduced to literary abstractions, as it is again in the conventionalities of the masque Prospero creates for Miranda and Ferdinand. When Ariel speaks in his own voice, it is of the enchantment of yellow sands and oozy bottoms where the alchemy of sea change makes precious stuff of human bones and eyes. Years on the island have not made Prospero responsive to the beauty of a flower; he does not speak of the music of sea and wind; he does not respond poetically to what is lovely and mysterious in nature. It is Caliban's lines, not Prospero's, that unfold the magic of the island:

> . . . the isle is full of noises,
> Sounds, and sweet airs, that give delight and hurt not.
> Sometimes a thousand twangling instruments
> Will hum about mine ears; and sometimes voices,

That if I then had wak'd after long sleep,
Will make me sleep again; and then in dreaming,
The clouds methought would open, and show riches
Ready to drop upon me, that when I wak'd
I cried to dream again.

(3.2. 135–43)

Like Caliban Ariel cannot be tamed; he can be taught to obey commands but
he cannot be domesticated. It is his nature to be free; he loves his master and
is eager to please him and be praised by him, but he keeps reminding
Prospero of his promised freedom despite Prospero's shows of annoyance.

Through Ariel, Prospero communes with the ineffable. Otherwise, his
imaginative reach is somewhat limited as is apparent in the masque he stages
for Miranda and Ferdinand as a "vanity of his art." Always on guard against
the excitements of passion, Prospero will allow nothing in the masque that
might heat the blood. Venus and Cupid are barred, Iris says, because they
intended "some wanton charm upon this man and maid." At this hymeneal
celebration only "cold nymphs" and chaste representations of fertility are
welcome: there are decorous country dances of reapers, but no antimasque
of satyrs as graces the sheep-shearing feast in *The Winter's Tale*. Nothing
wild and nothing erotic, not even a violet dim, is allowed in the natural
world that Prospero's lines invoke: all is orderly and cultivated. Fertility is
equated with bountiful harvests, not the desire for physical union that gives
Perdita's speeches their mythopeic beauty. The masque is imaginatively set in
a European landscape of fields and vineyards, and the classical deities who
are its characters are figures out of an Inigo Jones sketch, parts to be taken by
ladies-in-waiting at the court of Milan. The poetry is decorous and lacking in
spontaneity. If we did not know that the lines were Prospero's, we might
think they were the work of a minor Augustan poet with a taste for the
sententious:

> *Ceres.* Hail, many-colored messenger, that ne'er
>   Dost disobey the wife of Jupiter;
>   Who with thy saffron wings upon my flow'rs
>   Diffusest honey-drops, refreshing show'rs,
>   And with each end of thy blue bow dost crown
>   My bosky acres and my unshrubb'd down,
>   Rich scarf to my proud earth—why hath thy Queen
>   Summon'd me hither, to this short-grass'd green?
>
> (4.1. 76–83)

After these conventionalities, Prospero's great speech on the unsubstan-
tiality of experience is all the more stunning because it turns literary
platitudes into visionary insight. Prospero's anger at his forgetfulness is

understandable because it could have made him vulnerable to Stephano, Trinculo, and Caliban. Yet it is a more vehement response than the occasion warrants, one which Ferdinand notes and which Miranda has not seen before. The anger is directed, not at the drunken conspirators, but at the vanity that allowed Prospero to become absorbed in a display of his art. We could say that Prospero recoils from the sudden realization that his show is mere shadow, except that the speech is too splendid to be described as a cry of disillusion. At the moment Prospero realizes his vanity, he gains a largeness of vision that confirms the glory of the intellectual quest and power that he intends to renounce:

> You do look, my son, in a mov'd sort,
> As if you were dismay'd; be cheerful, sir.
> Our revels now are ended. These our actors
> (As I foretold you) were all spirits, and
> Are melted into air, into thin air,
> And like the baseless fabric of this vision,
> The cloud-capp'd tow'rs, the gorgeous palaces,
> The solemn temples, the great globe itself,
> Yea, all which it inherit, shall dissolve,
> And like this insubstantial pageant faded
> Leave not a rack behind. We are such stuff
> As dreams are made on; and our little life
> Is rounded with a sleep.
>
>   (4.1. 146–58)

Prospero's speech marks the end of the self-absorption that has kept him aloof even from Miranda and Ferdinand, to whom he now speaks of his age and vexed thoughts. If he were like Leontes, this moment of self-discovery would make him turn to others as Leontes turns to Paulina, but the habit of solitude is too strong in him, and, as his lines suggest, the world of his thought has become more real to him than the world in which others live— more real than the towers, temples, and palaces that are the enduring monuments of human achievement. After commanding through Ariel the forces that level mountains and erode the shore, Prospero is not awed by the unsubstantial pageantry of political greatness. He remembers the excitement of a power that could shake heaven and earth, dim the noontide sun, and raise the mutinous waves toward heaven. Now he must put aside "this rough magic" and relinquish his sway over all on the island. It never occurs to him to continue his studies in Milan, where they began, because the great adventure of his magic depended on Ariel, who was his link to mysteries that lie beyond human intellect. Thus when he sets Ariel free he also drowns his book, breaks his staff, and puts off forever his magician's gown.

Even before Prospero relinquishes his magical powers, the plot of *The*

Tempest anticipates a return to the mundane. Miranda and Ferdinand's declarations of love portend a great wedding to be celebrated in Milan or Naples; the conventionality of Prospero's nuptial masque brings that moment of pomp and ceremony closer in thought. In the last act there is little need of Ariel's power of enchantment. He plays the same practical joke on Trinculo, Stephano, and Caliban that Puck played on Demetrius and Lysander when he led them on a wild-goose chase in the Athenian forest. At the close Ariel has no function other than to be Prospero's valet and help him to dress again as Duke of Milan. The dimension of wonder on Prospero's island shrinks to the "astonishing" discovery of Miranda and Ferdinand playing chess, a most chaste recreation. For this kind of magic one needs only a stage and a bit of curtain, and an audience ignorant of the spectacle about to be revealed.

Awed by Ferdinand's resurrection, the cynical Sebastian proclaims it "a most high miracle." Miranda is astonished by the brave new world of Alonso's retinue, and Ferdinand declares that Miranda is his "by immortal providence." Gonzalo concludes that Prospero's fall was fortunate because though he was betrayed, nearly perished, and endured years as a castaway, his daughter will someday be Queen of Naples. In Gonzalo's worldview, a brother's villainy is providential if it leads to a daughter's elevation. Prospero does not join in the general rejoicing because he knows how these miracles were accomplished; he is not impressed by Miranda's prospects or eager to return to the ducal office that meant little to him before his exile.

Although psychological critics murmur of Prospero's somewhat incestuous love of Miranda,[8] he readily relinquishes her to Ferdinand. It is more difficult for him to part with Ariel, for whom he shows deep affection as the time approaches when he must set him free. Nothing that awaits Prospero in Milan can compensate for the loss of his "bird," his "delicate Ariel," his "chick," his "dainty," "tricksy spirit." Confined to an island, he found through Ariel a freedom from earthly limitations that makes the prospect of return to Milan drab, and he speaks of it only as a preparation for death. Since he never intended to revenge his wrongs, he is not exalted by the decision to release his enemies from their distraction. Ariel's compassion for the castaways does not move Prospero to be merciful. It makes him suddenly aware that years of isolation have made him somewhat indifferent to the anguish of others. The danger is not that he may punish his enemies but that he may remain apart from others and unable to think of them as fellow creatures. After deciding that "the rarer action is / In virtue than in vengeance," Prospero warmly embraces Gonzalo, greets Alonso courteously, and pays little attention to Antonio and Sebastian, who he knows are as unnatural as ever. His detachment from others in this scene suggests that he will never again be part of the world to which they belong. He acknowledges Caliban as a "thing of darkness," but of all the characters in *The Tempest,* the seemingly uneducable Caliban is the one most enlightened by what has happened. He had discovered the intoxication of revolutionary ardor as well as sack; he had made gods of a drunken butler and cook who he thought would free him from servitude to Prospero when all the time they were calculating the profit to be made from exhibiting him as a freak at country fairs. By the end of the play, Caliban has lost all illusions about the nobility of men; he will find freedom only when they leave the island, and he once again possesses an uninhabited realm.

The sadness that touches Prospero in the final scene will not allow us to sentimentalize *The Tempest* as a last exalted Shakespearean affirmation of the goodness of life. But neither does *The Tempest* record a final disillusionment with the unreality of art. If through Prospero Shakespeare makes a personal statement, it is about the price one may have to pay for great artistic achievement. We think of Shakespeare as one who, more than any other great writer, understood and enjoyed other people and was very much involved with and at home in his world. His masterpieces were, nevertheless, the work of an unassuming observer, an alert sympathetic listener, not a striking conversationalist; he was lovingly remembered by his colleagues for his gentleness, not his brilliance. He lived most intensely and fully perhaps in the hours he spent writing his plays and poems. When he laid down his pen, he no doubt found joy in the company of family and friends, but it is not likely that the ordinary experience of life was as vivid—as real—to him as the dream of art that ended with Prospero's farewell to Ariel.

15

Conclusion

The prefaces to Jonson's plays suggest that he rarely found audiences worthy of or sufficiently appreciative of his art. Shakespeare wrote no prefaces to his plays and nothing in them implies a superiority to his audiences; no prologue or epilogue speaks contemptuously of the unappreciative many or suggests that only a discerning few are the fit auditors of his comedies. Although he knew that some who came to see his plays were shallow in their perceptions and responses, he reached out to all. He was too wise to yearn for an audience of learned sophisticates, for they might find Bottom's artistic enthusiasms merely ludicrous and respond to Dogberry the way Antonio and Sebastian respond to Gonzalo. Critics may argue that this comedy or that one was intended for aristocratic listeners but none are caviar to the general. In performance, almost all the difficulties of language that confront a reader of the comedies disappear; even when audiences cannot follow the verbal acrobatics of *Love's Labor's,* they do not stir restlessly in their seats because they enjoy the gamesmanship of the ladies of France and the earnest, incompetent courtship of the gentlemen of Navarre.

The emphasis on "performance studies" in recent Shakespeare criticism is a useful reminder that interpretation should be consonant with the experience of the plays that an audience may have in the theater. When explanation of motive becomes arcane and subterranean, when the "essential reality" of characterization is too abstruse and involuted to be communicated by actors, criticism has lost its way. This does not mean, however, that the plays do not require thoughtful reflection or that one cannot deepen an awareness of Shakespeare's artistic purpose by pondering issues that only momentarily tease the mind when we watch a performance of a play. On stage, *The Merchant* can hardly fail to captivate and satisfy. While rereading the text, however, we are likely to pause over Jessica and Portia's responses to Shylock, be all too aware of the ironies of Antonio's idealism, and wonder about the "moral amnesia" of the final scene. Similarly, a reading of *Twelfth Night* prompts questions about Olivia's marriage to Sebastian that a stage production hardly allows to form. These questions are real and legitimate; by examining them we do not sacrifice or falsify the dramatic immediacy of Shakespeare's art. Rather we deepen our appreciation and understanding of his ability to fuse moral insight and aesthetic affect.[1]

The questions that absorb critics of Shakespeare differ from those that face critics of other Elizabethan and Jacobean playwrights because many plays of the period are as perplexing in the theater as in the study. A production of *The Changeling* does not convince us of the unity of its main and subplots any more than a production of *Bussy D'Ambois* establishes whether Bussy is a tragic protagonist or blustering poseur. Shakespearean drama challenges criticism to explain a reach of art that transcends ordinary logic, that convinces even though common sense declares that this dramatic portrait must be hopelessly contradictory or that handling of plot must be a gross violation of artistic decorum. Thus, we are tempted to invent ingenious rationalizations of the artistic flaws in non-Shakespearean plays, and we are tempted to argue that *Much Ado* and *All's Well* do not end well despite the evidence of their success in performance.

We oversimplify and distort the critical issues of the comedies when we conduct a moral audit of the plots and decide which characters are insufficiently noble or repentant to deserve the second chance at happiness that the plays allow. For the sense of the rightness of an ending is an artfully shaped emotional and aesthetic satisfaction that includes moral expectation and acceptance but is not reducible to a simple moral arithmetic. On the other hand, we will not appreciate the beauty and wholeness of form in a comedy if we declare that its emotional tensions are deliberately left unresolved or are incapable of resolution because the play offers dialectically opposed viewpoints and value judgments. While the history of Shakespeare criticism reveals continuing, often radical, disagreements about a handful of characters in a handful of plays, it also reveals the congruity of most interpretations and judgments—a congruity that testifies to the essential clarity and wholeness of Shakespeare's artistic vision.

Until the recent vogue of trendy productions of Shakespeare, eccentricity of interpretation was checked by awareness of the artistic unities of the plays, which demand that characterizations be seen in relation to one another and to the plot as a whole. Different actors may play Romeo with different emphases of personality, but if the play is to be convincing, Romeo must be at once intensely romantic and self-absorbed and yet manly enough to have Mercutio's friendship and admiration. He must have the courage to refuse Tybalt's challenge and yet feel compelled to fight Tybalt after Mercutio dies, even though he knows that by so doing he becomes fortune's fool. Romeo is not reckless from one perspective and noble from another—here a poetic fantasizer, there a virile swordsman. He is all of a piece, and his responses a revelation of the opposing claims of love and honor; and our response to him is all of a piece—we never think him unworthy of sympathy or too immature to rise to tragic heights. Similarly Julius Caesar must be a complex figure, one who is noble enough to merit Brutus's admiring love and vain enough to want Antony by his side as hero worshipper. Cassius cannot seem too Machiavellian because he must be noble enough to be a friend of Brutus and so hungry for Brutus's love that he repeatedly sacrifices his self-interest by bowing to Brutus's mistaken judgments. The greatest of Shakespeare's tragic figures are not differently conceived from Caesar, Brutus, or Cassius, but they challenge us to grasp profound paradoxes of human behavior: for example, the spiritual torment that precedes and accompanies Macbeth's murder of Duncan and that demands a greater brutality to follow.

Many of the comedies are as tightly and logically plotted as most of the history plays and tragedies; thus one can speak of the necessity that Claudio be uncertain of his judgment of women for the plot of *Much Ado* to be credible, just as Cassio must be devoted to Othello but vulnerable to Iago's wiles for the plot of *Othello* to be credible. Both are gallant soldiers who behave badly when their uncertainties of self are exploited by a cunning intriguer. Like Claudio, Antonio is explicable by reference to his role in *The Merchant* because his dramatic personality answers to the demands of plot and theme. He must be both noble and intolerant, generous and mean-spirited, selfless and unconsciously self-regarding. The characterization of Antonio in *Twelfth Night* is not so easily explicated. The plot demands that he be devoted enough to Sebastian to risk his safety by remaining in Illyria, but there is no reason why Antonio's need to be with Sebastian should be helpless and overwhelming. That intensity of devotion puzzles because it does not enlarge our understanding of the nature of love even though it echoes Olivia's desperate longing for Cesario; it seems out of size with Antonio's role in the dramatic action and indeed is all we know of him as a character.

The coarseness of Lavatch in *All's Well* is similarly opaque to critical understanding. It does not seem excessive in any respect or out of place in the scenes in which it is expressed, and yet one cannot say just what contribution it makes to the totality of the play. Indeed, attempts to explain the "necessity" for his obscene jests are more likely to exaggerate the supposed darkness of *All's Well* than to discover its imaginative coherences. It seems to me better to accept Lavatch's greasiness as a very minor element in a large composition than to "explain" it by distorting the tone of the play. Similarly, it is better to admit that the curious, languid villainy of Antonio and Sebastian in *The Tempest* is opaque to critical understanding than to exaggerate its significance by making it a final comment on political evil.

There are, I think, more characterizations in the comedies than in the tragedies and history plays that baffle one's desire to demonstrate the organicism of Shakespeare's art. They are a reminder that an understanding of his creative imagination is partial at best, and that his artistic vision is finally more idiosyncratic and mysterious than critical explanations suggest. He continually takes artistic risks that sensible people would avoid in writing plays. We would not make Orlando so utterly naive because we would have him a suitable match for the wise and witty Rosalind; we would not make Orsino so self-indulgent and narcissistic because we would have him more worthy of Viola's love.

Orsino is not a critical puzzle in the way that Prince Hal and Hamlet are. We do not wonder at his motivations or moral responses; we wonder instead why he is not more like Bassanio or Benedick and therefore more attractive as a romantic hero. Orsino tempts us to thoughts that are forbidden to critics, for we begin to imagine that Shakespeare would have made fewer artistic mistakes in his comedies if he had had the benefit of our refined judgments. It is worth noting that few if any of the supposed artistic miscalculations in the comedies are casual. Shakespeare goes out of his way to create the "problems" of The Merchant and All's Well by altering the characterizations that he found in his sources and by rewriting their plots. It would have been very easy, moreover, for him to have erased the artistic flaws critics perceive. A dozen lines that express a bit of regret or compassion for Shylock would make us think better of Portia, Antonio, and Jessica. A dozen lines that reflect deeper self-awareness would solve the "problem" of Claudio, Orsino, and Bertram; and the blotting out of a dozen lines by Toby and Feste would change the tonality of the final scene of Twelfth Night.

No one questions the bloody conclusions of the tragedies even when they depend (or seem to depend) on the accident of a message delayed, a single rapier thrust, a cup wrongly chosen, or a momentary forgetfulness about royal prisoners. For to wish that Laertes had not fatally wounded Hamlet or that Emilia had knocked sooner on the door of Othello's bedchamber is to reject the vision of tragedy. Less certain of what the vision of Shakespearean comedy is, critics are more inclined to reduce it to formulas and to grumble when a comedy does not end with the unalloyed triumph of love or festive release or a glimpse of the supposed green world. If we can rejoice in the affirmations of the spirit that the tragedies offer, we should be able to accept the note of sadness and awareness of human limitations that make the laughter of the comedies so much more precious and meaningful.

Notes

Chapter 1. Introduction

1. Barbara Everett has suggested that in the comedies Shakespeare creates a world in which women are often dominant figures and the embodiment of Shakespeare's humane principles (*"Much Ado About Nothing," Critical Quarterly* 3 [Winter 1961]: 334).

2. Noting that Lyly's comedies offer no heroines who can stand beside Shakespeare's, G. K. Hunter argues, however, that Lyly's emphasis upon female sensibility in his plays as well as his witty explorations of the meaning of love led the way to Shakespeare's romantic comedies (*John Lyly: The Humanist as Courtier* [Cambridge: Harvard University Press, 1962], 252–56). I would suggest that the romantic tonalities of Shakespeare's comedies are much closer to those of Elizabeth prose romance, pastoral narrative, and nondramatic love poetry than to the tonalities of Lyly's comedies. Although G. Wilson Knight suggests that love is a supreme value in Lyly's comedies ("John Lyly," *Review of English Studies* 15 [April 1939]: 146–63), Marco Mincoff more accurately speaks of the "comedy of love's foolishness" in Lyly's plays, a foolishness that lies "mainly in the desperate earnestness with which the lovers pursue what is mostly a very unsuitable affair" ("Shakespeare and Lyly," *Shakespeare Survey* 14 [1961]: 19). The view of love is ambivalent in most of Lyly's comedies and especially in *Endimion* and *Love's Metamorphosis.*

3. The memorable female characters of non-Shakespearean comedy are likely to be flamboyant figures like Moll of Middleton and Dekker's *The Roaring Girl* rather than romantic heroines of the temperament and stature of Portia and Viola.

4. Northrop Frye, "The Argument of Comedy," in *English Institute Essays,* ed. D. A. Robertson, Jr. (New York: Columbia University Press, 1949), 58–73.

5. C. L. Barber, *Shakespeare's Festive Comedy: A Study of Dramatic Form and Its Relation to Social Custom* (1959; reprint, Cleveland: Meridian Books, 1966), chaps. 1 and 2.

6. Ibid., chap. 3.

7. The identification of the "green world" of comedy with the idea of resurrection hints at the implicit theological basis of Frye's view of comedy ("Argument," 65–73).

8. Alexander Leggatt notes that the emphasis in *Errors* "is not on the creation of a new social unit (as in Northrop Frye's theory of comedy) but on the renewal of an old family unit" (*Shakespeare's Comedy of Love* [London: Methuen, 1974], 17). Similary R. A. Foakes points out that the designs of *As You Like It* and *Twelfth Night* do not conform to Frye's and Barber's ideas of comic release ("The Owl and the Cuckoo: Voices of Maturity in Shakespeare's Comedies," *Shakespearian Comedy,* ed. David Palmer and Malcolm Bradbury [London: E. Arnold, 1972], 141).

9. Leo Salingar notes the festive game-playing and carnival spirit of Italian Renaissance comedy in *Shakespeare and the Traditions of Comedy* (Cambridge: At the University Press, 1974), 191ff.

10. To argue for the fundamentally romantic impulse of Shakespeare's comedies is simply to restate a traditional viewpoint expressed by many earlier scholars, for example, Madeleine Doran in *Endeavors of Art: A Study of Form in Elizabethan Drama* (Madison: University of Wisconsin Press, 1954), 171–82. More recently the romantic nature of the comedies has been emphasized by Hallett Smith in *Shakespeare's Romances* (San Marino, Calif.: Huntington

Library Publications, 1972) and Howard Felperin in *Shakespearean Romance* (Princeton: Princeton University Press, 1972).

11. See the discussion of the Renaissance controversy about the nature of tragicomedy in Doran, *Endeavors of Art*, 190ff.

12. Most scholars agree that the extant text of *The Shrew* is very probably a revision of an earlier form of the play. I argue in the chapter on *The Shrew* that the earlier text was not written by Shakespeare but one obtained by his company about the same time it obtained *The Troublesome Reign*, on which *King John* is based.

Chapter 2. *The Comedy of Errors*

1. Modern editors generally assume that *Errors* was the first of the comedies, followed within a year or two by *The Shrew, Two Gentlemen*, and *Love's Labor's*. I think it possible, however, that the original composition of *Love's Labor's* preceded *Two Gentlemen*, partly because of the imitation of Lyly in the former and partly because the dramatic structure of *Love's Labor's* is more flawed than critics have generally noted. I place the discussion of *The Shrew* after the chapters on *Love's Labor's* and *Two Gentlemen*, not because I think it was written after them but because it is important to see that its treatment of love and marriage is diametrically opposed to that in the earliest of the comedies as well as that in *Much Ado* and *Twelfth Night*.

2. All quotations from Shakespeare's plays are from *The Riverside Shakespeare*, ed. G. B. Evans (Boston: Houghton Mifflin Co., 1974).

3. *The Alchemist, Elizabethan and Jacobean Comedy: An Anthology*, ed. Robert Ornstein and Hazelton Spencer (Boston: Heath, 1964), 150–51.

4. *Menaechmi*, 2.1, in *The Comedy of Errors*, ed. Harry Levin, Signet Classic Shakespeare (New York: New American Library, 1965), 124.

5. Compare Adriana's lines 2.2.125–29 with Antipholus S.'s lines 1.2.35–38.

6. Anne Barton speaks of Adriana's "possessiveness and jealous frenzy" in her introduction to *Errors, Riverside Shakespeare*, 81.

7. Ruth Nevo speaks of Adriana's "almost rapacious 'incorporation' of her husband into herself" (*Comic Transformations in Shakespeare* [London: Methuen, 1980], 26. I think the dignity of Adriana's character and the nobility of her view of marriage refute this suggestion of neurotic fixation, especially since man and wife are one flesh by religious doctrine.

8. Compare Adriana's response to Luciana with Bolingbroke's response to Gaunt's platitudes in *Richard II*, 1.3.294–303, and Brabantio's response to the Duke's platitudes in *Othello*, 1.3.210–19.

9. See Leggatt on the authority of the Abbess (*Shakespeare's Comedy of Love*, 16).

10. Because she does not catch the humor of the Abbess, Nevo says that she traps Adriana into a therapeutic self-confession (*Comic Transformations*, 28).

11. In *All's Well* as in *Errors*, the concluding scene dramatizes the hounding of an insensitive husband who is rescued from his ordeal by a woman: Bertram by Helena, Antipholus S. by the Abbess.

Chapter 3. *Love's Labor's Lost*

1. See Hunter, *John Lyly*, 315ff.; Mincoff, "Shakespeare and Lyly," 19ff.

2. Dover Wilson, among others, suggested that Shakespeare was alluding to an Elizabethan coterie of atheism that gained notoriety about 1593 (new Cambridge Shakespeare [Cambridge: At the University Press, 1923], xxviii–xxxiv). A more elaborate topical interpretation appears in Frances A. Yates, *A Study of Love's Labour's Lost* (Cambridge: At the University Press, 1936).

3. The demand for purity in those who search for the philosopher's stone is parodied in Jonson's *The Alchemist*.

4. See Barber's illuminating discussion of the treatment of language in the play (*Shakespeare's Festive Comedy*, 97–109).

5. Compare Romeo's description of Juliet, "she hangs upon the cheek of night / As a rich

jewel in an Ethiop's ear" (1.5.45–46), with his description of Rosaline, "O she is rich in beauty, only poor / That, when she dies, with beauty dies her store" (1.1.215–16).

6. The denouement of *As You Like It* also depends on the sudden arrival of a messenger with unexpected news, but the emotional resolution of the play is achieved before the characters learn of the conversion of Duke Frederick to a holy life.

7. The Princess invites Navarre to "come challenge me, challenge me by these deserts, / And by this virgin palm now kissing thine, / I will be thine (5.2.805–7). Juliet uses the same metaphor in sweetly putting off Romeo's desire for a kiss: "For saints have hands that pilgrims' hands do touch, / And palm to palm is holy palmers' kiss" (1.5.99–100).

8. Those who would justify the harshness of Rosaline's treatment of Berowne speak of his need for further chastening. Nevo, for example, says that he is still caught "in his web of self-regarding rhetoric" (*Comic Transformations,* 89).

9. Philip Edwards thinks the ending of *Love's Labor's* is flawed; see *Shakespeare and the Confines of Art* (London: Methuen, 1968), 47–48. Mincoff thinks that the abruptness of the ending almost suggests that Shakespeare "had suddenly lost patience with the very convention [of Lylyan love comedy] he had been exploiting" ("Shapespeare and Lyly," 19–20. An opposing view appears in B. Roesen (Anne Barton), *"Love's Labor's Lost," Shakespeare Quarterly* 4 (1953): 411–26, but her attempt to see the last act as a scene of lengthening shadows and increasing premonition of death seems to me unconvincing.

10. If, as Dover Wilson has suggested, the final lyric debate was added to the text in the revision and amplification of the play that preceded the 1598 Quarto, then it is quite possible that Shakespeare added the songs to round off a dramatic action that he recognized as lacking in emotional resolution. See Wilson, new Cambridge Shakespeare ed., 184.

11. It is puzzling to me that Barber omits *Much Ado* from his study of Shakespeare's festive comedies even though it has close affinities of plot structure with *Love's Labor's* and, indeed, has more festive occasions and observances than *Love's Labor's.* The festive spirit of the comedies, which Barber so cogently describes, does not depend on the dramatic use of holiday occasions and observances. There are, for example, more festive celebrations and game playing in *The Shrew* than in *Love's Labor's,* but Barber rightly omits *The Shrew* from his study of festive comedies because its "festive" occasions are moments of humiliation and subjugation.

Chapter 4. *Two Gentlemen of Verona*

1. See the discussion of the plotting of *Two Gentlemen* in Stanley Wells, "The Failure of *Two Gentlemen of Verona," Shakespeare-Jahrbuch* 99 (1963): 161–73. Wells, I think, undervalues the skill with which Shakespeare develops the ironic intrigues of the play, but he writes discerningly of its sketchy dramatic situations.

2. In Sidney's sonnet as in the first scene of *Two Gentlemen,* the power of love sweeps away the argument for honor and manly achievement, but the tone of the sonnet suggests that the opposing claims of love and honor are acknowledged by Astrophil as they are by Proteus. See David Kalstone's discussion of this thematic conflict in *Sidney's Poetry: Contexts and Interpretations* (New York: Norton, 1970), 150ff.

3. Another aspect of the use of sonnet themes in the play is suggested by Inga-Stina Ewbank in " 'Were man but constant, he were perfect': Constancy and Consistency in *Two Gentlemen of Verona,"* in *Shakespearian Comedy,* ed. Palmer and Bradbury, 51–57.

4. Julia tells Lucetta that the fire of her love cannot be quenched with words, the river of her love cannot be stopped. Proteus's looks are her "soul's food," for which she has long pined (1.7.9–38).

5. See Leggatt's fine commentary on Proteus and Valentine's glib casuistries (*Shakespeare's Comedy of Love,* 30–31).

6. The worldly cynicism of Proteus's advice is paralleled by the mock despair of the speaker in Donne's "Lovers' Infiniteness," who says that he cannot "breathe one other sigh to move, / Nor can intreat one other tear to fall, / And all my treasure which should purchase thee, / Sighs, tears, and oaths, and letters I have spent."

7. Shakespeare suggests the maturing of Julia under the pressure of unexpected calamity as

he suggests the maturing of Julia: by the riddling wit with which she responds to the news that she must marry Paris (3.5.88ff). Both heroines face the moment of crisis with a self-possession that allows a quiet ironic humor only they can appreciate.

8. See Leggatt's sensitive discussion of Julia (*Shakespeare's Comedy of Love*, 36–37).

9. Viola's riddling hints about her true identity recall the disguised Julia's hints of her relation to Proteus. The poignancy of her description of the fading beauty of Proteus's jilted lady is immediately echoed in Viola's fable of her lovelorn sister who sat like Patience on a monument and is transmuted by the gentle humor of Viola's account.

Chapter 5. *The Taming of the Shrew*

1. R. B. Heilman discusses the way farcical exaggerations of *The Shrew* insulate audiences against the grossness of Petruchio's conduct (introduction, Signet Classic Shakespeare (New York: New American Library, 1966), xxxiv–v).

2. Like many commentators, Anne Barton accuses Bianca first of "deviousness and cunning," and next of demonstrating a "streak of bawdry, willfulness, and arrogance" (*Riverside Shakespeare*, 108). But the only evidences of Bianca's shrewishness that critics can cite are a single, understandably annoyed remark she makes to her squabbling tutors (3.1.16–20) and her conduct in the final scene, which is discussed below.

3. See Peter Alexander, "The Original Ending of *The Taming of the Shrew*," *Shakespeare Quarterly* 20 (1969): 111–16, and the textual commentary in the new Cambridge edition of *The Shrew*, ed. J. D. Wilson (Cambridge: At the University Press, 1928).

4. R. A. Houk, "The Evolution of *The Taming of the Shrew*," *PMLA* 57 (1942): 1009–38; G. I. Duthie, "*The Taming of a Shrew* and *The Taming of the Shrew*," *Review of English Studies* 19 (1943): 337–56. H. J. Oliver supports this view in the Oxford edition of *The Shrew* (1982); Brian Morris argues for Alexander's view in the new Arden edition (1981).

5. For a contrary view, see G. R. Hibbard, new Penguin edition (Harmondsworth, 1968), 43–44.

6. J. W. Shroeder, "*The Taming of a Shrew* and *The Taming of the Shrew*: A Case Reopened," *Journal of English and Germanic Philology* 57 (1958): 424–43.

7. Quotations from *A Shrew* are from the modernized text edited by Alice Griffin, *The Sources of Ten Shakespearean Plays* (New York: T. Y. Crowell Co., 1966), 45–82.

8. See Nevo's astute discussion of the Kate of the early scenes (*Comic Transformations*, 41).

9. Only this scene supports Nevo's assertion that Petruchio's remedy for Kate's shrewishness is "an appeal to [her] intelligence" (ibid., 49).

10. Heilman writes, "The scene on the road to Padua (IV.v.1–78) is the high point of the play. From here on, it tends to move back closer to the boundaries of ordinary farce. When Petruchio asks for a kiss, we do have human beings with feelings, not robots; but the key line in the scene, which is sometimes missed, is Petruchio's 'Why, then let's home again. Come sirrah, let's away' (V.i.146). Here Petruchio is again making the same threat he made at IV.v.8–9, that is, not playing an imaginary game but hinting the symbolic whip, even though the end is a compliance that she is inwardly glad to give" (Signet Classic Shakespeare ed., xxxxix–xl).

11. Assuming that Petruchio becomes a "charming and affectionate gentleman" at the end of the play, Heilman remarks that such a person could not have played the tamer "so rigorously . . . to outbully the bully, especially when the bully lies bleeding on the ground" (xxxvii). Exactly so, but Petruchio is neither charming nor gentlemanly in the final scene of the play.

12. In *The Riverside Shakespeare*, Barton speaks of this Kate as "an integrated and quietly confident" woman (p. 107).

13. See Heilman's rejection of the possibility of ironic overtones in Kate's speech (Signet Classic Shakespeare, xl).

14. Leggatt, *Shakespeare's Comedy of Love*, 57.

15. See E. M. W. Tillyard, *Shakespeare's History Plays* (New York: Macmillan Co., 1946), 215, 232.

Chapter 6. *A Midsummer Night's Dream*

1. See David Young's detailed study of the imaginative structure of *A Dream* in *Something of Great Constancy: The Art of A Midsummer Night's Dream* (New Haven: Yale University Press, 1966), 86ff.

2. The ugliness of enforced marriage is a theme treated by Chapman, Tourneur, Jonson, and Ford as well as Shakespeare.

3. Young, I think, exaggerates the comic terror of the forest scenes when he speaks of the contrast between the "orderly society" of Athens and the "confusing wildness" the lovers encounter (*Something of Great Constancy*, 89).

4. Granville-Barker and Nevill Coghill have suggested that Titania's retinue may have been played by children on Shakespeare's stage, but Ernest Schanzer argues persuasively that Titania and Oberon could hardly have been played effectively by child actors. See Harley Granville-Barker, *More Prefaces to Shakespeare* (Princeton: Princeton University Press, 1974), 119; Nevill Coghill, *Shakespeare's Professional Skills* (Cambridge: At the University Press, 1964), 55; Ernest Schanzer, "*A Midsummer Night's Dream*," in *Shakespeare: The Comedies*, ed. K. Muir (Englewood Cliffs, N.J.: Prentice-Hall, 1965), 26–31. No child actor, of course, would be small enough for Shakespeare's conception of the fairies.

5. Hunter notes that Theseus dismisses himself in dismissing antique fables (*John Lyly*, 328).

6. Although some critics speak of Theseus's rational authority, others note the obvious limitations of his skeptical rationalism; see Leggatt, *Shakespeare's Comedy of Love*, 101; Young, *Something of Great Constancy*, 139.

7. Oberon's charms against birth deformities in the children of the newly married couples echo Titania's complaint that his brawls and their quarrelings had disordered nature and blasted harvests (2.1.81–117). With the blessing of the marriage beds, the fairies make restitution to mortals, and with the reconciliation of Titania and Oberon, fertility will return to the sodden fields of Athens.

8. See John Palmer on the centrality of Bottom in *Comic Characters of Shakespeare* (London: Macmillan & Co., 1946), 92–93.

Chapter 7. *The Merchant of Venice*

1. See the discussion of anti-Semitism in medieval and Renaissance Europe in E. E. Stoll's *Shakespeare Studies* (New York: G. E. Stechert, 1942; first edition 1927), 269–90.

2. Stoll mentions four Elizabethan plays that have anti-Semitic portraits of Jewish usurers apart from Marlowe's and Shakespeare's (*Shakespeare Studies* 272). His footnotes reveal, however, that two of these villains are not identified as Jews, and at least two are modeled after Shylock.

3. See Lawrence Danson's critique of Stoll's assumptions in *The Harmonies of "The Merchant of Venice"* (New Haven: Yale University Press, 1978), 133–34.

4. For a contrary view see Leggatt, who draws a sharp contrast between Belmont and Venice, which he calls a "world of need" (*Shakespeare's Comedy of Love*, 125).

5. See Danson's astute criticism of this view of Antonio (*Harmonies*, 34–36).

6. The desire of the receiver of generosity to be worthy of the gift is memorably expressed in George Herbert's religious poetry, especially "Love III."

7. For a portrait of a villainous usurer in later drama, see Sir Giles Ovvereach in Massinger's *A New Way to Pay Old Debts*. The malevolent Overreach has little in common with the Shylock of the first three acts.

8. Although Elizabethan law theoretically forbid all usury, severe penalties were set only for rates higher than ten percent, and commercial loans were a common business practice in Shakespeare's age.

9. See E. K. Chambers, *William Shakespeare: A Study of Facts and Problems* (Oxford: 1930) 2: 65–66.

10. Supposedly Portia gives away the answer to the riddle of the caskets by the song which rhymes "bred," "head," and "nourished" to draw Bassanio's attention to "lead."

11. The self-pitying tone of Antonio's letter is mirrored in the extreme self-abnegation of Sonnet 71, "No longer mourn for me." Some critics rejoice in the saintliness of attitude expressed in the sonnet, but its total denial of psychological reality, its hyperbolic command that not one tear be shed, seems to me to cry out for ironic interpretation.

12. See Nevill Coghill, "The Basis of Shakespearian Comedy," *Essays and Studies* (1950): 1–28. More intricate and ingenious in Barbara K. Lewalski's "Biblical Allusion and Allegory in *The Merchant of Venice*," *Shakespeare Quarterly* 12 (1962): 327–43.

13. It is almost commonplace for critics to suggest that Shakespeare made an artistic mistake in allowing Shylock to become too human and deserving of an audience's sympathies; see Barber, *Shakespeare's Festive Comedy*, 190–91; Nevo, *Comic Transformations*, 136ff. Palmer, on the other hand, notes the splendid comic balance of the portrait of Shylock, *Comic Characters*, 87.

Chapter 8. *Much Ado About Nothing*

1. The social realism of *Much Ado* is discussed by Barbara Everett, *"Much Ado About Nothing,"* 319–23, and by David Stevenson in the introduction to the Signet Classic Shakespeare edition (New York: New American Library, 1964) xxii–xxv.

2. Among those who emphasize the conventionality of the portraits of Claudio and Hero are Leggatt (*Shakespeare's Comedy of Love*, 157–58), and Nevo, who suggests that theirs is a "courtship of convenience" that produces a counterfeit match (*Comic Transformations*, 164–66).

3. Critical revulsion at Claudio reaches a climax in Bertrand Evans, *Shakespeare's Comedies* (New York: Oxford University Press, 1960), 80–86.

4. There is a close parallel between Beatrice's stunning response to Benedick's request, "bid me do anything for you," and Rosaline's stunning response to Berowne's request, "Impose some service on me for thy love." Shakespeare, it would seem, had the moment in *Love's Labor's* in mind when he wrote the later scene—an intimation of the possible connection he made between Beatrice and Rosaline, a connection broken by Beatrice's willingness to give up the pleasure of baiting Benedick. See Nevo's comments on the parallels between *Much Ado* and *Love's Labor's* (*Comic Transformations*, 92).

5. Palmer's usual appreciation of the psychological realism of Shakespeare's portrayal of character does not extend to Claudio and Don Pedro, who he thinks are sacrificed as characters to allow the melodrama of the denunciation scene (*Comic Characters*, 113).

Chapter 9. *As You Like It*

1. Leggatt observes that the Duke's and Oliver's "envy of those more popular than they" creates " a hint of pathos, of human vulnerability" *Shakespeare's Comedy of Love*, 186–87).

2. The "reality" that Ralegh opposes to Marlowe's pastoral dream is relentlessly sterile and grim:

> The flowers do fade, and wanton fields
> To wayward winter reckoning yields;
> A honey tongue, a heart of gall,
> Is fancy's spring, but sorrow's fall.
>
> Thy gowns, thy shoes, thy beds of roses,
> Thy cap, thy kirtle, and thy posies,
> Soon break, soon wither, soon forgotten:
> In folly ripe, in reason rotten.

"The Nymph's Reply to the Shepherd" stanzas 3 and 4.

3. See the fine discussion of Shakespeare's handling of the pastoral in Harold Jenkins, *"As You Like It," Shakespeare Survey* 8 (1955): 40–51.

4. John Palmer sees Jaques as an impercipient, amusing poseur (*Comic Characters*, 45–49).

Helen Gardner describes Jaques as "virtually a court entertainer" in her fine essay, *"As You Like It,"* in *More Talking of Shakespeare;* ed. John Garrett (New York: Arno, 1959), 31–32. Anne Barton, however, thinks that Jaques's pessimism poses a threat to the comic equilibrium of the play ("*As You Like It* and *Twelfth Night:* Shakespeare's Sense of an Ending," in *Shakespearean Comedy,* ed. Palmer and Badbury, 170–71).

5. Leggatt, however, speaks of Jaques' corruption (*Shakespeare's Comedy of Love,* 201).

6. See Leggatt's fine discussion of Rosalind's emotional exuberance (ibid., 204–5).

Chapter 10. *Twelfth Night*

1. Clifford Leech argues that Shakespeare "gives over the comic idea" in *Twelfth Night* (*"Twelfth Night" and Shakespearian Comedy* [Toronto: University of Toronto Press, 1965], 53). Anne Barton suggests that the last act of the play is a "desperate rearguard action against the cold light of day" ("*As You Like It* and *Twelfth Night,*" 176).

2. See Nevo's fine discussion of the scene (*Comic Transformations,* 205–7).

3. Like many other critics, Barber thinks that Malvolio is asexual, that he desires Olivia's wealth, not her person (*Shakespeare's Festive Comedy,* 255). When he fantasizes in the letter scene about marriage to Olivia, however, he imagines having left her asleep on a day-bed—that is, having made love to her of an afternoon.

4. In Sonnet 116, love is an "ever fixed mark / That looks on tempests and is never shaken . . . the star to every wand'ring bark."

5. Distinguishing the humor of the letter scene from that of the dark-room scene, Leggatt remarks that the "jokers' reaction when the victim is down is to hit him again" (*Shakespeare's Comedy of Love,* 243).

6. Compare Toby's sneering view of Andrew with Falstaff's contemptuous description of Shallow in *2 Henry IV,* 3.2. 300–302.

7. John Hollander discusses the Jonsonian qualities of *Twelfth Night* in "*Twelfth Night* and the Morality of Indulgence," *Sewanee Review* 68 (1959): 200–38.

8. E. M. W. Tillyard, *Shakespeare's Problem Plays* (Toronto: University of Toronto Press, 1950), 97.

9. Hollander argues that Orsino, like the others in the play, has been "surfeited of his vanity" by the final scene "Morality of Indulgence," 238. I see no change in Orsino's manner of speech, behavior, or self-awareness in the final scene, though his love of Viola is no doubt more genuine than his mooning over Olivia.

10. Joseph Summers writes sensitively of the mingled tonalities of the final scene in "The Masks of *Twelfth Night,*" *University Review* 22 (Autumn 1955): 31–32.

Chapter 11. *All's Well That Ends Well*

1. All references to Boccaccio's tale of Beltramo and Giletta are to the version in William Painter's *The Palace of Pleasure,* reprinted in the Signet Classic edition of *All's Well,* ed. Sylvan Barnet (New York: New American Library, 1965).

2. Tillyard finds the stiffness of Helena's lines a failure of Shakespeare's poetic imagination (*Problem Plays,* 91–92, 99–104). I think it is a revelation of a very particular mind and emotional being.

3. See Winifred Dodds's fine discussion of Angelo in "The Character of Angelo in *Measure for Measure,*" *Modern Language Review* 41 (1946): 246–55.

4. Signet Classic, 167.

5. For a view of Helena as social climber, see Clifford Leech, "The Theme of Ambition in *All's Well that Ends Well,*" *English Literary History,* 21 (1954): 17–29.

6. Ornstein, "Teaching *Hamlet,*" *Shakespeare in School and College* (Urbana: National Council of Teachers of English 1964), 30–36.

7. For a contrary view, see Tillyard (*Problem Plays,* 96).

8. Roger Warren notes that Shakespeare does not try to elevate Bertram's character to

provide a happy ending in "Why Does it End Well? Helena, Bertram, and the Sonnets," *Shakespeare Survey* 22 (1969): 88.

9. Tillyard suggests that Bertram needs Helena's "moral support with such pathetic obviousness that she never need fear his escape" (*Problem Plays*, 117).

10. In the absence of external evidences, the debate over the date of *All's Well* is bound to continue. Although some have argued that it was written in the 1590s, the scholarly consensus seems to be that it belongs to the period of *Measure for Measure* and probably preceded it.

Chapter 12. *Cymbeline*

1. Howard Felperin defends the artistic unity of Cymbeline in *Shakespearean Romance* (Princeton: Princeton University Press, 1972), 179ff.

2. That *Cymbeline* was influenced by Fletcherian romance was first argued by A. H. Thorndyke, *The Influence of Beaumont and Fletcher on Shakespeare* (Worcester, Mass.: Press of O. B. Wood, 1901) by detailed comparisons of the plots of *Philaster* and *Cymbeline* (pp. 152–54). H. S. Wilson has attempted to prove that there are no direct echoes of *Philaster* in *Cymbeline*, but his discussion ignores questions of tone and nuances of characterization ("*Philaster* and *Cymbeline*," in *English Institute Essays* [New York: Columbia University Press, 1951], 146–67). More recently Arthur Kirsch has pointed out the influence of Fletcher on *Cymbeline* in "*Cymbeline* and Coterie Dramaturgy," *ELH* 34 (1967): 294ff.

3. I discuss the evidence for Fletcher's hand in *Henry VIII* in *A Kingdom for a Stage: The Achievement of Shakespeare's History Plays* (Cambridge: Harvard University Press, 1972), chap. 9.

4. Since the date of *Philaster* is unknown, it is hypothetically possible that its resemblances to *Cymbeline* result from Fletcher's imitation of Shakespeare since Fletcher's imitation of other Shakespearean plays is beyond dispute. But whereas *Philaster* is akin to all of Fletcher's other plays in essential artistic respects, *Cymbeline* stands apart from the comedies that preceded it and the late romances that followed it precisely because of its Fletcherian mannerisms. Can we believe that in a singular aberration from his usual artistic practice, Shakespeare accidentally produced a play that inspired Fletcher's theatricalism? Or, as is far more likely, must we not regard *Cymbeline* as the one play of Shakespeare's sole authorship that mimics the new style of Fletcherian tragicomedy?

5. See Una Ellis-Fermor's excellent discussion of the sensibility of Fletcher's characters in *The Jacobean Drama*, 2d ed. (London: Methuen, 1947), 205–20.

6. Kirsch notes the resemblances of Posthumus's emotionality to Philaster's ("*Philaster* and *Cymbeline*," 295). See also Tillyard's remarks on Posthumus's soliloquy in *Shakespeare's Last Plays* (London: Chatto and Windus, 1938), 28–29.

7. An absurd eagerness to be slain by the man they love is shown by both heroines, Arethusa and "Bellario," in *Philaster*.

8. *Philaster*, in *English Drama 1580–1642*, ed. Charles F. Brooke and Nathaniel B. Paradise (Boston: D. C. Heath, 1933).

9. See Tillyard on the symbolic "Sidneyan" quality of these characters (*Last Plays*, 34–35).

10. Rashness of this sort is the very hallmark of Philaster, who stabs his beloved Arethusa in a moment of intense emotion.

Chapter 13. *The Winter's Tale*

1. See J. I. M. Stewart, *Character and Motive in Shakespeare* (New York: Barnes & Noble, 1969), 30–37, and the critique of this approach in Arthur Sewell, *Character and Society in Shakespeare* (Clarendon Press, 1951), 6–8, and in Meredith Skura's *The Literary Use of the Psychoanalytical Process* (New Haven: Yale University Press, 1981), 40.

2. R. A. Foakes comments that Leontes is "not presented as being fully responsible for his words or deeds, but rather as diseased or mad, before the arrival of the oracle" (*Shakespeare: The Dark Comedies to the Last Plays* (Charlottesville: University Press of Virginia, 1971), 126. I would say that Leontes' courtiers recognize that his jealous rage is an aberrant behavior but none suggests that he is, like Hamlet, "mad," or suffering from some mental derangement. On

the contrary, Paulina, the chief choric figure, insists that Leontes' acts are criminal.

3. See the fine discussion of the sophisticated wordplay in *The Winter's Tale* in M. M. Mahood, *Shakespeare's Wordplay* (London: Methuen, 1957). John R. Brown also writes discerningly of the sophistication of style in the early courtly conversations of the play in *Shakespeare and His Comedies*, 2d ed. (London: Methuen, 1962), 213–16.

4. J. A. Bryant, Jr., elaborating the biblical echoes in the play, comments that "fortunately Leontes has a St. Paul to help him to [self-understanding], for this is precisely the function of Shakespeare's Paulina" ("Shakespeare's Allegory: *The Winter's Tale*," *Sewanee Review* 63 (1955): 217). The most elaborate "Christian" interpretation of the play is S. L. Bethell's *The Winter Tale* (London: Staples Press, 1947).

5. It is not likely that Shakespeare knew the plot of Sophocles' *Antigone*, but I am struck by the parallel between Leontes' stubbornness in the face of all opposition and Creon's refusal to relent in *Antigone*. *Pandosto* does not tell of the king's denial of the oracle; that final arrogance is Shakespeare's invention and very like Creon's refusal to bow to religious values and prophetic warning.

6. Tillyard draws a sharp contrast between the worlds of Sicily and Bohemia in *Last Plays*, 77–78.

7. See Michael Goldman's discussion of the mingling of the natural and the artificial in the feast scene (*Shakespeare and the Energies of Drama* [Princeton: Princeton University Press, 1972], 131–35).

8. Tillyard suggests that Perdita is "the play's main symbol of the powers of creation" (*Last Plays*, 44).

9. William Matchett notes the significance of Hermione's fertility in "Some Dramatic Techniques in *The Winter's Tale*," *Shakespeare Survey* 22 (1961): 95–96.

10. See Matchett on Shakespeare's handling of audience expectation in the last scene in ibid., 102–3.

11. A. F. Bellette writes sensitively of the "miracle" of Hermione's resurrection in "Truth and Utterance in *The Winter's Tale*," *Shakespeare Survey* 31 (1978): 74–75.

12. According to Lawrence Stone, "there has always been a large element of make-believe" about lordly titles. Elevations to the peerage were "hastily made respectable by the fiction of gentle birth." See *The Crisis of the Aristocracy 1558–1641* [Oxford: Clarendon Press, 1965], 65.

Chapter 14. *The Tempest*

1. See A. D. Nuttall on Prospero's quirkiness in "Two Unassimilable Men," *Shakespearian Comedy*, 223–25. See also Tillyard, *Last Plays*, 53–54.

2. Fine discussions of the poetic evocativeness of *The Tempest* appear in Reuben Brower, "The Mirror of Analogy," *The Fields of Light* (New York: Oxford University Press, 1951), and Goldman, *Energies of Drama*, 137–50.

3. Philip Brockbank argues for a complex, multifaceted allegory in *The Tempest* in "*The Tempest*: Conventions of Art and Empire," *Later Shakespeare*, ed. Brown and Harris (London, 1966), pp. 183–84.

4. Bernard Knox suggests that the influence of Roman comedy on *The Tempest* extends beyond plot design to the characterizations of Ariel and Caliban, who he sees as sophisticated versions of the clever and oafish slaves of Plautus and Terence ("*The Tempest* and the Ancient Comic Tradition," *English Institute Essays* [1954], 55–71).

5. David Young notes that Prospero's art "consists mainly of shows and spectacles" (*The Heart's Forest* [New Haven: Yale University Press, 1972], 156).

6. See, for example, J. Hart, "Prospero and Faustus, *BUSE* 2 (1956): 197–206.

7. See Felperin's excellent discussion of the imaginative geography of Prospero's island in *Shakespearean Romance*, 252–57.

8. See the hint in Nuttall, "Two Unassimilable Men," 223.

Chapter 15. Conclusion

1. Ralph Berry also suggests that the comedies allow two levels of critical response in *Shakespeare's Comedies* (Princeton: Princeton University Press, 1972), 13–16.

Suggested Readings

Alexander, Peter. "The Original Ending of *The Taming of the Shrew.*" *Shakespeare Quarterly* 20 (1969): 111–16.

Barber, C. L. *Shakespeare's Festive Comedies: A Study of Dramatic Form and its Relation to Social Custom.* Princeton: Princeton University Press, 1959.

Barton, Anne (Roesen). *"Love's Labor's Lost." Shakespeare Quarterly* 4 (1953): 411–26.

———. *"As You Like It* and *Twelfth Night:* Shakespeare's Sense of an Ending." *Shakespearian Comedy.* Edited by David Palmer and Malcolm Bradbury. London: E. Arnold, 1972, 160–80.

Bellette, A. F. "Truth and Utterance in *The Winter's Tale.*" *Shakespeare Survey* 31 (1978): 65–75.

Berry, Ralph. *Shakespeare's Comedies.* Princeton: Princeton University Press, 1972.

Bethell, S. L. *The Winter's Tale: A Study.* London: Staples Press, 1947.

Bradbrook, Muriel C. *Shakespeare and Elizabethan Poetry.* London: Chatto & Windus, 1951.

———. *The Growth and Structure of Elizabethan Comedy.* London: Chatto & Windus, 1955.

Brockbank, Philip. *"The Tempest:* Conventions of Art and Empire." *Later Shakespeare.* Edited by J. R. Brown and B. Harris. London: E. Arnold, 1966: 183–202.

Brower, Reuben. "The Mirror of Analogy." *The Fields of Light.* New York: Oxford University Press, 1951.

Brown, John R. *Shakespeare and His Comedies.* 2d ed. London: Methuen, 1962.

Bryant, J. A. "Shakespeare's Allegory: *The Winter's Tale.*" *Sewanee Review* 63 (1955): 202–22.

Burckhardt, Sigurd. *Shakespearean Meanings.* Princeton: Princeton University Press, 1968.

Charlton, Henry B. *Shakespearian Comedy.* London: Methuen, 1938.

Coghill, Nevill. "The Basis of Shakespearian Comedy." *Essays and Studies* 3 (1950): 1–28.

———. *Shakespeare's Professional Skills.* Cambridge: At the University Press, 1964.

Danson, Lawrence. *The Harmonies of "The Merchant of Venice."* New Haven: Yale University Press, 1978.

Doran, Madeleine. *Endeavors of Art: A Study of Form in Elizabethan Drama.* Madison: University of Wisconsin Press, 1954.

Duthie, G. I. *"The Taming of A Shrew* and *The Taming of the Shrew." Review of English Studies* 19 (1943): 337–56.

Edwards, Philip. *Shakespeare and the Confines of Art.* London: Methuen, 1968.

Evans, Bertrand. *Shakespeare's Comedies.* New York: Oxford University Press, 1960.

Everett, Barbara. *"Much Ado About Nothing." Critical Quarterly* 3 (1961): 319–35.

Ewbank, Inga-Stina. " 'Were man but constant, he were perfect': Constancy and Consistency in *Two Gentlemen of Verona." Shakespearian Comedy.* Edited by David Palmer and Malcolm Bradbury. London: E. Arnold, 1972: 31–57.

Felperin, Howard. *Shakespearean Romance.* Princeton: Princeton University Press, 1972.

Foakes, R. A. "The Owl and the Cuckoo: Voices of Maturity in Shakespeare's Comedies." *Shakespearian Comedy.* Edited by David Palmer and Malcolm Bradbury. London: E. Arnold, 1972, 121–41.

———. *Shakespeare: The Dark Comedies to the Last Plays.* Charlottesville: University Press of Virginia, 1971.

Frye, Northrop. "The Argument of Comedy." *English Institute Essays.* Edited by D. A. Robertson, Jr. New York: Columbia University Press, 1949: 58–73.

———. *A Natural Perspective: The Development of Shakespearean Comedy and Romance.* New York: Columbia University Press, 1965.

Gardner, Helen. *"As You Like It." More Talking of Shakespeare.* Edited by John Garrett. New York: Arno, 1959.

Goldman, Michael. *Shakespeare and the Energies of Drama.* Princeton: Princeton University Press, 1972.

Gordon, George S. *Shakespearian Comedy and Other Studies.* London: Oxford University Press, 1944.

Heilman, R. B. "The *Taming* Untamed: or, The Return of the Shrew." *Modern Language Quarterly* 27 (1966): 147–61.

Hollander, John. *"Twelfth Night* and the Morality of Indulgence." *Sewanee Review* 68 (1959): 220–38.

Houk, R. A. "The Evolution of *The Taming of the Shrew." PMLA* 57 (1942): 1009–38.

Hunter, G. K. *Shakespeare: The Late Comedies.* London: Longmans, Green, 1962.

Jenkins, Harold. *"As You Like It." Shakespeare Survey* 8 (1955): 40–51.

Kermode, Frank. *Shakespeare: The Final Plays.* London: Longmans, Green, 1963.

Kirsch, Arthur. *"Cymbeline* and Coterie Dramaturgy." *ELH* 34 (1967): 285–306.

Knight, G. Wilson. *The Shakespearian Tempest.* London: Methuen, 1953.

———. *The Crown of Life: Essays in Interpretation of Shakespeare's Final Plays.* London: Methuen, 1947.

Knox, Bernard. *"The Tempest* and the Ancient Comic Tradition." *English Institute Essays.* New York: Columbia University Press, 1954: 55–71.

Leech, Clifford. *"Twelfth Night" and Shakespearian Comedy*. Toronto: University of Toronto Press, 1965.

———. "The Theme of Ambition in *All's Well that Ends Well*." *ELH* 21 (1954): 17–29.

Leggatt, Alexander., *Shakespeare's Comedy of Love*. London: Methuen, 1974.

Mahood, Molly M. *Shakespeare's Wordplay*. London: Methuen, 1957.

Matchett, William. "Some Dramatic Techniques in *The Winter's Tale*." *Shakespeare Survey* 22 (1969): 93–107.

Mincoff, Marco. "Shakespeare and Lyly." *Shakespeare Survey* 14 (1961): 15–24.

Nevo, Ruth. *Comic Transformations in Shakespeare*. London: Methuen, 1980.

Nuttall, A. D. "Two Unassimilable Men." *Shakespearian Comedy*. Edited by David Palmer and Malcolm Bradbury. London: E. Arnold, 1972: 210–40.

Palmer, John. *Comic Characters of Shakespeare*. London: Macmillan, 1946.

Salingar, Leo. *Shakespeare and the Traditions of Comedy*. Cambridge: At the University Press, 1974.

Shroeder, J. W. *"The Taming of A Shrew* and *The Taming of The Shrew:* A Case Reopened." *Journal of English and Germanic Philology* 57 (1958): 424–43.

Smith, Hallett. *Shakespeare's Romances*. San Marino, Calif.: Huntington Library Publications, 1972.

Stevenson, David L. *The Love-Game Comedy*. New York: Columbia University Press, 1946.

Stewart, J. I. M. *Character and Motive in Shakespeare*. New York: Barnes & Noble, 1949.

Stoll, E. E. *Shakespeare Studies*. New York: G. E. Stechart, 1942; first ed. 1927.

Summers, Joseph H. "The Masks of *Twelfth Night*." *University Review* 22 (1955): 25–32.

Thorndyke, A. H. *The Influence of Beaumont and Fletcher on Shakespeare*. Worcester, Mass.: Press of O. B. Wood, 1901.

Tillyard, E. M. W. *Shakespeare's Problem Plays*. Toronto: University of Toronto Press, 1950.

———. *Shakespeare's Last Plays*. London: Chatto & Windus, 1938.

Traversi, Derek. *Shakespeare: The Last Phase*. London: Hollis & Carter, 1954.

Warren, Roger. "Why Does it End well? Helena, Bertram, and the Sonnets." *Shakespeare Survey* 22 (1969): 79–92.

Wells, Stanley. "The Failure of *Two Gentlemen in Verona*." *Shakespeare-Jarhbuch* 99 (1963): 161–73.

Wilson, Harold S. *"Philaster* and *Cymbeline*." *English Institute Essays*. New York: Columbia University Press (1951): 146–67.

Yates, Frances A. *A Study of Love's Labor's Lost*. Cambridge: At the University Press, 1936.

Young, David. *Something of Great Constancy: The Art of A Midsummer Night's Dream*. New Haven: Yale University Press, 1966.

Index